THE
TRUTH
ABOUT
AMERICA'S
SCHOOLS

The Bracey Reports,
1991-97

Gerald W. Bracey

Phi Delta Kappa Educational Foundation
Bloomington, Indiana
U.S.A.

Cover design by
Victoria Voelker

Phi Delta Kappa Educational Foundation
408 North Union Street
Post Office Box 789
Bloomington, Indiana 47402-0789
U.S.A.

Printed in the United States of America

Library of Congress Catalog Card Number 97-69666
ISBN 0-87367-395-6

TABLE OF CONTENTS

FOREWORD

The public schools have always had their critics. But after the publication of *A Nation at Risk* in 1983, the critics of public education in America became more strident and more ubiquitous. Those critics eventually included three "Education Presidents," many public officials at all levels, the mass media, and even some education professionals — those who made careers of collecting grants to "fix" problems that had been magnified out of all correspondence with reality.

Hammered daily by statistics presented without the context that gives them meaning, most other Americans bought into the myth that the nation's public schools were in a state of collapse. It was a disheartening decade for many teachers and school administrators, who recognized the myth for what it was but whose voices could not be heard above the cacophony of the critics.

Then, in October 1991, the *Phi Delta Kappan* published Gerald Bracey's first data-based analysis of the condition of public education. Bracey's findings were in sharp conflict with the prevailing view. Instead of discovering an education system verging on total collapse, he found the schools to be about as effective as they had ever been (though the population they served had become dramatically harder to educate).

Not that Bracey started out to defend the public schools. Like most Americans in 1990, he thought that the schools his own children attended were "okay" but that other public schools across the nation were in serious trouble.

Indeed, as he explained in the prefatory note to *Final Exam: A Study of the Perpetual Scrutiny of American Education* (Technos Press, 1995), the first two Bracey Reports came about by acci-

1

dent. "Quite literally, if the *Denver Post* in late 1990 had not reprinted a Richard Cohen column that had appeared two months earlier in the *Washington Post*, 'Johnny's Miserable SATs,' the Bracey Reports would not exist," he said. Cohen's column aroused Bracey's curiosity, causing him to take a close look at SAT scores over the years in relation to demographic changes within the test-taking population. That analysis turned up a small drop in the verbal SAT score over time and no drop in the math score — a much healthier situation than Cohen and most other commentators had led us to believe.

Bracey published the results of his analysis in *Education Week*, and that article — "SATs: Miserable or Miraculous?" — prompted colleagues across the nation to send him other data that corroborated his findings. Those colleagues included a group of systems engineers at Sandia National Laboratories in Albuquerque, whose own conclusions regarding the condition of public education in America matched Bracey's — but whose report of those conclusions had been suppressed by "internal politics."

Out of all these data came the initial article, "Why Can't They Be Like We Were?" The publication of that piece in the *Kappan* brought Bracey more new data from colleagues — enough to merit a second Bracey Report (a title coined by the editors when it became clear that the reports would be an annual feature). And that second Bracey Report spawned subsequent ones. The initial Bracey Report, which footnoted the third draft of the Sandia Report, also made pirated photocopies of the Sandia Report hot items across the nation. Now the secret was out: The American system of public education was *not* in the state of collapse.

Since 1991, the national dialogue about the condition of public education has shifted — albeit glacially — from the notion of total collapse to the view that U.S. public schools will not be good enough for the 21st century. That's a position that Bracey endorses. As he noted in the introduction to *Transforming America's Schools*: *An Rx for Getting Past Blame* (American Association of School Administrators, 1994), "One need not assume school failure to propose school reform."

Meanwhile, as long as the new data merit them, Bracey will continue to write his annual reports on the condition of public education for the *Kappan*. He has proven to us time and again that he is data-driven. No one "owns" him; as an independent agent, he single-mindedly pursues whatever truth can be derived from empirical evidence. When he errs in his interpretation of the data (which happens only rarely), he publicly admits his mistake and corrects it. And when others ignore or misuse data to tell a tale about American public education that simply isn't so, he doesn't pull his punches in publicly calling those individuals to task. It was Bracey, you may remember, who coined the label "data-proof ideologues."

While taping a radio show recently with John Merrow, Bracey noted that, when he embarked on his study of the condition of public education, he had "no position."

"Do you have one now?" Merrow asked.

Bracey paused, and then replied: "Yes, in the sense that I am more convinced now that my original conclusions were correct. But no, in the sense that all last year [1996] I told audiences all over the country that, if the Third International Mathematics and Science Study proved to be a credible study and showed that American kids really looked lousy when matched against their peers in other countries, then that is what the next Bracey Report would say."

Trained as a developmental and cognitive psychologist, Bracey remains true to the principles of his profession. He is not an "apologist" for the public schools. He is not a "revisionist" of education history. He is a truth-teller.

And, when the history of my editorship of the *Kappan* is written, I believe that the journal's role in bringing Bracey's views to public attention will be perceived as one of the *Kappan*'s proudest accomplishments.

Pauline B. Gough
Editor, *Phi Delta Kappan*

WHY CAN'T THEY BE LIKE WE WERE?

October 1991

Schools stink. Says who? Virtually everyone. When George Bush announced America 2000, he said that we've "moved beyond the days of issuing report after report about the dismal state of our schools." The opening sentence of Edward Fiske's recent book is succinct: "It's no secret that America's public schools are failing."[1] Chester Finn, former assistant secretary for research and improvement in the U.S. Department of Education, is no kinder: "[These] examples [of educational shortcomings] are so familiar we're tempted not to pay them much heed. Why make ourselves miserable?"[2] And, at the opening session of the annual Conference on Assessment sponsored by the Education Commission of the States, Lauren Resnick, former president of the American Educational Research Association and co-director of a foundation-funded effort to establish national standards and examinations, said, "We all know how terrible we are."

"Why Can't They Be Like We Were?" was published in the October 1991 issue of the Phi Delta Kappan *and became the first Bracey report on the condition of public education.*

5

Reports about how awful we are have always issued forth with some frequency, but they began pouring in after 1983. In that year the National Commission on Excellence in Education, assembled by then Secretary of Education Terrel Bell, declared us to be "a nation at risk," awash in "a rising tide of mediocrity."[3] Since then, we have been deluged with a flood tide of reports criticizing curriculum, administrators, teachers, parents, and students. "Johnny's Miserable SATs" screamed the headline of a 1990 diatribe by *Washington Post* columnist Richard Cohen.[4]

So many people have said so often that the schools are bad that it is no longer a debatable proposition subject to empirical proof. It has become an assumption. But it is an assumption that turns out to be false. The evidence overwhelmingly shows that *American schools have never achieved more than they currently achieve.* And some indicators show them performing better than ever.

From the moment that *A Nation at Risk* appeared, I had my doubts about all the talk about mediocrity and decline. The conclusions of the Bell commission simply didn't ring true to my experiences as an educator, as a parent, or, for that matter, as a student.

As a parent, I watched my son and his buddies set off in the eighth grade in an ordinary Virginia public school to follow a course of mathematical study that would land them in calculus as high school seniors. In my own academic career, my high school math followed the usual (for then) four-year trajectory: algebra I, plane geometry, algebra II, and solid geometry and trigonometry. Calculus was considered so difficult and arcane that I had begun my sophomore year in college before I was permitted to explore the deep mysteries of derivatives and integrals.

Then came my daughter, plowing through the works of Ibsen — part of a regular offering to juniors at her Colorado public high school. Her own social condition, rather advanced when compared with that of Ibsen's heroines, prevented her from relating well to their cultural straitjackets, but neither the prose nor the themes posed any comprehension problems for her. As with calculus, Ibsen and I had not crossed paths until my college years.

Finally, each spring as the aspen leafed out in the Rocky Mountains, so did displays of paintings, sculpture, and science projects appear in the foyers of the administration building of the Cherry Creek (Colorado) School District. Many paintings revealed highly sophisticated techniques applied with considerable skill. The science projects spoke in tongues: they rendered the once-familiar dialects of physics, chemistry, and biology as strange as the Russian I had briefly explored 25 years earlier. Light years removed from the simple machines, simple equations, and phyla to be memorized in my high school days, these displays presented complicated explorations of protein absorption, gene splicing, immunological reactions, nucleic acids, and so on. Certainly, these exhibits represented the best that the district's high schools had to offer, but they were nonetheless the works of *high schoolers.*

As I absorbed these personal collisions with the Bell commission's findings, I began to bump up against statistics that contradicted the findings as well. These numbers dealt with general trends and spoke to what was happening in the nation at large, as well as in my family. The clang of these data against the Bell commission's assertions affirmed that my experiences were neither idiosyncratic nor bound by my middle-class milieu. The many allegations that the education system has tumbled constitute "The Big Lie" about education. In short, the Bell commission blew it.

What do the various indicators of quality *really* say about the health of U.S. education? High school graduation rates are at an all-time high. The proportion of 17-year-olds who complete high school rose from 10% in 1910 to about 75% in 1965 and has remained at similarly high levels since. In 1989 about 83% of all students received a diploma 12 years after beginning school.[5]

Ironically, it is likely that this very success has contributed to the perception of decline. Many of the current crop of school critics wistfully recall a "golden age" of American education, usually when they themselves were in school. But, on examination, this enlightened epoch actually turns out to be a time when fewer than 50% of the class graduated, when minorities were invisible, and when "special education" meant keeping both physically and mentally disabled students out of sight.

In those days of the golden age, "book learnin'" was clearly recognized as only one kind of learning and was often contrasted with the learning that would happen later in the "real world." There was plenty of meaningful work for high school dropouts, and little stigma was attached to leaving school early. Indeed, dropouts constituted the group from which emerged the popular American cultural hero, the "self-made man."

In those days, too, the channeling of students into college-bound and vocational tracks often amounted to virtual segregation into two schools. Moreover, such tracking often became sex segregation, since many fewer girls than boys headed for college; as late as 1965, boys outnumbered girls in college by seven to four. Of course, segregation by race was the norm everywhere.

Yet even today's 83% graduation rate is misleadingly low. It takes account only of those who graduate "on time" — those who begin in kindergarten or grade 1 and receive their diplomas 12 or 13 years later. But, unlike many countries, the United States operates "flexible reentry" schools. People are permitted to come back and finish school almost any time they choose. And come back they do. In 1989, 87% of Americans between the ages of 25 and 29 held high school diplomas or GED (General Education Development) certificates, up from about 73% only 20 years earlier. Similarly, 91% of the class of 1980 had completed high school or its equivalent by 1986.[6]

Recently, there has been much weeping and gnashing of teeth over dropout rates. "The dropout problem has engaged the minds and hearts of Americans. Parents, educators, business executives, and policy makers all believe that leaving school profoundly handicaps the dropouts themselves and the entire Nation."[7] (This sentiment is typical, although I should point out that many jobs in this country virtually *require* dropouts because people with more education don't care to do them.)

However, if completion rates are high, then dropout rates must be low. They are, and they're declining for all ethnic groups except Hispanics, for whom the rate is steady. Moreover, the true figures for Hispanics are probably lower than they appear to be. In some reports that calculate dropout rates, a *dropout* is any person without a high school diploma who is not in school. Thus many undereducated *adults* who have immigrated recently from South and Central America are labeled as dropouts from a system that they never entered.

Even our notions about who drops out are off. Contrary to the popular stereotype of dropouts as largely blacks and Hispanics, 66% of dropouts are white. Sixty-eight percent come from two-parent families, 42% come from suburban high schools, 71% never repeated a grade, and 86% live in homes where English is the native language.[8]

Blacks drop out at a somewhat higher *rate* than whites, and Hispanics drop out at a much higher *rate* than members of any other group; but the *number* of white dropouts is much larger because whites are still the dominant population group in the country.

Why then do we hear so many lamentations about dropout rates? I expect that many people find it genuinely horrific that some people don't finish high school and thus effectively cut themselves off from their best chance at the good life. But I believe that some of the sorrow reflects a certain amount of opportunism, even cynicism. When the applicants outnumbered available jobs and college desks, dropouts could be ignored. Now that the baby boomers are entering their fifth decade, young workers are becoming scarce. As a result, employers have suddenly discovered dropouts and the need to save them. At the same time, colleges have discovered "nontraditional" students.

Of course, it matters little that so many people are walking across the stage at commencement if we are simply handing out diplomas to functionally illiterate know-nothings who have been passed through the system by grade inflation and social promotion and who have earned their sheepskins for "seat time" served. Many articles have asserted that this is the case, but an examination of trends in test scores reveals otherwise.

We have three major sources of test information: commercial, standardized, norm-referenced achievement tests, such as the Iowa Tests of Basic Skills (ITBS); the tests administered by the National Assessment of Educational Progress (NAEP); and college admissions tests, such as the Scholastic Aptitude Test (SAT). Let us examine each source separately.

After falling in the 1960s and early 1970s, scores on standardized tests began rising in the mid-1970s — and, by 1986, some stood at a 30-year high.[9] Scores on standardized tests have continued to rise since then.[10]

It is extremely difficult to locate the causes of either the decline or the subsequent rise. About all we can say is that we cannot ascribe much of either trend to *educational* factors. This conclusion follows from the rather unusual shape of the curves of test score trends.

When we graph test scores across time, we notice a peculiar phenomenon. Suppose a group of students in one elementary grade scores higher than the previous year's students in the same grade scored. This new group then takes its higher scores along with it for the rest of its years in school. That is, if a group of fifth-graders scores higher in one year, eighth-grade scores will rise three years later, and 12th-grade scores will rise seven years later. The changes in test scores ripple up the grade ladder like waves.[11]

Changes in school factors can hardly produce such grade-by-grade progression, because any change in the school should affect all grades equally. Or, if the rise were caused by some special program that teachers in a particular grade cooked up, then the scores should fall again when the students move on. The age-related ripple effect that we observe in the achievement test data must derive from some change in broader demographic characteristics — family size, income level, and so on — of the nation.

In recent years, some observers have alleged that much of the rise in achievement test scores stems from questionable practices on the part of teachers and administrators.[12] And it is true that shady practices have occurred and that scores are higher than they would otherwise be. Under pressure to get scores up, schools have aligned their curricula with the tests, emphasized test-taking skills, and even cheated. But such practices cannot account for the age-related ripple effect, because such practices should affect all scores, not just those of a particular age group. (Many fingers have been wagged at teachers and administrators for cheating on tests. CBS News considered it a sufficiently serious problem to merit one-quarter of a "60 Minutes" program. Less outrage has been expressed over the fact that flight times between cities got longer when airlines began to be rated on the percentage of on-time arrivals. The simple fact is that all public indicators of performance tend to be corrupted when pressure is brought to make them look good.)

Because standardized tests are subject to manipulation, many people put more stock in the results of the NAEP, commonly known as "the nation's report card." The NAEP hires and trains test administrators and maintains tight security, rendering administrative goofs, curricular alignment, and cheating all highly improbable. The NAEP also attempts to get beyond the rote recall of tiny factoids so characteristic of commercial, standardized achievement tests and instead to measure higher-order skills. Some people cite the NAEP results as proof of the decline of education.

The NAEP began in 1969. So what do 20-odd years of NAEP results look like? Overall, they are very stable. The percentage of white students scoring at the three levels of reading achievement— basic, proficient, and advanced—has remained constant since 1971. The scores of blacks and Hispanics have *risen* during the same period. Scores in writing have not changed since 1974, and those in math have remained constant since 1973. Between 1969 and 1982, scores on the NAEP science assessment fell for 17-year-olds but have risen slightly since. For 9-year-olds, science achievement was the same in 1986 as in 1969, and for 13-year olds the decline is so slight as to be well within the range of possible measurement error.

Here's how the 1990 NAEP publication, *Accelerating Academic Achievement,* put it:

> Across all three ages assessed, over-all reading performance in 1988 was as good as, if not slightly better than, it was nearly two decades ago. . . . In 1986, mathematics [achievement] had changed very little from the levels achieved in 1973. . . . Viewed as a whole, science achieve-

ment in 1986 remained below levels attained in 1969. Trends at ages 9 and 13 are characterized by a decline in the early 1970s, stable performance at that lower level of achievement through the 1970s, and improvement in the 1980s. With these gains, average proficiency at age 9 returned to that of the first assessment in 1970, but average proficiency at age 13 remained slightly below the 1970 level. At age 17, science performance dropped steadily from 1969 to 1982, but improved significantly from 1982 to 1986.[13]

The National Center for Education Statistics (NCES) calls these results "stagnation at relatively low levels" of achievement.[14] Let me observe here only that such an interpretation is subject to debate.

While NAEP results provide more reliable trend information than do standardized tests, no trends in test scores have received more publicity than those of the SAT. In 1977, after 14 consecutive years of "decline" (decline *is* in quotes because, as will become apparent, no decline exists or ever existed), the Educational Testing Service (ETS) appointed a commission to figure out why. Although the commission report ascribed a lot of the decline to changes in the population of test-takers, it also offered nearly as many potential reasons as there were points in the decline.[15] This fact alone should have tipped us off that something other than the quality of schooling was at issue here. (Of course, ETS and the College Board rightly maintained all along that the SAT *was not* an index of school quality and should not be used as such.)

Since the 1977 report, every one- or two-point change in SAT scores has been front-page news. This is more than a little surprising, given the fact that each of the two tests that make up the full SAT has a range of *600 points*. Less has been made of the fact that blacks, Asian-Americans, Native Americans, Mexican-Americans, and Puerto Ricans *all* scored higher on the SAT in 1990 than in 1975. This is true despite the fact that many more students, from all socioeconomic levels, are taking the SAT today and that many more students with bad grades in school are taking the test. As we would expect, students in the lower half of their high school class do not dazzle on the SAT. (Why are many more students taking the SAT? Because more colleges are *requiring* it, even as there is less evidence that they are actually *using* it, now that colleges have to *recruit* students rather than *select* them. A low-scoring student in 1990 had a much better chance of getting into college than a low-scoring student in 1965.)

As with achievement tests, we must exercise caution when interpreting SAT scores or changes in SAT scores. The average score on the SAT is determined by whoever shows up on Saturday morning to take the test. If the characteristics of these test-takers change over time — and they do — then interpretation of simple averages gets iffy. For example, if we look at a group of students who took the SAT in 1990 and compare them to a group with the same ethnic and gender mix that took the test in 1975, the "average" scores of the 1990 group rise significantly.

Even if we are cautious in our interpretations, we can conclude that there has not really been a decline in SAT scores. It only appears that way because people have made apples-to-oranges comparisons using simple averages. To understand this point, recall that the standards on the SAT were set in 1941. In that year, those who got an average number of questions correct were assigned a score of 500, and all scores were scaled to fit into a range from 200 to 800. There is nothing magical about these numbers; they were chosen so that they would not be confused with I.Q. scores or with scores on any other existing test. All subsequent SATs are equated with this first administration. A 500 in 1991 means the same things in terms of skill levels as a 500 did in 1941.

Thus the question becomes, How similar are today's test-takers to that standard-setting group? If the students who huddle in angst over their test packets on Saturday mornings now have the same characteristics as those who filled in answer sheets in 1941, then any increase or decrease in the scores would be real.

But today's SAT-takers scarcely resemble those of 1941. In 1941 an elite group of 10,654 mostly white, mostly male, mostly Northeastern students, mostly headed for Ivy League and other

13

prestigious private universities, sat down to take the SAT. During the 1989-90 school year, 1,025,523 students (about 42% of the entire senior class) paid for that privilege. Fully 27% of the 1989-90 test-takers were members of minority groups; many others were from lower socioeconomic groups. They came from Austin and Boston, from Orlando and Sacramento. Fifty-two percent were females, who, for unknown reasons, have not scored as well as males on the SAT. (Some argue that the test is biased against women; others contend that the males and females taking the test differ on many socioeconomic variables.) The median class rank of test-takers has fallen from the 79th percentile in 1971 to the 73rd percentile in 1989.[16]

The College Entrance Examination Board, which commissions ETS to produce the SAT, no longer has exact information about the characteristics of the 1941 group, so we can't make an exact comparison with a sample of 1990 test-takers. But we can find a sample of today's test-takers that resembles those of 1941. A group that reasonably approximates the original test-takers would be the group of white students who come from homes in which at least one parent has obtained a bachelor's degree.[17] In 1990 this group, of whom a majority were female, scored 454 on the verbal subtest of the SAT and 505 on the mathematics subtest. The drop in verbal scores from the 500 of the standard-setting group is smaller than it appears. By 1951, long before the spread of mass televiewing and other distractions, average verbal scores had stabilized at around 475.[18]

The *average score,* compiled from the scores of everyone who takes the test, has gone down because, since the 1960s, that average has included more scores of white students with lower grade-point averages and more scores of groups that have traditionally been excluded from higher education: blacks, Hispanics, and women. These groups have not traditionally scored well on the SAT, nor do they now. Yet, as the doors to our colleges and universities have opened ever wider, more and more of them have had to take the test.

Sadly, the gains that minorities have registered in the past 15 years obscure the fact that the scores of all ethnic groups (except

Asians) remain depressingly low on standardized tests, on the NAEP, and on the SAT. Although the College Board and ETS like to tout the gains of minorities on SAT scores as evidence of the narrowing gap between minorities and whites, blacks have raised their percentile scores relative to those of whites by only 5% in 15 years. At that rate they will need another 50 years or so to catch up. I doubt that we have that much time. (Those who would explain the low scores of blacks and Hispanics in terms of "bias" inherent in the test are left with the difficult — I would say impossible — task of explaining the extraordinary performance of Asians. Else they must hold the equally implausible view that a test developed for a middle- and upper-middle-class white Anglo-Saxon culture just happens to fit well with the variegated cultures of the Pacific Rim.)

Data concerning the Preliminary Scholastic Aptitude Test (PSAT), a short version of the SAT, bolster the conclusion that SAT scores have not declined. Unlike the SAT, whose average depends solely on who takes the test in a given year, the PSAT is occasionally normed on a representative group of students. From the initial PSAT norming in 1960 to the most recent in 1983, the lines on a graph of average scores on the PSAT are as flat as the surface of a frozen lake. Nowhere is there any hint of a decline.[19]

In this discussion, I have not touched on one area of testing: namely, all those recent geography tests — some national, some local — that show alarming numbers of children unable to find Mexico on a map. Alas, no such tests were administered in the past. My guess is that geography is a special case and that it has always been so.

In our isolated and isolationist nation, we have always been ignorant of geography. I recall a poll taken at the height of the Vietnam War in which a certain percentage of Americans misidentified the Viet Cong. A poll taken during the Gulf War showed similar confusions about who was who and what was where in the Middle East. A poll conducted by Harrison Salisbury that appeared in the June 1957 issue of *McCall's* found that only 71% of American *college graduates* could name the capital of the Soviet

Union, that only 21% could name a single Russian author, and that only 24% could name a single Russian composer.[20] This geographical obliviousness is certainly no source of national pride, but it is a condition of long standing. Who else but Americans could be laughed at by people in other countries as "innocents" or decried as "ugly"?

It would not surprise me to learn that teachers — with a finite amount of time to teach and with health education, sex education, drug education, AIDS education, and many other educations added to the curriculum — have reduced the time allotted to geography. Since schoolchildren tend to learn what they are taught, it seems likely that a great deal of geography hasn't been taught.

The various test scores that we have been considering point, perhaps more emphatically than any other information, to the conclusion that achievement in American schools is as high as it has ever been. Many argue that to stay competitive internationally we have to raise achievement, and this may be true. But to say that is to say something quite different from what critics and would-be reformers have been saying.

One final possible contention about test scores deserves some consideration. Some would concede that average test scores have held steady or risen slightly, but they wonder about the issue covered in a recent ETS publication, *Performance at the Top.*[21] After all, one definition of *mediocre* is average. If average scores are holding steady but our highest scorers are regressing toward the mean, then this wave could define the rising tide of mediocrity that the Bell commission thought it saw.

In fact, if we look at the top scorers, the evidence once again shows us mostly steady or rising performance. It doesn't seem to matter whether we define "top performance" as the average performance of the select group of students taking the toughest tests or as the percentage of students scoring at the highest levels on those tests. Consider the following:

- From 1981 to 1990 the percentage of students taking the general test of the Graduate Record Examinations (GRE) rose 16%. Scores on most tests decline as the number of test-takers grows, but GRE subscores have all risen: the verbal score by eight points, the quantitative score by 36 points, and the analytical score by 30 points.

- The number of students taking the Graduate Management Admission Test (GMAT) also rose over the last decade. But average GMAT scores rose as well, from 481 to 503.

- The percentage of students scoring above 600 (above the 84th percentile) on the verbal subtest of the SAT fell until 1975 and then stabilized. The percentage of students scoring above 600 on the math subtest fell until 1975 and has recently returned to a level slightly above that of 1972. Currently more people score above 600 on the math subtest than one would expect, given the characteristics of the normal curve — and substantially more than would be expected score above 700. The percentage of students scoring above the 84th percentile on the American College Testing (ACT) Program tests has fallen for math since 1973 but has risen for English during the same period. The percentage receiving a composite score equal to or higher than the 84th percentile has been steady since 1973.

- The percentage of high school students taking the achievement tests offered by the College Board has also risen since 1977 — and so have their achievement test scores (from 533 to 546) and their SAT scores. Since 1977 the SAT verbal scores of those taking achievement tests have risen from 504 to 515; their SAT math scores have risen from 553 to 585.

- The number of students taking College Board Advanced Placement (AP) tests rose from 90,000 in 1978 to 324,000 (who took some 481,000 tests) in 1990. Yet the average score on these exams dropped only 11 one-hundredths of a point (from 3.16 to 3.05 on a five-point scale). Moreover, these changes cannot be explained simply by citing increases in the number of high-scoring Asian students taking the tests. While the percentage of Asians taking AP tests tripled from 1978 to 1990, the percentage of blacks doubled, and the percentage of Hispanics quadrupled.

- On NAEP assessments, the percentage of 17-year-olds who show advanced proficiency in reading has declined from 6.6% in 1971 to 4.8% in 1988. The percentages of students at advanced levels in math (7.4% in 1971, 6.5% in 1988) and in science (8.5% in 1971, 8.2% in 1988), however, have been relatively steady.

The authors of *A Nation at Risk* launched a crusade for school reform by claiming that America was drowning in "a rising tide of mediocrity." *There is no such tide.* Those who penned this document were sometimes merely naive in their interpretations, but at other times they verged on being criminally uncritical about the misinformation they were fed. (One wonders whether they understood it.)

Not only are students completing high school and scoring higher on most tests, but more and more of them are pursuing degrees beyond a high school diploma.

They don't all do this immediately upon finishing high school, but they are chasing higher degrees despite having to cope with considerable economic hardships to do so. (At the same time, a report from the National Center for Education Statistics cites a decline in the number of universities offering remedial help to all students.[22])

The number of high school graduates peaked in 1977, then began a decline that is expected to last until the mid-1990s. As baby boomers passed into adulthood, fewer and fewer 18-year-olds were available to roam the groves of academe. One might have expected college enrollments to shrink as a result, but enrollment in higher education now stands at an all-time high. Between 1965 and 1987 the number of males enrolled in college rose from 3.6 million to six million; the number of females skyrocketed from 2.1 million to 6.9 million.[23]

How can this be? Simple. Rather than shut down or cut staff positions after the baby boomers had passed through, universities began admitting higher percentages of applicants. Nothing is held to be more sacred by a college than maintaining its enrollment.

When my peers and I applied to colleges, we waved flags in front of admissions offices, flaunted our grade-point averages and SAT scores (if we had them), and still suffered from anxiety and insecurity about whether or not we would be allowed to attend the colleges of our choice. As my children rose to their junior year in high school, with decent but not outstanding academic records, our mailbox literally overflowed with thick, glossy, full-color booklets explaining why Old Ivy U was the perfect choice for them.

One recent fall I had occasion to conduct a survey among a sample of university admissions officers. A number responded quite late, offering by way of apology the fact that fall was the height of their recruiting season. They made college admissions sound like a sport. However, the sport consists largely of beating the bushes for warm bodies; the average four-year college, public or private, now admits nearly 80% of its applicants. Only a small number of mostly small schools admit fewer than half of those who apply. Naturally, professors complain bitterly and loudly that these students do not compare with the high-quality undergraduates of the good ol' days. (But what professor doesn't prefer less able students to no students at all?)

Universities have also kept their enrollments up and their faculties employed by recruiting nontraditional students. Currently, almost 30% of full-time college students are over 22 years of age. More than 80% of part-time college students are over 22. Only 62% of all college students attend school full-time, and only 43% obtain the baccalaureate four years after high school graduation. The typical American family is no longer the Nelsons, or the Cleavers, or even the Huxtables; and the typical American college student is no longer a callow youth.[24]

Despite the changing population, the percentage of 22-year-olds obtaining bachelor's degrees increased from 21% in 1970 to 26% in 1987. The latter figure compares well with those of Canada (25%), Japan (21%), France (14%), Great Britain (14%), and what was in 1987 West Germany (13%). Despite concern about our need to be competitive in science and technology in the future, more 22-year-olds in the U.S. obtain bachelor's degrees in science and engineering than in any of these countries. The rate of growth in the number of science and engineering degrees awarded since 1970 is higher in the U.S. than in any industrialized country except Japan.[25]

If we conducted a poll, we would probably find that most people believe that *everyone* ought to earn a college degree — or, at the very least, ought to have a chance to try. America holds this educational goal so dear and so universal that a recent report on the educational needs of those who *don't* aspire to a bachelor's degree referred to them as "the forgotten half." Ignoring for the moment the question of whether everyone has the *talent* for college, we seldom ponder the ramifications of what would happen if everyone *did* earn a B.S. or a B.A.

Overeducation poses queasy social problems because well-educated people tend to shy away from occupations that require them to sweep the streets, unclog sewers, scrub toilets, pick up trash, bus tables, or mop floors — no matter what the wages. Moreover, they don't even like to *see* these jobs being done. When I lived in Scandinavia in the mid-Seventies, the highly educated Danes and Swedes had imported uneducated Yugoslavs and Turks to do the "dirty jobs." (And, on occasion, typical racist remarks about how these two nationalities were contributing to the deterioration of the social fabric could be heard as part of "polite" dinner conversation.)

In the U.S., we avoid discussing the implications of overeducation because we fear that we may reach conclusions that clash with our ideal of equal opportunity for all. But until everyone owns a humanoid robot, as well as a car and a color television, some *person* will have to do the "dirty jobs." Until then, however loath we are to admit it, we must continue to produce an uneducated social class that will do what Kurt Vonnegut referred to in *Breakfast of Champions* as "the nigger work."

At this point, some readers might be willing to concede that scores are up and more people are in college. However, given the amount of money we spend on education, they might also contend that we ought to see even *higher* scores and *better* college performance. I recall a picture of former Secretary of Education Lauro Cavazos standing in front of a chart showing the soaring costs of education. Overlaid on the spiraling costs was a chart of SAT scores looking lamely the same, year after year. We're not getting our money's worth, Cavazos said. That's what most people believe. But it's not true.

Only if we examine all costs lumped together does education appear to be a fiscal black hole. If we sort out the costs of *special education* from those of regular K-12 education, however, a very different picture emerges of how costs have increased in recent years. Everyone acknowledges that special education costs a great deal more than regular education. But not everyone realizes that the usual method of figuring pupil/teacher ratios for special education makes those costs look deceptively low. If a regular teacher teaches six children for six periods on one day, she is said to have taught six students. That's straightforward and is sometimes expressed by saying that the teacher had 36 pupil-contact hours (six students times six hours).

If a special education teacher teaches six children, one at a time, for one hour *each,* she, too, is said to have taught six children, though she has had only six pupil-contact hours. In addition, school systems often figure special education programs as marginal, "add-on" costs, incorporating none of the expenditures for overhead incurred simply by operating a school.

When we properly account for the number of children actually taught in the various "educations," we find that the cost of regular education (in constant 1988 dollars) has risen scarcely at all since 1970. In 1988 that cost stood at about $2,500 per pupil, up from $1,800 in 1960 and $2,400 in 1970.[26] This contrasts sharply with the current average annual per-pupil expenditure on a special education student of $17,600.[27] When we acknowledge that federally supported special education programs today enroll more than 12% of all students, we should no longer be confused by where all the dollars have gone.

A similar analysis of teacher salaries leads to similar results. Although legislators and governors have regaled us lately with tales of how much new money they have plunked into the pot of teacher salaries, teachers' annual incomes actually fell between 1973 and 1982 (in constant 1989 dollars). Since then, teacher salaries have risen at a rate very close to that for the cost of living.[28]

Other ways exist to measure costs, and only one approach makes education look at all overpriced: in raw *numbers* of dollars, the U.S. coughs up a lot for its schools . However, as a *percentage* of the gross national product (GNP), we shell out a good deal less on K-12 education than many other nations. From 1970 to 1987, public school expenditures as a percentage of GNP fell from 4.2% to 3.6%. A recent study by the American Federation of Teachers found similar results. Although the U.S. has the highest gross domestic product (GDP), as well as the highest GNP, it finished 12th among 16 developed countries in terms of expenditure for K-12 education as a percent of GDP.[29] Educators did not reap the fruits of the longest peacetime economic expansion in history.

As a percentage of per-capita income, expenditures for education rose rapidly in the 1960s, almost entirely as a result of new federal programs that were aimed at poor, minority, and handicapped students. In an interesting variation on the theme of federal involvement, the Heritage Foundation blamed the "decline" of the schools on the increased federal presence, with its attention to the "special students" and the inevitable centralization produced by federal involvement. The "proof' for this claim consisted of a chart plotting both increasing federal funds for education and declining SAT scores.

Expenditures as a percentage of per capita income rose only slightly during the 1970s and hardly at all during the 1980s. Finally, if you compare the U.S. to other countries in terms of "purchasing power parity" — that is, how much education can be bought for a specific number of dollars (or yen or marks) — the U.S. is about average among other industrialized nations.[30]

Overall, as we scan from the federal government to the state capitals to the local town halls, there is little evidence of largesse from any governing body or of increased burden on the taxpayer for general education.

Some readers might now object to the limited geographical scope of my analysis so far. In the global village, in the highly competitive international marketplace, the only indicators really worthy of our attention are those that compare the performance of our system of education with that of systems in other countries.

Unfortunately, such comparisons of national *systems* of education do not exist. Nor is it hard to see why. To compare systems both within and across national contexts would be very complicated and difficult — and it just might prove meaningless as well. Education has different functions in different societies. Thus an appropriate exercise might be to compare how well education serves each nation within the context of its larger culture. To pull education out of its cultural contexts might destroy its meaning altogether. Whatever the value of such analyses might be, to date we have had only much more modest, limited, and error-prone comparisons of the performance of students from various nations on tests. Such comparisons have generated much heat, but very little light.

Still, in recent years the school critics bashing educators and students have used no set of numbers to greater effect than those that come from these narrow studies of achievement. It was bad enough to fall behind the Japanese and the West Germans; after all, we had made them what they are today. But American students often show up trailing their counterparts from Third World nations. Such humiliation is intolerable.

Although many people continue to cite these studies, the comparisons are so flawed as to be meaningless. American students may or may not stack up well against students from other countries; but, in the studies done to date, the students are not comparable, the curricula are not comparable, the schools are not comparable, and the tests are not comparable. Even in such "straightforward" subjects as science and math, test questions do not travel well.

It should surprise no one that Japanese students, who attend school for some 243 days a year, who go to school on Saturdays, who attend "after-school" schools, and who have mothers at home pressuring them to do well, score higher than American youngsters.[31] (Whether or not American students should be in school for 243 days a year is a legitimate question that can be debated. But the simple-minded, context-free comparisons of narrow measures of achievement distort the situation.)

Likewise, it should surprise no one that Korean children, who traipse off to school for 220 days a year, score higher on the tests than their American counterparts. In addition to sitting in class 40 more days, the Koreans approach the tests differently. In one study, as each Korean student's name was called to come to the testing area, that child stood and exited the classroom to loud applause. What a personal honor to be chosen to perform for the honor of the nation!

For American students, this kind of test is a yawn. It comes into his or her life one day, then exits an hour later like a cognitive neutrino — a chargeless, massless, unnoticed particle of information. The American student won't even get the scores — nor will the teacher or the student's parents. American students won't be praised for how well they do or scolded for how poorly. Ho hum.

Two problems concerning language differences affect these international comparisons as well. First, the language used in the examination might not be the language that all people of a given nation speak. The Second International Assessment of Educational Progress (IAEP-2), in an assessment of math and science achievement that was conducted in March of 1991, tested Soviet students in Russian and tested Chinese students in Mandarin. As reasonable as this sounds at first, these are the languages in which the *better-educated* citizens of both nations tend to be most comfortable.

Second, there is the problem of translation. Anyone familiar with a language other than English knows that translations can be tough — a word with a given meaning in English might be rendered by several different words in, say, French. Moreover, each of those French words would have a meaning somewhat different from that of the single English word.

In past comparisons, some words in English simply didn't exist in other tongues. For example, on a test requiring students to judge two words as either near synonyms or near antonyms, only about

50% of Americans chose the correct alternative for the pair "pessimistic-sanguine." Ninety-eight percent of Finnish students got it right. On further examination, researchers discovered that Finnish has no equivalent for the word *sanguine* and that the word substituted for it was the dead giveaway *optimistic*. About such problems, a spokesperson for the International Association for the Evaluation of Educational Achievement (IEA), an organization that conducts many of these comparisons, has noted, "We can only hope that the tests are equally unfair to most cultures."[32]

The international comparisons lead us farthest astray, however, when they compare American youngsters, almost all of whom are in school, with a highly selected group of students from other countries. Most countries have massive dropout rates, with many students dropping out at the end of elementary school. The IAEP-2 in math and science conducted last March will include results for students in Brazil, Mozambique, and China. Only 35% of the young people in Brazil are still in school at age 13; only 5% of the elementary students in war-ravaged Mozambique stay around long enough to reach eighth grade.[33] And China hopes to have universal education through the *sixth grade* by the end of the century.[34] While it is easy to describe (and locate) a representative sample of American students, in some countries the census data are so inaccurate and unreliable that no one can say with any certainty what a representative sample would even look like.

Moreover, many nations that do educate more than a small fraction of their students to levels beyond the early grades, such as Great Britain and Germany, make life-directing decisions early and track students into academic or job-related programs around age 13. According to the IEA, this selectivity greatly affects what it calls the "opportunity to learn." Whether the selection comes about through dropping out or through tracking, we should not compare the resulting elite groups of students to a sample of American students that represents virtually everyone.

Even where there are similar percentages of students enrolled in the same grades, we cannot assume that they are studying the same things. A far smaller percentage of students in Hong Kong study advanced math in the 12th grade than do so in either Japan or the U.S. It is thus no accident that, in international comparisons, those nations that enroll the fewest students in a given area of study score the highest: A small elite will always outperform a large mass of students.[35]

And even the way in which the tests are administered varies from nation to nation. Most countries do not use standardized tests to the extent that we do in the U.S. Giving students a few extra minutes to work on a standardized test can elevate scores substantially. Proctors who are not paying close attention to time limits have contributed to the degradation of international comparisons.

Where the curriculum itself is concerned, the U.S. differs from other countries — and not just because, as some believe, we use watered-down textbooks, assign mindless worksheets, and subject students to lectures. For example, in many countries what is judged important must be taught before eighth grade in order to ensure that most students will be exposed to the material. Thus, in some nations, eighth-graders have been taught much more geometry than have American students. While we weave geometric concepts into the curriculum at all grade levels, we *choose* to teach geometry as a course of study primarily in the 10th grade, knowing that nearly all U.S. students will still be around to take it if they want to — or if their parents or counselors say they must. Many countries cannot afford the luxury of waiting, and so their students appear to know more than American students precisely because of their higher dropout rates.

President Bush and the nation's governors decided that one of the national goals for education should be to make the U.S. first in the world in math and science by the year 2000. They appear to want to base this competition on test results. But if we consider indicators other than test scores, we can argue, without puffery, that the U.S. *already* leads the world in science, mathematics, and technology. Moreover, it has done so for some time and shows no sign of losing ground.

I will ignore data on the dominance of the U.S. in the Nobel Prize competition because some might object that this reflects immigration just prior to and during World War II. (Still, many winners were educated in this country, and one must wonder how such a terrible system failed to cripple them, much less managed to produce them.) However, a variety of other indicators put the U.S. out in front in math and science.

A 1976 study estimated that there were more than 40,000 professional journals in the sciences and that researchers were pumping articles into those journals at the rate of one article every 30 seconds, seven days a week, 24 hours a day, 365 days a year.[36] Americans accounted for between 30% and 40% of *all* publications in those journals of engineering, mathematics, biomedical research, physics, earth/space sciences, chemistry, and biology. No one else even came close: Great Britain, Japan, and the Soviet Union all tied for second at 8%. What's more, these figures have remained stable since 1973.[37] If our schools provided a sow's-ear education in science and math, would it be possible for our universities to turn it into such a scientific silk purse?

In a related matter, concern has been expressed in many quarters that U.S. students are not choosing to study science and engineering and that these departments in our universities are being swamped by foreigners. But our schools of science and engineering are not on the wane. The number of degrees awarded in engineering, in physical science, and in mathematics has grown from 90,000 in 1977 to 175,000 in 1987, *despite* the shrinking population of traditional college-age students.[38] (An aside from the past: the baby boomers of the Sixties scarfed up engineering degrees like no other group in history, peaking in 1970. And you thought the Sixties were all sex, drugs, and rock 'n' roll.)

In the field of engineering there is also news to cheer about concerning minority participation: *all* minority groups showed greater increases than did whites in the rate at which they obtained engineering degrees. The differences range from a low for Native Americans (who doubled the rate of increase for whites) to a high for Asians (whose rate of increase was seven times that for whites).[39]

Moreover, we remain among the most technologically oriented of countries. Only Japan and the former West Germany have comparable numbers of engineers per 10,000 workers: Japan, 188; U.S., 184; West Germany, 182. By contrast, Great Britain has 132, and France has 104.[40]

It is true that U.S. universities currently award about 50% of all doctoral degrees in engineering to foreigners. But this constitutes a great brain drain *into* the United States, for a majority of foreign doctoral recipients continue to work in this country either on permanent or temporary visas. Less than half hop a plane back to their native countries after receiving their degrees. When it comes to the world of engineering, we educate the world, and we keep the best and the brightest.

Reading about jobs in the future could lead one to think that all workers will need engineering degrees. *A Nation at Risk* referred fearfully to jobs that "will involve laser technology and robotics." It continued, "Computers and computer-controlled equipment are penetrating every aspect of our lives."

In fact, the shape of the workforce our schools are producing matches pretty closely the shape of the workforce needed in the future (which is a good thing, since 71% of the workers for the year 2000 are already in the workforce). The two studies that give evidence of how much education it will take to do the jobs of the future and how much education our students will need differ, but neither gives particular cause for alarm.

In 1985 the Hudson Institute projected that, between 1985 and 1999, 19% of the new jobs that will be created could be performed by high school dropouts.[41] Seventeen percent of U.S. students drop out (though, as noted above, not necessarily permanently). Sixty-one percent of the new jobs will require a high school diploma and up to three years of college; 60% of our current crop of young people meet this requirement. Only 20% of newly created jobs will require a college degree, and 26% of our current high school graduates obtain bachelor's degrees.

A more recent study by the National Center on Education and the Economy finds a more even distribution, with 34% of new jobs projected to require less than a high school diploma, 36% a diploma and up to three years of college, and 30% a college degree.[42]

By this estimate, overeducation seems to be a more pressing problem than insufficient education.

As with analyses of dropout rates, much of the discussion surrounding the future skill levels of the workforce confuses *rates* with *numbers*. It is true that the occupations predicted to have the greatest growth between 1988 and the year 2000 will require greater than average skills. But these occupations account for less than 4% of all jobs. Moreover, the projected increase is based on generous assumptions about how fast the economy will grow; and, even if those assumptions prove correct, by the year 2000 three out of four jobs will still demand less than a college education.[43]

While some surveys find employers concerned about the lack of "basic skills" that students bring with them to the workplace, other surveys find employers more sanguine. Only 5% of employers believe that education and skill requirements are increasing significantly. Only 15% report difficulty finding skilled workers, and these shortages are generally in the chronically underpaid "women's positions," such as nurse and secretary, which might be a reflection of the times. Women can now aspire to be the doctor, not the nurse; the executive, not the secretary.[44]

Listening to the rhetoric of the reports, the legislators, and the media pundits, we would conclude that virtually all our graduates leave school functionally illiterate. Eighty percent of employers *do* express concern about the "skills" of young workers — but not primarily about the academic skills they bring from school. Instead, they complain that young people lack a work ethic: They don't show up on time or don't show up at all, and they don't work hard when they're present (teachers complain about the same things). Moreover, they don't have the social skills to deal with customers and co-workers, and they don't speak proper (i.e., standard) English.

Given these complaints, it is interesting to see where business puts its money for training. While 34% of all jobs are categorized as unskilled labor, only 15% of training dollars are spent on such jobs. Skilled labor takes up another 36% of jobs, and these jobs get 20% of the training dollars. Jobs that require a college education account for the remaining 30% of jobs — but 65% of all training dollars are spent on workers in these positions.[45] The push for training in business — if dollars spent are any gauge — is not to increase the basic skills of unskilled or skilled labor but to augment the skills of the most highly trained personnel.

What's more, I wonder about the complaints that I do hear about the skills of workers. While employers talk a great deal about pushing decisions down in the hierarchy, my experience is that the relationship between most employers and their employees is only slightly different from that of a plantation owner and a slave. Indeed, the fact that only 5% of employers foresee increasing skill requirements for jobs in the future reflects this relationship and is a source of worry to the people at the Hudson Institute and at the National Center on Education and the Economy who collected the data. They argue that the only way for the U.S. to become more productive — and so more competitive — is to increase the skill levels of our non-college-bound graduates.

While the analyses above do not convey unmitigated good news, they do convey a view of education quite different from what one typically sees in print. As readers of the notes to this article can see, the data I cite come primarily from sources available to any interested person. I can only assume that people have heard the opposite so often and for so long that they have come to assume it to be true.

Still, a number of possible rejoinders might be made to my analysis above. I will consider four here.

1. The trends for most indicators are stable because American schools are mediocre and always have been mediocre. One author has written of the crisis in education:

> The facts of the school crisis are all out in plain sight and pretty dreadful to look at. First of all, it has been shown that a surprisingly small percentage of high school students is studying what used to be considered basic subjects. . . . People are complaining that the diploma has been devalued to the point of meaninglessness. . . . To revitalize America's educational dream, we must stop kowtowing to the mediocre.

Although this quote has quite a contemporary ring to it, the words were penned by novelist Sloan Wilson for the 24 March 1958 issue of *Life* magazine.[46] Wilson decried social promotion, the decline of standards, automatic graduation, grade inflation, the proliferation of electives, and the neglect of intellectually gifted students. He seems not to have been aware that, in the late Fifties, fewer than half of all U.S. students finished high school.

Wilson's essay was the culmination of the first segment of a four-part series on the "Crisis in Education." The remainder of the first part compared American schools to their Russian counterparts. The results sound very much like current comparisons of American and Japanese schools. It seemed clear that, without massive reform, the Russians would deliver on Khrushchev's boast and bury us.

So it may be that to say nothing much has changed in the last 33 years leaves us still "kowtowing to mediocrity." But those who would hold this view and at the same time hold the view that education is linked to international competitiveness face the difficult task of explaining how mediocrity in one generation was linked to international economic ascendance and in another generation to international economic decline. In fact, the link between our education system and our economic productivity is tenuous at best. The connection has often been alleged, but it has never been demonstrated.

2. *The indicators are not sufficiently sensitive to detect the changes that have occurred.* This argument puts the burden of proof on its proponents, because the indicators discussed above represent a wide sampling of the only indicators we have. In fact, many of these indicators have been used to argue *for* educational decline. As we have seen, the evidence from SAT scores and from NAEP assessments does indicate a small decline in verbal skills. But this drop is scarcely the enormous calamity that the purveyors of the crisis rhetoric would have us believe.

There is a problem with most of the indicators: They rest on "passive" performance — that is, on multiple-choice tests. Multiple-choice tests have so dominated the field of testing in the U.S.

that many people believe they have shaped the form of instruction as well. Reports abound that teaching sometimes looks like preparation for the ITBS or for the California Achievement Tests. At the same time, more people are in college than ever before, and scores on the GRE are up.

Unfortunately, historical databases on performance assessments do not exist. This means that those who argue that today's performance is down must rely on conjecture, unless someone can develop a means for estimating performance in years gone by.

3. *The performance of the education system over time is not the issue. Level performance is not good enough; the rules have changed, and — to stay competitive internationally — the education system must do better.* Here I would defer to the experts in international affairs, but it doesn't seem obvious to me that the decline in our economic standing stems from problems in the schools — or will be reversed merely by solving them. Are the schools responsible for the management decisions that kept Detroit turning out self-destructing, two-ton gas guzzlers until it lost its dominance of the market? Did the schools' sloppy pedagogy prevent industry from automating until it was too late? Does the schools' failure to teach students to delay gratification explain why far too many business people keep their eyes focused on the quarterly profit sheet and not on the strategic plan? Did the lack of emphasis on basic skills produce the savings-and-loan debacle and its coming cousins in the banking and insurance industries? Did U.S. schools somehow decree that Korean workers would toil for low wages?

To reread *A Nation at Risk* eight years after its publication is to see it as a xenophobic screed that has little to do with education. Consider the now-familiar opening:

> Our Nation is at risk. Our once unchallenged preeminence in commerce, industry, science, and technological innovation is being overtaken by competitors throughout the world. . . . What was unimaginable a generation ago has begun to occur — others are matching and surpassing our educational attain- ·ments.[47]

"Surpassing" is surely questionable and so is "unimaginable a generation ago," when, of course, our bugaboo was the Soviets and their schools. And elsewhere this first paragraph does acknowledge that education is only one of "many causes and dimensions" of the problem, though one that "undergirds American prosperity, security, and civility." But the real question to ask of the Bell commission is, Why on earth would we expect anything else?

The Marshall Plan was designed to get countries that were defeated in World War II back on their feet. Should it surprise us that our "preeminence," established largely through military success, should have faded somewhat as other countries began to strive for the "good life" as America has defined it? Certainly it would have been silly to expect anything else. The Bell commission makes it sound as though our "unchallenged preeminence" should remain unchallenged forever, calling to mind the Manifest Destiny that fueled our push to the Pacific more than a century ago.

Whatever the failings of our schools, one thing is clear: The link between education and international competitiveness is as tenuous as that between education and economic well-being.

4. After almost a decade of reform, test scores should be going up, not merely remaining stable. This is a charge that cannot be answered at this time. It is probably too early to tell with any certainty just what came of the reforms of the Eighties, although three authors from widely disparate political positions have judged the reforms to have produced little or nothing.[48] Linking changes in the indicators I've cited here to reforms involving some form of "restructuring" is still more difficult. On curricular reforms, such as those undertaken by California or those recommended by the National Council of Teachers of Mathematics, data are not yet available.

There are plenty of problems in education that we ought to be working on. But we should be dealing with them because, like Everest, they are there. Americans have a natural inclination to seek improvement that often tumbles over into perfectionism. Good! Let's work to make things better. But let's not do it while telling people in the schools what a crummy job they're doing.

A snippet from *Bye, Bye, Birdie* forms the title of this essay. The entire refrain goes, "Why can't they be like we were, perfect in every way? Oh, what's the matter with kids today?" Listening to many of the critics of the schools sets me to humming this ditty. Given that it was written in 1960, when many of us were kids, shouldn't we be just a little more reluctant about pointing out what's wrong with the current crop of kids?

Notes

1. Edward B. Fiske, *Smart Schools, Smart Kids: Why Do Some Schools Work?* (New York: Simon & Schuster, 1991).
2. Chester E. Finn, Jr., *We Must Take Charge: Our Schools and Our Future* (New York: Macmillan, 1991), p. 14.
3. National Commission on Excellence in Education, *A Nation at Risk: The Imperative for Educational Reform* (Washington, D.C.: U S. Government Printing Office, 1983), p. 5.
4. Richard Cohen, "Johnny's Miserable SATs," *Washington Post,* 4 September 1990, p. A-19.
5. National Center for Education Statistics, *The Condition of Education 1991, Vol. 1, Elementary and Secondary Education* (Washington, D.C.: U.S. Department of Education, 1991), p. 27.
6. Ibid.
7. *Dealing with Dropouts* (Washington, D.C.: Office of Educational Research and Improvement, U.S. Department of Education, November 1987), p. 1.
8. *Report on Dropouts: 1988* (Washington, D.C.: Office of Educational Research and Improvement, U.S. Department of Education, November 1989).
9. *Trends in Educational Achievement* (Washington, D.C.: Congressional Budget Office, April 1986), p. xvii; and *Educational Achievement: Explanations and Implications of Recent Trends* (Washington, D.C.: Congressional Budget Office, August 1987), p. 14.
10. Gerald W. Bracey et al., *Report on Standardized Testing* (Englewood, Colo.: Cherry Creek School District, 1987-90).
11. *Trends in Educational Achievement.*
12. John J. Cannell, *National Norm-Referenced Elementary Achievement Testing in America's Public Schools: How All Fifty States Are*

Above the National Average (Charleston, W.Va.: Friends of Education, 1987).

13. *Accelerating Educational Achievement* (Princeton, N.J.: Educational Testing Service, 1990), p. 31.

14. National Center for Education Statistics, *The Condition of Education 1990, Vol. 1, Elementary and Secondary Education* (Washington, D.C.: U.S. Department of Education, 1990), p. 9.

15. Willard Wirtz et al., *On Further Examination: Report of the Commission to Examine the Decline in SAT Scores* (New York: College Board, 1977).

16. *College Bound Seniors, 1990* (New York: College Board, 1990).

17. This comparison derived from a conversation with William Angoff at ETS headquarters in October 1990.

18. Thomas F. Donlon and William H. Angoff, "The Scholastic Aptitude Test," in William H. Angoff, ed., *The College Board Admissions Testing Program: A Technical Report* (New York: College Board, 1971).

19. "Scholastic Ability," *Policy Notes,* Educational Testing Service, Fall 1989.

20. Harrison Salisbury, "What Americans Know About the Soviet Union," *McCall's,* June 1957, pp. 40-41.

21. *Performance at the Top: From Elementary Through Graduate School* (Princeton, N.J.: Educational Testing Service, 1991).

22. National Center for Education Statistics, *College-Level Remedial Education in the Fall of 1989* (Washington, D.C.: U.S. Department of Education, May 1991).

23. C. C. Carson, R. M. Huelskamp, and T. D. Woodall, "Perspective on Education in America," Third Draft, Sandia National Laboratories, Albuquerque, N.M., May 1991.

24. National Center for Education Statistics, *The Condition of Education 1991, Vol. 2, Postsecondary Education* (Washington, D.C.: U.S. Department of Education, 1991), pp. 220-21.

25. Ibid., pp. 36-37.

26. "Analysis of the U.S. System of Education," Second Report, Sandia National Laboratories, Albuquerque, N.M., January 1991.

27. Carson, Huelskamp, and Woodall, pp. 80-81.

28. National Center for Education Statistics, *The Condition of Education 1991, Vol. 1,* p. 234.

29. "International Comparison of Public Spending on Education," American Federation of Teachers, Washington, D.C., February 1991.

30. National Center for Education Statistics, *The Condition of Education 1991, Vol. 1,* p. 230.

31. Michael J. Barren, "The Case for More School Days," *The Atlantic,* September 1990, p. 78.

32. "Technical Issues in International Assessments," a symposium at the annual meeting of the American Educational Research Association, Chicago, 1991.

33. Iris C. Rotberg, "I Never Promised You First Place," *Phi Delta Kappan,* December 1990, p. 298.

34. Lun Bing and Yang Zhi-Ling, speech delivered at Phi Delta Kappa International Headquarters, Bloomington, Ind., 9 January 1990.

35. Rotberg, p. 297.

36. Michael Mahoney, "Open Exchange and Epistemic Progress," *American Psychologist,* January 1985, pp. 29-39.

37. Rotberg, p. 300.

38. Carson, Huelskamp, and Woodall, pp. 58-59.

39. Ibid., pp. 62-63.

40. Ibid., p. 107.

41. Ibid., pp. 126-27.

42. Ibid., pp. 128-29.

43. Ibid., pp. 126-27.

44. Ibid., pp. 128-29.

45. Ibid., pp. 134-35.

46. Sloan Wilson, "It's Time to Close Our Carnival," *Life,* 24 March 1958, pp. 36-37.

47. National Commission on Excellence in Education, p. 5.

48. Fiske, op. cit.; Finn, op. cit.; and Thomas Toch, *In the Name of Excellence: The Struggle to Reform the Nation's Public Schools. Why It's Failing, and What Should Be Done* (New York: Oxford University Press, 1991).

THE SECOND BRACEY REPORT ON THE CONDITION OF PUBLIC EDUCATION

October 1992

Just about the time Adam first whispered to Eve that they were living through an age of transition, the Serpent doubtless issued the first complaint that academic standards were beginning to decline.[1]

This issue of the *Kappan* [October 1992] marks the anniversary of the publication of the first "Bracey Report," titled "Why Can't They Be Like We Were?" In that article I presented a mass of evidence to show that schools were not in the state of collapse some observers had claimed. Times since then have been anything but dull. No one expected so many strong reactions to that essay, to the Sandia report, or to articles by Harold Hodgkinson and by Iris Rotberg, all of which appeared at about the same time and arrived at similar conclusions.[2] The responses have proved interesting, sometimes troubling.

In front-page stories, *Education Week* dubbed the three of us and the Sandia researchers "revisionists," while *USA Today* hailed us as "Defenders of U.S. Schools."[3] Removed from the front page, but still in Section A, a piece in the *New York Times* tagged us "renegade researchers."[4]

37

At a presentation to the Forum of Education Organization Leaders, the executive director of the American Association of School Administrators called me a hero for writing the article. At the time, I did not think writing an article compiling research required much courage. However, when I returned home, I found a letter from a professor friend applauding the article but commenting that "the American common school is an endangered species. The wimps in education will not defend it. They are afraid of losing their federal dollars or access to the corridors of power." Another professor friend, commenting on the article's role in my dismissal from the staff of the National Education Association, wrote that "it probably wasn't a good time to stick your head up out of the trench."

When I told yet another friend about these letters, he remarked that, after he himself had raised some controversial issues, he received letters from professors — full professors with tenure — encouraging him to speak out more. At the same time, several Washington firms told me that they could not hire me, the article having rendered me "politically incorrect" (their phrase). They worried that my presence might endanger their contracts with the Department of Education or with the Department of Health and Human Services. In sum, it began to seem that courage may be in short supply in the education research community.

Also at the Forum of Education Organization Leaders, I was asked if I had been contacted by any of the then-numerous Democratic candidates for President. I had not and have not been contacted nor, to the best of my knowledge, have any of the other so-called revisionists.

The silence of the Democrats is a bit odd since members of the Bush and Reagan Administrations have been actively assaulting us in public, which should have at least piqued the curiosity of the opposing party. On the op-ed page of the *Washington Post,* Assistant Secretary of Education Diane Ravitch labeled us messengers of complacency.[5] In *USA Today,* former Secretary of Education William Bennett dismissed our findings, saying, "If the area was drugs, you'd call it denial."[6] In reaction to an oral presentation by the Sandia engineers, Deputy Secretary of Education David Kearns said, "You bury this, or I'll bury you." Ravitch later denied in a public forum that Kearns had uttered those words, but persons in the room — other than the Sandia presenters — have stated that he did, although none are in a position to go on record at this time.

By the time the weather had finally turned warm this spring, however, the world had begun to move our way. David Berliner and Richard Jaeger had added their voices and had supplied much additional data to support our contentions.[7] Elliot Eisner had raised a host of important questions that have not even been considered in the present federal reform effort.[8] In his *New York Times* column of May 10, Albert Shanker wrote, "People who say that U.S. schools are performing better than ever in most respects are correct." Along the way the nation had discovered that the long-predicted, long-feared shortage of scientists had not developed and did not seem likely to do so, since the forecasts had been based on faulty assumptions. Indeed, there was even a surplus of mathematicians.[9] With the end of the Cold War, existing surpluses should grow, for one-third of our scientists and engineers work for the Pentagon.

Not everyone took these signs as indicators that things were better than had been thought, however. In April 1992 Marc Tucker was quoted in the *New York Times* as saying of this body of data, "It's true but irrelevant"[10] — a comment that reflects what might be called the critics' "new orthodoxy" about what's wrong with the schools. (I will deal with the relevance or irrelevance of this truth below.) And many people still wrote articles and editorials that assumed school failure and often stated that test scores were still falling. For example, in his column of August 4, *Washington Post* columnist Richard Cohen stated that, during the Reagan/Bush years, "the country got . . . dumber on just about every achievement test the kids could take."[11] But scores are rising and have been for some time.

It seems to me that *Washington Post* columnist William Raspberry made the most complete and interesting turnabout with regard to the supposed failure of the schools. On 12 October 1991, in the opening paragraph of a column on different conceptions of intelligence, Raspberry mentioned "the bewildering failure of American education." It was a throwaway line, a simple fact of life, unchallengeable. Naturally, I sent him my *Kappan* article. He summarized it in his column of October 28 and challenged readers to show him how I had bamboozled him.[12] I guess no one did (though Ravitch tried), because by February 1992 Raspberry had this to say: "[We] knew it all along. . . . American schools are doing a pretty good job of teaching children who arrive at school ready to learn."[13] Ah, yes, children ready to learn. Therein lies the rub.

At the 1992 meeting of the American Educational Research Association (AERA), where in a symposium I debated Ravitch and Lauren Resnick on the condition of education, Berliner contended from the floor that we ought to be able to advance an agenda of what we want schools to be — without, in the process, having to bash them for what they are. Resnick and Ravitch immediately "signed on" to this perspective and course of action. I urged the audience to watch what they did, not what they said.[14]

So there you have it. In the course of a year, those who were disparaging the schools have come to acknowledge that schools are performing as well as or better than ever, and we can hope that the days of school-bashing are over. However, the most common reaction to this news is that of Tucker: it's irrelevant. The new orthodoxy contends that, no matter how good the schools are, they are not good enough. "It is not good enough to be as good as we were in 1940 or in 1970," Ravitch told the AERA symposium. And she is not alone in espousing these views. "If I buy a car, I don't give a damn if it's better than the 1970 model," said Shanker. "I care whether it's better than the Japanese car across the street."[15] The general argument runs along these lines: The rules have changed; we've got to do more to stay competitive internationally; we need a more highly skilled work force.

Before I address these arguments, I would first like to present data that have come to light since my October 1991 article appeared. These data supply additional evidence that the education system — as a system — continues to perform better than ever, an amazing finding given the severe decline in other social institutions. The data point to the need for a different reform strategy, one that is better focused than the one currently in place, which assumes that the typical school is failing and that the typical student is getting dumber each year. The data strongly imply that "choice" will not affect the schools that need help the most and that these "needy" schools will find the results of the New Standards Project irrelevant — high standards are meaningless in the absence of textbooks and other materials that schools serving the middle class take for granted. The data reveal that the U.S. continues to have the highest productivity in the world and in some quarters is becoming more competitive internationally. Such improvements stem from better decisions by a newly awakened management, not from an increasingly skilled work force.

Achievement Test Scores

I made little of achievement test scores in my initial article for two reasons. First, I don't think they measure particularly important outcomes. Second, I was aware that testing's "Lake Wobegon Effect" — all the children are above average — had diminished the credibility of test scores.

Yet even as I wrote last year's article, data in hand showed test scores rising in ways that cheating or curriculum alignment could not account for. The 1989 Iowa Tests of Basic Skills (ITBS) for the schools in Cherry Creek, Colorado, had been scored using four sets of norms: 1978, 1982, 1985, and 1988. Each newer set of norms was designed to be "harder" than the previous one: that is, a given raw score translated into a lower percentile rank for each of the more recent sets of norms. Students had to run faster to stay in the same place.

More dramatic trends come from Iowa, where a low-stakes testing program has been in operation since 1934. Trendlines in Iowa show scores falling in the late Sixties and early Seventies, then rising again. By 1991 the ITBS scores for grades 3 through 7 were at all-time highs, and grade 8 was nearing an all-time high. Grades 9, 10, and 11 were at all-time highs on the Iowa Tests of Educational Development (ITED), and grade 12 was close.[16]

These results would be of limited importance if they pertained only to Iowa. However, when results of national norming studies of the ITBS and ITED are placed on the Iowa trend lines, they fit well: The phenomenon appears to be nationwide. Robert Linn and his colleagues have found similar, although somewhat smaller, results for a large array of standardized tests.[17] In the case of Iowa, it should be noted that, while the ITBS measures "basic skills," the ITED is a difficult test. Thus one cannot make the argument that children are learning "the basics" at the expense of higher-order skills.

In a different curriculum arena, when Diane Ravitch and Chester Finn asked in the title of their 1987 book, *What Do Our 17-Year-Olds Know?* their answer was "not much." "If there were such a thing as a national report card for those studying American history and literature, then we would have to say that this nationally representative sample of 11th-graders earns failing marks on both subjects," they wrote.[18] However, Dale Whittington has observed that their item selection techniques guaranteed low scores. Ravitch and Finn set the pass/fail score at 60%; then they used norm-referenced items that, on average, half of all test-takers get wrong. A test made up of 100 such items would yield an average score of 50. No doubt Ravitch and Finn would have been equally dismayed at how many students missed each item, but their item selection method, coupled with the cutoff score they set, insured failure for most students.

More important, Whittington reviewed other studies of student achievement in American history from 1917, 1933, 1944, and 1964, taking as much care as possible to insure comparability of coverage. She found no decline over time and concluded:

> [E]ach group [of test-takers] performed about the same on
> the particular set of test questions designed for them to take.
> . . . Comparisons of student performance on test questions
> that matched the content of specific questions in the test used

by Ravitch and Finn seem to confirm the results of this study that, for the most part, students of the 1980s are not demonstrably different from students of their parents and grandparents' generation in terms of their knowledge of American history. . . . Indeed, given the reduced dropout rate and less elitist composition of the 17-year-old student body today, one could argue that students know more American history today than did their age peers of the past.[19]

Anecdotally speaking, Americans' ignorance of history and geography is legendary. Surely it is nothing to be proud of, but there appears to be no slippage. Given not only the less elitist student body, but also a curriculum crowded with new roles for teachers and with sex education, drug education, computer education, health education, parenting education, and so forth, holding one's own once again looks like running faster to stay in place.

Whittington's results are not unique. "Then-and-now" studies of test scores typically favor the now, no matter how we define the terms *then* and *now.* Carl Kaestle and his colleagues reviewed many then-and-now reading studies in *Literacy in the United States.* They found these studies "fraught with design and interpretation problems" but still ventured an "educated guess that schoolchildren of the same age and socioeconomic status have been performing at similar levels throughout most of the twentieth century."[20]

International Comparisons

In February 1992, with much attendant publicity, the Educational Testing Service (ETS) released the findings of the Second International Assessment of Educational Progress (IAEP-2).[21] Because the samples from various countries were not comparable, ETS cautioned against ranking nations. Of course, the press proceeded to rank them anyway — as ETS did in the body of its report. American 9-year-olds finished third among the 10 participating nations in science and ninth in mathematics. American 13-year-olds finished 14th of 15 nations in science and 13th of 15 in math. "An 'F' in World Competition," blared a headline in *Newsweek*. Indeed, *Newsweek* even tried to discount the third-place finish of 9-year-olds in science.[22] Good news is apparently no news.

The *Newsweek* coverage reflects the perverse attention that education gets from the media — when it gets any attention at all. And this perversity has been documented in George Kaplan's *Images of Education*. The media do not focus similar attention on other social institutions.[23] For example, the Children's Defense Fund reports that the U.S. ranks 19th in the world in infant mortality, 19th in the mortality of children before age 5, and 28th in the incidence of low birth weight infants.[24] These are much worse finishes than those in the testing olympics, but nowhere does one see the media indicting doctors and complaining about our dreadful hospitals. Indeed, these devastating figures are scarcely reported.

Newsweek also quoted Secretary of Education Lamar Alexander as saying that the U.S. spends more money on education than any other country. Misleading statements such as this one led Berliner to title the paper he presented to the February 1992 meeting of the American Association of Colleges for Teacher Education "Educational Reform in an Age of Disinformation."[25] Secretary Alexander's comment is true only if we include the costs of higher education. The U.S. spends a bundle on higher education because higher education costs more and because the U.S. sends almost twice as many high school graduates on to college as the next-highest nation. Currently, 68% of college-age students are enrolled in postsecondary institutions. This is double the rate for Japan and Germany and triple the rate for the United Kingdom.[26]

Per-pupil expenditures for elementary and secondary education can be calculated in a variety of ways. But no matter which method is used, the U.S. never finishes better than average and often places near the bottom.[27]

The IAEP-2 was the most sophisticated of the international studies to date; yet one is left wondering what it means. Rotberg has pointed out that the people who conduct these studies are very much aware of the problems; they simply haven't been able to solve them.[28] The problems are beyond the reach of sophisticated research design. Shanker and others have contended that 20 years' worth of studies showing American students finishing poorly can't be wrong.[29] But such an argument confuses reliability with validity. Rotberg has observed that the consistency of the findings means that all the studies have the same shortcomings.

The IAEP-2 and other international comparisons generally leave several other questions unanswered. Is a multiple-choice test the most appropriate measure of a nation's achievement? Even if it is, is there any relationship between test scores at ages 9 and 13 and later accomplishments by individuals or by nations? Is it wise to give weight to the scores of 13-year-olds? If you ask teachers in this country how students of different ages represent the achievements of the education system, they might well rank age 13 next-to-last — ahead of only the seniors, who don't take tests seriously. Teachers feel that many American 13-year-olds' cognitive development is in "mental pause."

The impact of motivation should not be underestimated. American students are the most tested in the world, bubbling in 100 million answer sheets a year. It takes some urging to get their enthusiasm up for yet another round of answer sheets. On the other hand, Archie Lapointe, executive director of IAEP-2, discovered a somewhat different attitude among top-ranked Korean children. When their names were called, they stood and exited for the testing room to the applause of their classmates.[30] Such an honor to perform for the nation! Lapointe described this anecdote in a manuscript written before the IAEP-2 tests were administered, so one wonders when it actually took place. In any event, I can attest that when the schools in Cherry Creek participated in the state-by-state National Assessment of Educational Progress (NAEP) in math and science, no such motivating factors were at play. Half of the teachers who had administered the tests stated in a debriefing that they had trouble keeping the children on-task.

Differences in motivation can seriously affect even familiar tests. One year, a computer program to detect cheating in Virginia state testing programs spit out the name of a mostly rural district. No

45

cheating had occurred, but the new superintendent, observing that few of his students went on to college, had decided the tests held little interest for them. To make the tests relevant, he had cast them as analogous to an athletic contest. Just as in football or basketball, students should give their all in order to beat the adjacent, arch-rival county. The week of testing, teachers dressed as cheerleaders and led pep rallies. Scores rose between 20 and 30 percentile ranks.

It is not clear how nations can use the results of international comparisons, and they may not do so wisely. Lapointe observed that some countries are sending delegates to ETS to study the goals of IAEP-2 and to examine areas in which their students did poorly, while Taiwan has adopted the goals of IAEP-2 as its curriculum to be emphasized.[31] High-stakes testing on a global scale! The U.S. Department of Education examined results from six international studies and reached the stunning conclusion that "the more students are taught, the more they learn.[32] Although this seems banal at first, it could be dangerous, implying as it does that we should unthinkingly teach more and faster. But we know that this practice backfires in Japan, where, when students reach college, they simply stop working and often don't bother to go to class.[33]

Also on the international front, *The Learning Gap,* by Harold Stevenson and James Stigler, did little to reassure anyone who even looked at it, much less read it. Its cover read, in its entirety, "Why Our Schools Are Failing and What We Can Learn from Japanese and Chinese Education." Its opening sentences sounded the alarm once more: "It is no secret by now that American education is in crisis. . . . Our children's academic achievement is in decline. We pour money into our schools, but we don't see a corresponding improvement in quality."[34]

Given the all-time high scores on achievement tests, coupled with rising scores on the College Board Achievement Tests, stable Advanced Placement tests in spite of many more test-takers, and stable NAEP results, one can certainly question the accuracy of the charge that "academic achievement is in decline."[35] The notion that we "pour money" into schools in greater amounts than other developed nations was dealt with above. Indeed, the costs of education have risen only modestly when the cost of special education is factored out.[36]

When data leave the research laboratory and enter the public domain, they invariably get romanticized. The conclusions of the authors of *The Learning Gap* with regard to academic achievement rest largely on two studies: one comparing students in Minneapolis with students in Taipei and Sendai, Japan; another measuring students in Chicago against those in Beijing.[37]

In spite of its inflammatory cover and opening fusillade, *The Learning Gap* does not look at "schools." It does not thoroughly scrutinize the entire system of education from kindergarten through graduate school in all curriculum areas. Stevenson and Stigler limit their discussion almost entirely to mathematics in grades 1 and 5. (Another of their studies did look at kindergarten, and there is apparently an 11th-grade follow-up of the Minneapolis study about to be published.)

In one of their studies, Stigler and his colleagues did collect reading and vocabulary test data.[38] American students equaled Japanese students in reading, and Americans outperformed their Japanese counterparts on a vocabulary test. Certainly one can wonder about the cross-cultural comparability of these tests, but one can also wonder why Stevenson and Stigler ignored these positive outcomes while touting the negative results in mathematics to lay and professional audiences alike.

Methodological problems too numerous to consider in detail afflict these studies. For example, in the Beijing/Chicago comparison, Chicago families had incomes from $0 to more than $60,000, with about 13% below $10,000 and the same number above $60,000 — many poor families and no really wealthy ones. Fifty percent of the Chinese children had at least one grandparent living with them, while grandparents resided in only 10% of the Chicago homes. The Chinese children were typically only children, an outcome of China's harsh policies of population control, while the Chicago households averaged nearly three children. Anecdotes abound about how these only children are highly valued in China.

The Chinese children thus live among a great many adults and probably receive a great deal more adult attention than do the American children. Nowhere do Stevenson and Stigler discuss these differences.

Moreover, the Chicago sample was 39% black or Hispanic, hardly representative of the nation. In addition, 84% of the Hispanic families, 13% of the white families, and 2% of the black families — 20% of all families — do not speak English at home. Stevenson and Stigler do not report how many Beijing families do not speak Mandarin at home, but the number is probably negligible.

Thus the Chicago and Beijing samples are in no way comparable. The Chicago sample is not representative of the U.S. and is characterized by many attributes associated with low achievement. It is impossible to say what the comparative achievement data mean, if anything.

Stevenson and Stigler have asserted that American children think they're good at math when they're not, while Asian children think they're not good when they are. Stevenson and Stigler have also stated that American children see successful performance as a result of ability, while Japanese children see success as a result of effort. The first assertion is problematic; their own results prove the second one false.

Stevenson and Stigler's questions did not directly ask the children whether they think they are good at math, so it is difficult to judge how they feel. In addition, these results don't seem to accord with those found by the American Association of University Women. (I say "seem" because the studies are not directly comparable.) The AAUW study found large percentages of children, especially girls, who do not think they're competent at math.[39] The percentages increased with age.

Moreover, anyone who has ever lived in the Orient knows the endemic modesty of the peoples there. One does not brag about anything, least of all about personal qualities. When I lived in Hong Kong, Chinese friends would recommend a restaurant with something like, "I think you might find that you will be given a reasonably acceptable meal there." And I would drool, knowing I had just received the Cantonese equivalent of a five-star rave review. It is odd that Stevenson and Stigler nowhere discuss these characteristics, especially considering that Stevenson has visited Japan off and on since 1949. These considerations also point to difficulties in international comparisons that no research design, no matter how sophisticated, can take into account.

As for the views of young people with regard to ability and effort, it is true that children in Beijing put their money on effort, but Stevenson and Stigler's own data show that American children rate effort just as high! They do give ability much more importance than Japanese children, but they still give it slightly less importance than effort. American children rank both ability and effort very high and almost equal in importance.[40] As one trained in developmental psychology during the height of the nature/nurture controversy, I would have to say that American children have a much better grasp of reality about this issue than do Japanese children. Ability counts. So does effort. And American kids know it. No wonder Berliner is concerned about disinformation.

The Learning Gap is not the only international report that requires closer scrutiny. Ian Westbury decided that all was not what it seemed with the Second International Math Study (SIMS).[41] The researchers had administered an algebra test to eighth-graders and a calculus test to 12th-graders, creating a test/curriculum mismatch for many American students who often take algebra in the ninth grade and calculus in college.

Westbury reanalyzed the SIMS data comparing American students in a variety of math classes with those in Japan, almost all of whom take algebra. American students in remedial and regular eighth-grade math performed below the Japanese. Students in classes labeled "enriched" equaled the Japanese, and the 20% of our eighth-graders who are actually taking algebra surpassed them.

Of course, comparing 20% of American students, presumably the top 20% academically, with all Japanese students creates a large selection bias in our favor. Therefore, Westbury compared American eighth-graders taking algebra with the top 20% of Japanese students. Once again, the American students performed better, although the difference is so small that "no difference" is the appropriate conclusion. Similar analyses of the data for calculus show greatly reduced differences between Americans and Japanese.

Westbury's analysis does not take American schools off the hook, but it does recast the question. As he points out, American teachers are doing a good job of teaching the curriculum they are asked to teach, and American students are doing a good job of learning the curriculum they are taught. The appropriate questions to ask are, What should we teach? When? And to whom? Should all American eighth-graders be taught algebra? By what rationale? Algebra currently functions as a "gatekeeper," but would it play that role if all students took it? And is that any reason to require it? Or consider the converse. By what criterion do we fail to give 80% of our eighth-graders the opportunity to learn algebra? These questions are not answerable with data.

Westbury seems to favor the "algebra-for-all" approach of Europe and Asia, but at least one professor of mathematics, Underwood Dudley, has argued for less algebra on the grounds that it is irrelevant to most people, that it is taught so poorly as to subvert its avowed goals, and that those for whom it will be relevant also show obvious talent for it.[42] Dudley writes lightheartedly, but he may be on to something serious. The *Washington Post* of May 15 described a public school program in Fairfax County, Virginia, in which parents returned to school to relearn algebra.[43] They had taken it in high school, had had no subsequent use for it, had forgotten it, and so couldn't help their children who were now struggling with it. This may tell us something about the relevance of algebra to life after school.

While the Council for Basic Education recently made the preposterous claim that in the near future " 'minimum competency' will come to mean knowledge of advanced algebra," the state department of education in New York analyzed the job demands of 1,400 jobs and found that 78% of them required no algebra; only 10% required more than just a little.[44] I updated Dudley's arguments with these and other facts and published them in the *Washington Post*.[45] Calls and letters pro and con ran about even. (Favorable calls might well have been a majority, but the headline writer, perhaps having suffered too much as a child at the hands of the binomial theorem, changed my mild, Dudleyesque title to "Cut Out Algebra!")

Dudley also argued that algebra does not discipline the mind (an argument supported by psychological research), because it is generally taught through rote memorization and the application of rules. The original *Washington Post* article stated that the teacher taught rules by invoking "the gods of algebra," who decree what can and cannot be done — hardly a prescription for building mental muscle.

If we decide to teach algebra to all eighth-graders, it might not turn out to be so traumatic for them. Thomas Romberg, a math educator at the University of Wisconsin, claims that we already ask students in seventh grade to do mathematical tasks that are more difficult than those required in algebra I.[46] However, he considers "calls to teach the traditional course to younger students ludicrous" and supports the teaching of algebraic concepts "integrated throughout the curriculum beginning in the early grades."[47]

Richard Jaeger (in the October 1992 *Kappan)* takes a different research tack. He examined nations' scores on the SIMS together with their scores on the First International Mathematics Study and found them strongly correlated with such variables as mean percentage of children living in poverty, mean percentage of children living in single-parent families, and mean percentage of youths who work. The correlation between test scores and the percentage of children living in poverty is a whopping .99, and the U.S. has the highest percentage of poor children among the countries in Jaeger's study. Admittedly, there are only a few data points — but even so, such a figure speaks volumes. Jaeger's findings may be explained in part by our low taxes: the U.S. placed 24th of 25 nations in terms of taxes as a percentage of gross domestic product, finishing just above Turkey.[48]

Other Social Institutions

During the past year we saw disturbing evidence — in the form of data and riots — of how far many social institutions have

51

declined. "In our time," wrote sociologist Todd Gitlin, "America has become a land of marauding gangs, of desperate homeless, and general surliness. The achievement of the last decade of American government has been to persuade a majority that this situation is normal."[49] In the dark shadows of these changes, the performance of education looks unusually bright, almost miraculous. Even in schools where the impact of social decline has not been the greatest, it is still felt. Guy Kelly, a reporter for the *Rocky Mountain News,* observed a team-taught class in a middle school in Aurora, Colorado. The school was 28% minority and about 50% middle class, hardly a decaying inner-city school. Kelly's three-part series begins:

> Donna Beck and Toni Lyman love to teach. Too bad things keep getting in the way.
>
> Instead of teaching, their days are filled with crisis intervention, counseling, parenting, and repeated doses of emotional first aid for children going through one of the most difficult periods of their lives.
>
> "There are days when you want to scream: Leave me alone and let me teach!" Lyman said.[50]

Recall that in one year these struggling children will reach the age most frequently tested in international comparisons. Even the *Wall Street Journal,* never an apologist for schools, recognized the conditions against which many schools must struggle:

> The problems of America's schools stem in large part from causes deep in the national experience: urban blight, the erosion of the family, and the long-standing failure to devote sufficient resources to the schools. In the face of these pressures, schools have been called upon to take over roles formerly played by the family, churches, and other agencies, ranging from sex education to housing and feeding children from dawn to dusk, well beyond school hours.
>
> We should stop pushing the corporate model on our schools. Competition, after all, produces losers as well as winners. Mr. Alexander might more usefully spend his time and influence supporting Headstart and other successful early-child-

hood education programs, getting beginning teachers' pay above the poverty level, . . . and placing the "funding of education," not merely "education," in the high position it ought to occupy on our national agenda.[51]

Perhaps the single most interesting way of looking at social decline is Fordham University's Index of Social Health, sometimes referred to as the Dow Jones of the Soul, which fell to an all-time low in 1989, the latest year for which figures are available.[52] The Index combines 17 indicators — such as infant mortality rate, food stamp rate, homicide rate, and so on — into a single scale that takes on the values between 0 and 100. The Index peaked at 72 in 1976 and plummeted to 32 in 1989. It averaged a miserable 38.6 for the decade of the Eighties, and its producers are confident that it will sink even further when the numbers for 1990 and 1991 arrive.

The only educational indicator in the Index is the dropout rate, which has been stable or improving. It is not the schools that are dragging the Index down.

In a separate Urban Index in the same report, the Fordham researchers use five indicators — homicide, infant mortality, poverty, child abuse, tuberculosis — to track social health in three cities: New York, Chicago, and Los Angeles. Never as high as the Index for the nation as a whole, the Urban Index improved in the early Eighties, then reversed course and also fell to an all-time low in 1989. On page 10 of the report, the Fordham researchers note: "The Urban Index presents a picture of substantial decline in the social health of the cities. . . . Most significant is the steep downward trend of the final two years of the study, 1988 and 1989, where the social health of the three cities declined by 19 points, an extraordinary drop for a two-year period." Considering the state of the Index of Social Health, it comes as no surprise that Phi Delta Kappa's study of children at risk not only found large percentages of children in that category but also found that children at risk on one indicator are often at risk on many others: "Children who hurt, hurt all over. Children who fail often fail at everything they do. Risk is pervasive. If a student is at risk in one area, that student is very likely to be at risk in many other areas; thus efforts to help may be confounded because other problems are involved." For example, a student who had excessive absences from school was also much more likely to get low grades, have a father with a low-level job, move frequently, and, generally, score worse — often much worse — on all of the 33 indicators of risk identified in the study than a child without excessive absences.[53]

The Bush plan for education reform, America 2000, ignores all these problems. I cannot improve on Henry Giroux's description of the plan:

> Organized around the imperatives of choice, standardized testing, and the reprivatization of public schools, [America 2000] displays no sense of urgency in addressing the importance of schooling for improving the quality of democratic public life. Not only does it suffer from a curious form of historical amnesia by refusing to build on the gains of programs that have been quite successful in addressing the needs of children from subordinate groups. . . . but it also has written out of its script some of the most pressing difficulties facing administrators and teachers in America's schools.
>
> America 2000 ignores such problems as child poverty at a time when 40% of all children are classified as poor; it ignores the pressing problem of unemployment when the unemployment rate among black male teens in March 1991 was 38.4%. It ignores issues of health care, teenage pregnancy, drugs, violence, and racial discrimination at a time when these issues play a central role in defining the quality of life for increasing numbers of students in this country. Instead of addressing how these issues impact upon schools and undermine how children learn, America 2000 focuses on issues such as testing and choice.[54]

Through a quirky historical coincidence, Giroux's article appeared just days before the Los Angeles riots.

An idea of how America 2000 ignores pressing social problems can be gleaned from the U.S. Department of Labor's *What Work Requires of Schools: A SCANS Report for America 2000.* Before

54

setting out its recommendations for curriculum and instruction, SCANS (the Secretary's Commission on Achieving Necessary Skills) presents several vignettes that illustrate the need for the required skills. Here is part of one:

> Luretta is the registrar in the emergency room of City Hospital, a large public facility on the West Coast serving a diverse, urban population. She is the first person patients meet when they enter the hospital. Stress in the emergency room is almost tangible, particularly on weekends. Residents of nearby low income neighborhoods use the facility for routine health care; accident victims from all over the area are frequently brought to City; and gang violence produces many severely wounded patients. . . . As Luretta takes a breather, an ambulance crew brings in a local college student suffering a drug overdose. As the LPS leaves, a gunshot victim staggers in on the arm of a friend. . . ."[55]

Set aside any question about whether public hospitals these days are providing "routine health care" to low-income patients. From this scene it would not be too much of an exaggeration to say that SCANS fiddles as the country burns. No doubt this description accurately represents current urban reality, but SCANS accepts the drugs, gangs, and guns — it cares only that Luretta have the skills to do her job.

As if to underscore Giroux's assessment of America 2000, in July 1992 President Bush proposed giving $1,000 in tuition grants to allow children to attend any legally operating school — public, private, or religious. The program has been dubbed the "G.I. Bill for Children." Shanker promptly and accurately labeled it "G.I. Bull."[56] The Administration argues that the program would help both public and private schools. (Interestingly, according to the most recent analysis of NAEP data, public and private schools differ little, in spite of the enormously advantageous circumstances private schools enjoy.[57])

Bush's program seems all the more curious in view of data from the 1990 Census showing that more children than ever are falling behind grade level.[58] And this is true in spite of the achievement increases discussed earlier. Those most affected, of course, are the children of the poor and minorities. We shouldn't be surprised by these data, of course: Whenever city test scores are disaggregated by ethnic group, the advantages of white students over black and Hispanic students are huge. If I assume for the moment that the international comparisons are valid, it astonishes me that Bush and Secretary of Education Lamar Alexander rail at relatively small differences between the U.S. and other countries and maintain a stony silence on the enormous gaps in achievement test scores between rich and poor students, between black and white students, and between Hispanic and white students right in our own backyard.

Education, Productivity, and International Competitiveness

As an incisive general comment on education, productivity, and economic competitiveness, the following statement by Lawrence Cremin cannot be improved upon.

> American economic competitiveness with Japan and other nations is to a considerable degree a function of monetary, trade, and industrial policy, and of decisions made by the President and Congress, the Federal Reserve Board, and the federal departments of the Treasury and Commerce and Labor.
>
> Therefore, to contend that problems of international competitiveness can be solved by educational reform, especially educational reform defined solely as school reform, is not merely Utopian and millennialist, it is at best foolish and at worst a crass effort to direct attention away from those truly responsible for doing something about competitiveness and to lay the burden on the schools. It is a device that has been used repeatedly in the history of American education.[59]

Certainly Cremin's words refute Alexander's bizarre remark that "for the country to change, the schools have to change."[60] The nation as dependent variable. What a concept! Still, Cremin's analysis needs specific data to demonstrate its veracity and to show that the role of the education system in the competitiveness crisis exists primarily in the minds of school critics.

For example, a graph in *Newsweek* depicted the defect rate of American and Japanese automobile manufacturers between 1981 and 1991.[61] In 1981 American cars had three to four times as many defects as Japanese vehicles. But American cars improved sharply over the decade, and by 1991 little difference could be seen among all companies. According to the bad-schools-produce-bad-workers theory, this curve should not exist. If declining schools affected the workforce in any way during the 1980s, we might argue from this curve that we should encourage further decline.

As winter 1991 approached, arguments over competitiveness polarized into what *Education Week* called "a think tank war."[62] One side, represented by the Hudson Institute's *Workforce 2000* and *America's Choice: High Skills or Low Wages,*[63] espoused the bad-schools-produce-bad-workers position. The other side, inspired by Lawrence Mishel and Ruy Texeira in *The Myth of the Coming Labor Shortage,*[64] argued that industry had used schools as "an avenue of convenience" to hide its failure to innovate. "Employers would choose the high-skill, high-wage track to economic development if the education system allowed it," said the Hudson Institute's Arnold Packer. "An intelligent labor policy would create skilled jobs, not expect them to happen by themselves. I can't support the 'blame the schools' view," countered Mishel.[65]

Data on productivity support Mishel's view. The publication *Got to Learn to Earn* set the productivity of the American worker at 100 and found German workers scoring 77 while Japanese workers scored 73.66. When equated for the longer hours of Japanese workers, that figure falls to 57 — barely half of the productivity of the American laborer.[66]

As a minor digression, it is sometimes hard to get a good fix on what is happening with regard to productivity. A headline over a graph in *Workforce 2000* reads: "Productivity Has Declined Considerably." However, the label on the ordinate of the graph clearly indicates that it represents the rate of productivity *improvement.*

So productivity is not declining; we are simply getting better more slowly. According to economists, so is the rest of the world, and this is normal. It was the high rate of productivity growth from the end of World War II into the 1970s that was abnormal.

Aggregate productivity statistics also show that other countries are undergoing changes similar to those in the U.S. According to economist William Baumol, Europe is moving toward a service economy even faster than the U.S., and Japan is not far behind. Said Baumol, "During the time our productivity growth fell 65%, the Japanese growth rate fell 66%.[67]

Although the U.S. still leads everyone in measures of aggregate productivity, such statistics may no longer be meaningful. More and more economists now argue that we should replace overall productivity scores, such as those given above, with measures of productivity in different sectors of the economy. Countries specialize in different activities, after all. In such an analysis, the *New York Times* found the United States with higher productivity in all but one of seven large areas analyzed.[68] In insurance and real estate the Germans came out ahead. Breaking down the large area of manufacturing into smaller areas, the *Times* found the U.S. ahead in seven categories, Japan in four, and Germany in none.

America's Choice argues that America must produce a highly skilled work force if it is to compete with the rest of the world. Such a strategy would require U.S. business to invest more in people. Yet a recent study reported in *Education Week* found the number of people working for low wages to be growing, which suggests that business has yet to make such an investment.[69] Moreover, Harold Hodgkinson reports that, while the three fastest-growing job areas will create about 600,000 new, skilled jobs by the year 2000, the top three job areas in terms of numbers of new jobs (salesclerks, janitors, and waiters) will create 10.4 million.[70] Not exactly a recipe for a rising standard of living!

On another front, the *New York Times* found that, in 1990, 12% of those earning doctorates in physics received no job offers.[71] Hodgkinson reports that 26% of those graduating from college in 1991 accepted jobs that they could have obtained with only a high school diploma.[72] One wonders what kind of alienation this mismatch between skills and jobs will ultimately produce.

Economist Robert Samuelson argues that we should abandon our usual ways of thinking about international competitiveness. We play it as a zero-sum game; if Japan wins, we lose. This is false, says Samuelson, and only distracts us from more important internal social problems:

> What we're being asked to believe is that if another country (say, Japan) pioneers a new technology, we won't benefit. This defies logic and history. After World War II, the United States led in most technologies. That hardly prevented Europe and Japan from rapidly raising their living standards. Just the opposite: the availability of proven U.S technologies accelerated their economic growth.[73]

Samuelson argues that solving our internal problems (and, it must be said, he thinks schools are one of them) will do more to help our international standing than direct competition in technological races. "It matters more that we control health costs than [that we] regain global dominance in machine tools. . . . The race we need to win is not against others but against ourselves." From this perspective, Marc Tucker's assertion — that data showing schools improving are irrelevant — rings false.

By the spring of 1992 the revisionists seemed to have the upper hand. Jonathan Weisman, a reporter who had written objectively about the controversy in the fall of 1991, took sides with the revisionists.[74] Articles documented improvements in industry that were unrelated to education. A typical example from the *New York Times* reported that the head of the European Division of General Motors would take over that company's U.S. operations.[75] GM in Europe makes almost as much money as GM in the United States loses. The article described how GM in Europe became profitable by dumping its incestuous and inefficient practice of buying components only from internal operations. It discussed in some detail how such practices would be applied to U.S. plants. The quality of the workforce was not mentioned once. Moreover, BMW now plans to build a plant in the U.S., not because of the skilled work-force but because it is cheaper to build cars here than in Germany.[76] This argues against those who hold that industry will pay higher wages to highly skilled workers, as does the flood of jobs flowing from this country to the border towns of Mexico, where wages average $27.50 a week.

Indeed, criticism of the work force might actually reflect a problem in management. General Motors closed its Fremont, California, plant, declaring the workers there to be the worst in the country. Toyota reopened the plant, hired 80% of the GM workers, and soon pronounced that plant as productive as any in Japan. This turnaround may be partly due to differences in worker training: Japanese automakers provide Japanese workers with 350 hours of training and provide workers in their American plants with 300 hours. American automakers provide only 50 hours.[77]

Epilogue

The data and policy issues that have come to light since "Why Can't They Be Like We Were?" appeared in October 1991 suggest that, in that article, I may have erred in two ways. First, I clearly erred in the attribution of its title (a mistake that many, many people hastened to point out to me). I said that the title came from *The Fantasticks*. It came, of course, from *Bye, Bye, Birdie*. At least I got the year right. [Ed. note: The first report was corrected for this volume.]

Second and more important, linking the essay to a musical comedy may have made the situation seem less serious than it is. The true crisis of education in America is that it is trying to function not only in an era of disinformation but also in a time of social decline that sometimes looks like collapse. And it is trying to function in spite of an Administration with a misguided agenda for education reform. Henry Giroux speaks of a crisis not of education, but of democracy itself. As of the middle of last summer, over 80% of the population said they believed that the country is headed in the wrong direction, and at one point more people said they would vote for Ross Perot than for the incumbent Republican President or his Democratic challenger.

Staying within our own bailiwick, there are, as I said a year ago, plenty of problems to work on in most schools. Schools truly in crisis, such as those described by Jonathan Kozol in *Savage Inequalities* and those serving the rural underclass, need immediate, intensive, and extensive help.[78] A group about half the size of the urban underclass, the rural needy have fewer resources and suffer even more intractable problems than people in the cities. They get less attention, though, because they are dispersed across the land, invisible to the network TV news cameras that reside in our cities.

A recent story described how school officials in Gary, Indiana, who used to send dog-eared textbooks to Africa, are now sending them to Mississippi and Alabama, where they are received as a godsend.[79] Accompanying the books, many of them published in the 1950s, are desks and chairs. The story quotes the superintendent of schools in Walker County, Alabama, as saying, "This past year we didn't have enough desks and chairs for all our students." It also states that the couple responsible for the charity were "moved to tears" when they first saw the terrible conditions of the schools. What on earth can the National Standards Project, with its "world class" standards and assessments, mean to people working in these conditions? That is a question that Resnick and Tucker, co-directors of the project, cannot answer.

Urgent societal problems — and not just those highlighted by the Los Angeles riots — cry out for solutions (and money). George Will reported that we spend $11,000 a year on every American over 65, but only $4,200 on every American under 18.[80] Perhaps that's why Ernest Boyer reports that children are arriving at school today less ready to learn than in the past. He offers this ominous observation:

> America is losing sight of its children. In decisions made every day we are placing them at the bottom of the agenda, with grave consequences for the future of the nation. It's simply intolerable that millions of children in this country are

physically and emotionally disadvantaged in ways that restrict their capacity to learn, especially when we know what a terrible price will be paid for such neglect, not just educationally, but in tragic human terms as well. . . . In our search for [school] excellence, children have somehow been forgotten. We have ignored the fundamental fact that to improve the nation's schools, a solid foundation must be laid. We have failed to recognize that the family may be a more imperiled institution than the school and that many of education's failures relate to problems that precede schooling, even birth itself.[81]

So let's get to work on the real problems — of education and of society. There is certainly no dearth of them, nor are they small. Surely we can proceed without bashing the schools or the people in them.

Notes

1. Lawrence A. Cremin, *Popular Education and Its Discontents* (New York: Harper & Row, 1989), p. 7.
2. C. C. Carson, R. M. Huelskamp, and T. D. Woodall, "Perspectives on Education in America," Third Draft, Sandia National Laboratories, Albuquerque, N.M., May 1991; Harold Hodgkinson, "Schools Are Really Awful, Aren't They?" *Education Week,* 30 October 1991, p. 32; Iris Rotberg, "Myths in International Comparisons of Science and Mathematics Achievement," *The Bridge,* Fall 1991, pp 3-10; and idem, "I Never Promised You First Place," *Phi Delta Kappan,* December 1990, pp. 296-303. Although widely disseminated, the Sandia report has never officially been published, and there have been allegations that it has been suppressed and censored. See Julie A. Miller, "Report Questioning 'Crisis' in Education Triggers an Uproar," *Education Week,* 9 October 1991, p. 1.
3. Robert Rothman, "Revisionists Take Aim at Gloomy View of Schools," *Education Week,* 13 November 1991; and Dennis Kelly, "Defending U.S. Schools," *USA Today,* 7 November 1991, p. D-l.
4. Susan Chira, "Renegade Researchers Offer Rebuttal: U.S. Schools Are Better Than Many Think," *New York Times,* 8 April 1992, p. A-23.

5. Diane Ravitch, "U.S. Schools: The Bad News Is Right," *Washington Post,* 14 November 1991, p. C-7.
6. Quoted in Kelly, op. cit.
7. David Berliner, "Education Reform in an Era of Disinformation," paper presented at the annual meeting of the American Association of Colleges for Teacher Education, San Antonio, February 1992; and Richard Jaeger, "'World Class' Standards, Choice, and Privatization: Weak Measurement Serving Presumptive Policy," vice presidential address to the annual meeting of the American Educational Research Association, San Francisco, April 1992.
8. Elliot W. Eisner, "The Federal Reform of Schools: Looking for the Silver Bullet," *Phi Delta Kappan,* May 1992, pp. 722-23.
9. Boyse Rensberger, "Scientist Shortfall a Myth," *Washington Post,* 9 April 1992, p. A-l; and Michael Schrage, "Mathematics Remains a Crucial — and Misapplied — Key to Economy," *Washington Post,* 13 September 1991, p. D-2.
10. Quoted in Chira, op. cit.
11. Richard Cohen, "Blame Reagan Too," *Washington Post,* 4 August 1992, p. A-19.
12. William Raspberry, "The Secret of Smart," *Washington Post,* 12 October 1991, p. A-25; and idem, "U.S. Schools: Better Than We Think," *Washington Post,* 28 October 1991, p. A-21.
13. William Raspberry, "Teachers Can't Be Proxy Parents," *Washington Post,* 17 February 1992, p. A-29.
14. Gerald W. Bracey, "The Greatly Exaggerated Death of Our Schools," symposium presented at the annual meeting of the American Educational Research Association, San Francisco, April 1992. Lauren Resnick and Diane Ravitch were respondents, and the entire symposium is available on tape from AERA.
15. Quoted in Rothman, op. cit.
16. H. D. Hoover, personal communication, January 1992.
17. Robert L. Linn, M. E. Graue, and N. M. Sanders, "Comparing State and District Test Results to National Norms: The Validity of Claims That 'Everyone Is Above Average'," *Educational Measurement: Issues and Practice,* Fall 1990, pp. 5-14.
18. Diane Ravitch and Chester E. Finn, Jr., *What Do Our 17-Year-Olds Know?* (New York: Harper & Row, 1987), p. 1.
19. Dale Whittington, "What Have Our 17-Year-Olds Known in the Past?" *American Educational Research Journal,* Winter 1992, pp. 776, 778.

20. Carl F. Kaestle et al., *Literacy in the United States: Readers and Reading Since 1880* (New Haven, Conn.: Yale University Press, 1991), p. 89.

21. Archie E. Lapointe, Nancy A. Mead, and Janice M. Askew, *Learning Mathematics* (Princeton, N.J.: Educational Testing Service, Report No. 22-CAEP-01, February 1992), and Archie E. Lapointe, Janice M. Askew, and Nancy A. Mead, *Learning Science* (Princeton, N.J.: Educational Testing Service, Report No. 22-CAEP-02, February 1992).

22. "An 'F' in World Competition," *Newsweek,* 17 February 1992, p. 57.

23. George R. Kaplan, *Images of Education: The Mass Media's Version of America's Schools* (Washington, D.C.: National School Public Relations Association and the Institute for Educational Leadership, 1992).

24. *The State of America's Children 1991* (Washington, D.C.: Children's Defense Fund, 1991).

25. Berliner, op. cit.

26. National Center for Education Statistics, *Digest of Education Statistics* (Washington, D.C.: U.S. Department of Education, 1991), pp. 396-97.

27. Jaeger, op. cit.

28. Iris Rotberg, "The Questions No One Has Been Afraid to Ask," presentation to the U.S. Department of Education, March 1992.

29. Albert Shanker, personal communication, April 1992.

30. Archie E. Lapointe, "Scientific Sample but Plenty of Differences," Educational Testing Service, Princeton, N.J., February 1992.

31. Archie Lapointe, personal communication, June 1992.

32. National Center for Education Statistics, *International Mathematics and Science Assessments: What Have We Learned?* (Washington, D.C.: Office of Educational Research and Improvement, U.S. Department of Education, January 1992).

33. Ken Schooland, *Shogun's Ghosts: The Dark Side of Japanese Education* (New York: Bergin and Garvey, 1990).

34. Harold Stevenson and James Stigler, *The Learning Gap* (New York: Summit Books, 1992).

35. These results were discussed in Gerald W. Bracey, "Why Can't They Be Like We Were?" *Phi Delta Kappan,* October 1991, pp. 104-17.

36. Carson, Huelskamp, and Woodall, op. cit.

37. James Stigler et al., "Curriculum and Achievement in Mathematics: A Study of Elementary School Children in Japan, Taiwan, and the United States," *Child Development,* June 1982, pp. 315-22; and Harold Stevenson et al., "Mathematics Achievement of Children in China and the United States," *Child Development,* vol. 61, 1990, pp. 1053-66.

38. Stigler et al., op. cit.

39. *Shortchanging Girls, Shortchanging America* (Washington, D.C.: American Association of University Women, 1991).

40. Stevenson and Stigler, p. 102.

41. Ian Westbury, "Comparing American and Japanese Achievement: Is the United States Really a Low Achiever?" *Educational Researcher,* June/July 1992, pp. 18-24.

42. Underwood Dudley, "Living Without a Firm Grasp of Algebra," *DePauw Alumnus,* Winter 1984, pp. 10-11.

43. DeNeen L. Brown, "Doing Class Work to Master Homework," *Washington Post,* 15 May 1992, p. D-1.

44. Pane Barth, "When Good Will Be Good Enough," *Basic Education,* December 1991, p. 1; and "Report to the Board of Regents on Career Preparation Validation Study," New York Department of Education, Albany, n.d.

45. Gerald W. Bracey, "Cut Out Algebra!" *Washington Post,* 12 June 1992, p. C-5.

46. Thomas Romberg, personal communication, April 1992.

47. Thomas Romberg, personal communication, August 1992.

48. Michael Wolf, "Walking Small at Munich," *Washington Post,* 5 July 1992, p. C-3.

49. Todd Gitlin, "Uncivil Society," *San Francisco Examiner Image,* 19 April 1992, pp. 13-17.

50. Guy Kelly, "Real World Interrupts Learning," *Rocky Mountain News,* 1 May 1991, p. 8; idem, "A Day in Spinning Classroom," *Rocky Mountain News,* 2 May 1991, p. 8; and idem, "Nobody Gets a Chance to Flunk," *Rocky Mountain News,* 3 May 1991, p. 8.

51. R. W. Carr, "Markets Can't Fix Schools," *Wall Street Journal,* 2 May 1991, p. A-17.

52. "1991 Index of Social Health: Monitoring the Social Well-Being of the Nation," Fordham University Institute for Innovations in Social Policy, Tarrytown, N.Y., 1991.

53. Jack Frymier et al., *Growing Up Is Risky Business, and Schools Are Not to Blame: Final Report — Phi Delta Kappa Study of Students at Risk, Vol. I* (Bloomington, Ind.: Phi Delta Kappa, 1992), p. 10.

54. Henry A. Giroux, "Educational Leadership and the Crisis of Democratic Government," *Educational Researcher,* May 1992, pp. 4-11.

55. *What Work Requires of Schools: A SCANS Report for America 2000* (Washington, D.C.: U.S. Department of Labor, n.d.), p. 8.

56. Albert Shanker, "G.I. Bull," *New York Times,* 5 July 1992, p. E-7.

57. Albert Shanker, "Public Vs. Private Schools: What Education Gap?" *Washington Post,* 2 February 1992, p. C-3.

58. Peter Schmidt, "Census Data Find More Are Falling Behind in School," *Education Week,* 10 June 1992, p. 1.

59. Lawrence Cremin, *Popular Education and Its Discontents* (New York: Harper & Row, 1989), p. 103.

60. Lamar Alexander, "McNeil Lehrer News Hour," 7 July 1992.

61. *Newsweek,* 30 March 1992, p. 51.

62. Jonathan Weisman, "Some Economists Challenging View That Schools Hurt Competitiveness," *Education Week,* 13 November 1991, p. 1.

63. *Workforce 2000* (Washington, D.C.: Hudson Institute, 1988); and *America's Choice: High Skills or Low Wages* (Rochester, N.Y.: National Center on Education and the Economy, 1990).

64. Lawrence Mishel and Ruy Texeira, *The Myth of the Coming Labor Shortage* (Washington, D.C.: Economic Policy Institute, 1991).

65. Both are quoted in Weisman, op. cit.

66. *Got to Learn to Earn* (Washington, D.C.: George Washington University, 1991), p. 16.

67. Quoted in Michael Schrage, "The Hopeless Downward Spiral of U.S. Productivity Isn't as Bad as It Looks," *Washington Post,* 13 December 1991, p. D-3.

68. Sylvia Nasar, "Cars and VCR's Aren't Necessarily the First Domino," *New York Times,* 3 May 1992, p. 6-E.

69. "Low Earnings and Education," *Education Week,* 27 May 1992, p. 3.

70. Harold Hodgkinson, "A Demographic Look at Tomorrow," Institute for Educational Leadership, Washington, D.C., 1992.

71. Malcolm W. Browne, "Amid 'Shortage,' Young Physicists See Few Jobs," *New York Times,* 10 March 1992, p. C-1.

72. Harold Hodgkinson, personal communication, July 1992.

73. Robert J. Samuelson, "Taking Competitiveness Too Seriously," *Washington Post,* 30 May 1992, p. A-23.

74. Jonathan Weisman, "Skills and Schools," *Washington Post,* 29 March 1992, p. C-l; and idem, "The Education Smokescreen," *Phi Delta Kappan,* May 1992, p. 721.

75. Roger Cohen, "GM Europe Revolutionizing Its Parent," *Dallas Morning News,* 14 June 1992, p. 7-H.

76. "Bavaria Meets the Blue Ridge," *U.S. News & World Report,* 6 July 1992, p. 20.

77. Weisman, "Some Economists . . . ," p. 1.

78. Jonathan Kozol, *Savage Inequalities* (New York: Crown, 1991); and William P. O'Hare and Brenda Curry-White, "The Rural Underclass: Examination of Multiple-Problem Populations in Urban and Rural Settings," Population Reference Bureau, Washington, D.C., January 1992.

79. William Booth, "Rustbelt's Outdated Books Are 'Godsend' in the South," *Washington Post,* 13 July 1992, p. A-l.

80. George F. Will, "Stressed Out in America," *Washington Post,* 16 January 1992, p. A-27.

81. Ernest L. Boyer, *Ready to Learn* (Princeton, N.J.: Carnegie Foundation for the Advancement of Learning, 1991), p. 3.

THE
THIRD
BRACEY REPORT ON
THE CONDITION
OF PUBLIC EDUCATION

October 1993

In the "Second Bracey Report on the Condition of Public Education," I wrote: "We can now hope that the days of school-bashing are over."[1] Naive, was I, and not forward looking either. While the departure of George Bush and his Department of Education appointees (the schools-are-for-knocking crowd) did indeed result in much less negative noise from the politicians, the media picked up the cudgels and banged the drum of failure with them. And had I but looked ahead a few months, I would have noticed looming on the horizon the cruelest month, an April that marked the 10th anniversary of "a rising tide of mediocrity." The 10th jubilee of the document I had called a "xenophobic screed" in the First Bracey Report[2] was too juicy a target for the press pundits to pass up.

Indeed, April 1993 was the occasion for a new flood tide of negative columns, many of them inaccurate. "Our schools have barely improved," lamented William Kristol and Jay Lefkowitz in the *New York Times.*[3] In the *Rocky Mountain News,* Edward Lederman declared that it didn't matter what indicator you looked at, they'd all gotten worse in the last decade.[4] The *News* at least had the courage to feature my rejoinder in a prominent place in a Sunday edition.

Not so the *Washington Post.* The *Post* labeled schools "dismal" (a favorite adjective of both the *Post* and *Newsweek)* and mentioned stagnant Scholastic Aptitude Test (SAT) scores.[5] It followed up three days later with a long article by former *New York Times* education writer Edward Fiske, whose essay concluded that the value of *A Nation at Risk* was to show that, "so far as the quality of American public schools was concerned, the emperor had no clothes."[6] And three days after that, Robert Samuelson weighed in on the op-ed page of the *Post* with "Let's grant that lots of our schools are lousy."[7] The *Post,* as has been its custom in the two years I have lived in the D.C. area, declined to publish my rebuttals to these pieces. Indeed, the *Post's* refusal to print anything contrary to its steady message of failure reminds me of the controlled information policies we usually associate with totalitarian regimes. Only *USA Today,* in a special education supplement, provided a balanced view of events since April 1983.[8]

Unfortunately, the *Post* was not alone. *Scientific American* offered a scary example of bias in American media. The December 1992 issue featured an article by Harold Stevenson that once more propagated his findings of school failure,[9] findings that I critiqued in the Second Bracey Report. I offered the editors a rebuttal, declaring that had Stevenson conducted precisely the same studies but found American students scoring higher than Asian students, those who now quote him would have rejected his findings outright because of the many methodological flaws in the work.

David Berliner of Arizona State University took a different tack in countering Stevenson's article. In a letter to the editor of *Scientific American,* Berliner offered to accept Stevenson's data as reported but then challenged the interpretations of those data. Berliner offered compelling analyses — and has since changed his mind about the quality of the data as well — and he closed with the comment that "to uncover cultural differences and then decide that one group is deficient requires a completely different form of scholarship than that offered by Dr. Stevenson. He is no more qualified to make that argument than the typical American parent."

Neither Berliner nor I received any response from the editors of *Scientific American.* I dispatched a second letter and repeated my offer of a rebuttal. This time, I received a form rejection postcard.

The contagious mindset of failure infected even writers whose expertise is in education. On June 27 Albert Shanker opened his weekly *New York Times* column with, "The achievement of U.S. students in grades K-12 is very poor."[10] This opening volley seemed particularly gratuitous since the rest of the column was about grade inflation in colleges. Shanker continued the fireworks the following week, however, opening his Independence Day column with, "American students are performing at much lower levels than students in other industrialized nations."[11] He proffered no data in support of that conclusion. Shanker's first sentence in his July 11 essay — the final fusillade of his three-part attack — declared that "international examinations designed to compare students from all over the world usually show American students at or near the bottom."[12] Again, no data were provided. Data provided in the Second Bracey Report and those to be presented later in this article show that Shanker's statement is simply not true.

The perception of catastrophe has loomed so large that people have interpreted good news badly and printed false bad news simply because they "knew" it must be true. For example, when a virtually invisible international reading study found American 9-year-olds ranking second among students of 31 nations and American 14-year-olds ranking ninth, the November 1992 issue of the *American School Board Journal* ran the story under this headline: "Good News: Our 9-Year-Olds Read Well/Bad News: Our 14-Year-Olds Don't." In a comparison where 16th place is average, how can ninth place be deemed bad? More important, looking at the actual scores of the 14-year-olds reveals that they are close to the top — almost as close as the second-place 9-year-olds.

Other "truths" about school failure have entered the popular culture and become so pervasive that it's hard to combat them. I am reminded of the saying of Josh Billings, the 19th-century American humorist: "It's better to know nothing than to know what ain't so." A lot of people in the past year have claimed to know what ain't so.

Katherine Merseth's March 1993 *Kappan* article about mathematics instruction illustrates the problem well. She declared that in this country "effort receives little credit for contributing to successful learning in mathematics — or, for that matter, in any subject. For example, American, Japanese, and Chinese mothers were asked what factors among ability, effort, task difficulty, and luck made their children successful in school. American mothers ranked *ability* the highest, while Asian mothers gave high marks to *effort*."[13]

Merseth was only the latest of many to mouth this apparent verity, which also derived from the work of Stevenson. But it ain't so. Although the text from which Merseth was working certainly seems to say that, it really doesn't. The accompanying graphs resolve any ambiguity: American mothers ranked ability as more important than Japanese or Taiwanese mothers, yes; but they also thought that effort was more important than ability or any other factor. So did their children. Although the scale of the graph misleadingly makes the differences look large, the differences among mothers' rankings on the four factors in the three countries are quite small.[14] The largest difference is about one point on a 10-point scale, and most are smaller. One wonders if such small differences translate into any behavioral difference whatsoever. Merseth's article — and Stevenson's article on which it was based — gives the impression that the differences are enormous and that they affect classroom outcomes.

In a similar misreport, the 10 February 1993 edition of *Education Week,* "America's Education Newspaper of Record," as the masthead proclaims, got the record wrong.[15] The editors' lead essay in their special report, "From Reform to Renewal," claimed that "the proportion of American youngsters performing at high levels remains infinitesimally small. In the past 10 years, for instance, the number and proportion of those scoring at or above 650 on the verbal or math section of the Scholastic Aptitude Test has actually declined." Later in the section, a table listed numbers that confirmed the text. It's something everyone "knows." But it ain't so.

In the last decade, the number of scorers above 650 on the SAT has grown on both the verbal section and the math one. And while the proportion of students scoring at this level on the verbal section has remained relatively stable across the 10 years, the proportion of high scorers on the math section has grown from 7% in 1982 to 10.1% in 1992.[16] The explanation for *Education Week's* error? The numbers reported for 1982 were accurate, but the figures for 1992 included only students scoring between 650 and 690. (The College Board reports results in 40-point intervals, except for the last one, which is 50 points.) It seems that someone forgot to include those who scored above 690.

As for this still being an "infinitesimally small" proportion, the editors seem not to understand that few people can score high when statisticians impose a normal curve on the results, as they did when the SAT was first constructed. In fact, given the mathematical properties of the normal distribution, we know that, when an all-white, mostly male, Northeastern elite set the standards on the SAT in 1941, 6.68% of them scored above 650. (On the SAT 650 is 1.5 standard deviations above the mean — or it was then — though the standard deviation has grown to 112 on the verbal section and 123 on the mathematics section.) In 1992 the majority female, mixed-socioeconomic-status, polyglot pool of test-takers had 10.1% of their numbers above 650 — a 51% increase over a group headed largely for Ivy League and Seven Sisters Colleges. Incidentally, the growth in the number of high scorers cannot be explained in terms of the recent influx in Asian immigrants. While they do score well above other ethnic groups, they constitute too small a group — 8% of all test-takers — to account for the rise.

In the past year noneducators often reported statistics that made U.S. schools look bad, while ignoring those that made them look good. On the op-ed page of the *Washington Post,* Jessica Mathews, vice president of the World Resources Institute, made much of the oft-repeated "fact" that only 1% of American students score as well in mathematics as 50% of Japanese students.[17] Mathews, like many other Americans, had absorbed this figure from an article by Harold Stevenson.

But it ain't so. Or, more precisely, only Stevenson finds it so. If that conclusion were accurate, surely we should stand in breathless awe before the Japanese and maybe begin a search for a "math gene" that only they possess. If it were accurate, we would have to acknowledge that, in spite of a 50% increase in the number of Americans scoring above 650 on the SAT mathematics test, only 1% of all our students would be able to maintain the class average in Japan. Fortunately, there are data that offer direct refutation.

In the Second International Assessment of Educational Progress (IAEP-2), the 95th percentiles of almost all nations are virtually identical for both science and mathematics and for both 9-year-olds and 13-year-olds.[18] Top-ranked Korea did finish noticeably higher than the rest, and it may even have a higher average than recorded, as there is some indication of a ceiling effect for Korean students. Jordan's bottom rank on everything stood out from the crowd, too, but the countries in between were bunched in a very narrow range. In fact, the 95th percentile for the U.S. was higher than that of some countries that had higher average scores. Moreover, as noted in the Second Bracey Report, a reanalysis of the Second International Mathematics Study found that American eighth-graders who had taken algebra scored higher than even the top 20% of Japanese students.

Meanwhile, writers at *Newsweek* went so far as to invent a statistic to demonstrate how awful the situation is. In an appendix to a story on the nature of genius, reporters Pat Wingert and Melinda Beck wrote that "SAT scores have dropped most precipitously for the best students."[19] Of course, no data exist that would allow them to calculate such a drop. The writers may have had in mind the drop in the proportion of high scorers on the SAT (see above). Since the decline of the national average SAT scores began back in 1963, the proportion of high scorers on the verbal section has fallen, but the proportion on the mathematics section has not. However, that is certainly not what the sentence in *Newsweek* says.

Media Coverage

The First Bracey Report did not capture the media's attention, even though a news release preceded it. Except for columnist

William Raspberry, very few commentators found it worth noting. The three articles that did discuss it (in the *New York Times, USA Today,* and *Education Week)* all had bundled it together with discussions of work by Harold Hodgkinson, Iris Rotberg, and the engineers at Sandia National Laboratories. All these articles devoted ample space to rebuttals. The Second Bracey Report generated even less interest from the media, despite the fact that the *Kappan* had paired it with an impressive corroborative treatise by Richard Jaeger. National Public Radio reporter Claudio Sanchez interviewed me on "Morning Edition," with Archie Lapointe, the executive director of the National Assessment of Educational Progress (NAEP), adding commentary and Diane Ravitch and Marc Tucker brought in to rebut.[20]

NBC television officials said that they couldn't do such a story as news because they would have to bring in people for rebuttal and didn't have that kind of time on news programs. They referred me to a producer for the "Today Show," who never returned calls. After the Second Bracey Report, I was referred to another producer who seemed interested and whose assistant called every few weeks to say that the producer would get back to me. She never did.

"Sixty Minutes" showed some interest — until the election was over and the Bush crowd exited, taking their antischool rhetoric with them. In one conversation, a producer said, "I'm having a hard time finding the story in this. This looks like issues. We don't do issues. We do stories."

My lack of success with the media led me to write an article titled "The Media's Myth of School Failure." Naturally, no one in the general media would publish it. The *Columbia Journalism Review* editors said that, "sadly," they had heard the sentiments often. They declined to print it. The Association for the Advancement of International Education featured it in the summer issue of its periodical, *Inter Ed.*[21] A longer, more current version will appear in a forthcoming issue of *Educational Leadership.* My experiences with the media seemed only to confirm the gloomy view expressed by George Kaplan in *Images of Education: The Mass Media's Version of America's Schools.*[22]

Other New Data

As mentioned earlier, in July 1992 the International Association for the Evaluation of Educational Achievement (IEA) released a report comparing reading skills of 200,000 students in 31 countries.[23] No one noticed. Although the IEA put out a press release, not one print or broadcast agency covered the data. Robert Rothman, a writer for *Education Week,* told me that he knew of the study but did not know about its findings until September 1992, when a European friend sent him a copy of the report from Germany. Naturally, *Education Week* carried a front-page article on the study.[24] Following its usual practice of providing broad if not deep coverage of education issues, *USA Today* picked up on the *Education Week* article and ran another front-page story.[25] But that was about it. In November, the *American School Board Journal* printed the good news/bad news headline and story referred to above.

The Bush Administration didn't help, of course. While it had orchestrated a large press conference on the release of the IAEP-2, no such event heralded the IEA reading study. Indeed, the *USA Today* story carried a comment from Francie Alexander, who was then deputy assistant secretary of education, in which she dismissed the study as irrelevant.

The study found American 9-year-olds reading better than anyone in the world except Finnish 9-year-olds. Using a scale identical to that of the SAT — with the mean set at 500 and the standard deviation set at 100 — American 9-year-olds averaged 547, while the high-flying Finns came in at 569. American 14-year-olds finished ninth, with an average score of 535. These results illustrate the hazard of such rankings: ranks obscure performance. When people are ranked, someone always finishes last, even in the Olympics. The American 14-year-olds actually scored almost as close to first place as the 9-year-olds. The difference between the American teenagers and the second-place French is only 14 points on a 600-point scale. "Bells should have gone off all over the country," said Archie Lapointe of the study's findings. Yet hardly a tinkle was heard anywhere in the nation.

German education has been the subject of encomiums in recent years in this country, so it is interesting to observe that German youngsters at both ages finished in the middle of the pack. The German Research Service reported these findings with some anxiety, appearing especially concerned that "German standards were exceeded . . . even in the USA."[26] Even. German authorities placed the blame squarely on German families' neglect of books.

The 1992 National Assessment of Educational Progress in mathematics showed a statistically significant gain from the 1990 math assessment.[27] Given that 250,000 students were involved, it is hard to say whether this means anything in practical terms. (Tests of statistical significance were designed for groups of about 30; with a sample of 250,000, tiny differences will be statistically significant.) Most stories about the results mentioned the increase but emphasized the paucity of students who scored high.

Apropos of the NAEP, people continue to make inappropriate statements about what students at various levels of proficiency can and cannot do. This is the case despite Robert Forsyth's definitive analysis showing that such statements are invalid.[28] The National Assessment Governing Board (NAGB) persisted in making such claims, using its flawed standard-setting procedure. When a team of evaluators, headed by Daniel Stufflebeam, declared the standard-setting procedure invalid in 1991, NAGB's response was to summarily fire the evaluators. Last summer, a General Accounting Office (GAO) report declared NAGB's procedures much improved but still not valid for talking about what children can and cannot do. While the GAO found that the levels do represent the quality of performance on the NAEP tests, "they do not necessarily imply that students have achieved the item mastery or readiness for future life, work, and study specified in NAGB's definitions and descriptions."[29]

More reanalyses of the Second International Mathematics Assessment (SIMS) appeared in the past year — and offered competing claims. David Baker challenged Ian Westbury's earlier reanalysis, and Westbury responded.[30] Baker argued that "Japan teaches more mathematics effectively to more of its students in elementary and secondary school." Baker's analysis used the entire mathematics curriculum of eighth grade. Westbury countered that this was inappropriate. "Outside the American algebra tracks," he wrote, "the intentions of the U.S. and Japanese curricula are so different they cannot be meaningfully compared. Given this, and given that achievement is similar in both Japan and the United States when intentions are similar, I asked what reason there is to believe that American teachers working outside the Grade 8 algebra course might not do as well as other countries' teachers if the curriculum was better, or differently, crafted."

As I noted in the Second Bracey Report when I discussed Westbury's reanalysis of the SIMS data, his research does not take American mathematics curriculum builders and teachers off the hook. It simply changes the focus. As Westbury said in his exchange with Baker, "The curriculum offered the majority of U.S. Grade 8 students . . . is a poorly realized last year of an elementary arithmetic curriculum that does not cover much algebra or measurement, includes virtually no geometry, and offers little new material, even in arithmetic, to students."

Westbury's new analysis of Japanese and American performance looked at the SIMS scores in terms of the scores of students in the top and bottom half of classes in the two countries. For the American classes, he further categorized scores in terms of whether the class was remedial, regular, enriched, or algebra. For those classes in the top half that were regular, the average score was 60; for enriched, 67; for algebra, 76. The remedial classes that were in the top half of classes scored 61, but there were only four such classes. The Japanese students in the top half of all Japanese classes averaged 66. Thus, within each country, classes that finished in the top half of all classes appear comparable. As with the earlier analysis, American students taking algebra scored above the Japanese average.

In the classes in the bottom half, though, a different picture emerges. The Japanese students in these classes average 55, not terribly far from the 66 average posted by students in the top half of classes in Japan. But American students in lower-half classes categorized as remedial scored only 28; those in lower-half regular classes, 39; those in lower-half enriched classes, 37; and those in lower-half algebra classes, 42.

These results illustrate something both Baker and Westbury discuss: the extraordinarily large variance of American scores, something apparently unique to this nation among SIMS participants. One of Baker's graphs showing differences between pretest and posttest scores is particularly striking. The gains for Japanese students are tightly bunched around the average. American students who gained the most also gained much more than even the best Japanese students, while American students who gained the least gained much less than their Japanese counterparts. Indeed, some even lost ground during the course of the year.

These results would seem to confirm both a Japanese saying and a common observation about American classrooms. The Japanese saying goes, "The nail that stands out gets hammered down." Observers of American classrooms have noted that the cognitively rich get richer, while the cognitively poor get poorer. On the other hand, all of the students in Japanese schools are ethnic Japanese. Virtually all the children in Finnish schools are ethnic Finns. In the U.S., large districts strive to teach students who speak as many as 108 languages other than English as their native tongues. Such a diverse and polyglot nation is not likely to show homogeneity on any variable. Still, these and other data indicate something Harold Hodgkinson and I have been saying to each other and in our speeches around the country: The top third of our students are world class, however one defines that squishy concept; the second third are not in any serious academic trouble; the bottom third are in terrible shape.

The data comparing American students to Chinese students in Beijing purport to show the Chinese students ahead. But these data are of questionable validity for a variety of reasons cited in the Second Bracey Report. In addition to the methodological flaws noted there, we really do not know how representative the Beijing schools are of either the city or the nation. Reports from Lena Sun in the *Washington Post* suggest that they are certainly not representative of the nation.[31] Sun describes China's new "schools for aristocrats" — private schools that charge a lot of money for tuition and have lots of amenities, such as air conditioning and color televisions. "By contrast, many state-run schools, especially in poor, rural areas, have no heat and sometimes no electricity," according to Sun. "Some students have to share notebooks, use pencils with no points, and sit on hard, backless wooden planks. Education is such a low priority in some areas that classrooms are used as cowsheds." Not exactly a students' paradise.

In the same article, Sun cites an editorial in a Chinese newspaper that expressed the worry that students attending the "schools for aristocrats" might become "willful." The quote makes it sound like "willful" is about the worst thing a Chinese child can become, and in a later article Sun describes the extraordinary lengths to which Chinese parents and educators go to ensure conformity.

> In [a Chinese preschool], if it is time to color, the children sit at their desks with crayons in hand. If it is time to listen to the teacher read a story, the boys and girls are seated, all in a row, in their tiny chairs. After lunch, every child gets his or her cot ready for the required nap, whether they are sleepy or not. There is virtually no unstructured time. . . . Even toilet breaks are scheduled into the day; the children squat together over one long trough in the communal bathroom. . . . Even at an exclusive private school in Sichuan Province that has American teachers, youngsters march in formation to wash their hands and are not allowed to talk during lunch.[32]

During the year since the Second Bracey Report, other descriptions of Japanese schools emerged, portraying at least the secondary system as something less than a pleasant place. The *New York Times* featured an article on *ijime,* the bullying that takes place in Japanese schools.[33] According to this article, which begins with the bullying death of a middle school student, those most vulnerable are students who are wealthier and brighter, yet fail "to be part of the group in a society that demands conformity."

In the Backtalk section of the March 1993 *Kappan,* Peter Boylan punctured a few balloons about the Japanese system. Intrigued by his letter, I wrote to him, enclosing the Second Bracey Report. His reply is an even fiercer indictment:

> There is one important effect of Japan's education system that is not addressed: the incredible stunting of the students' social and psychological development. My students have all the emotional maturity of American elementary school students. If I ask a girl a question, often she will sink to the floor in embarrassment at being asked to answer a question. These are 19-year-old high school seniors I'm talking about. The boys aren't so dramatic; they just pretend that the teacher doesn't exist if they are unsure about things. Socially, these students are almost incapable of doing anything on their own. . . . I close with this comment. I consider the Japanese schools to be a national, institutionalized system of child abuse.[34]

Events

Several events that took place in 1992-93 bore directly on the shape of education reform. In October 1992 the Economic Policy Institute sponsored a conference in Washington, D.C., titled "Choice: What Role in American Education?" Although the various descriptions of programs in different American cities and states painted differing pictures of choice programs, the general tone was not encouraging. Some choice programs had been found to siphon off the abler students, leaving the neighborhood schools to cope with a greater number of problems. Some programs found that choices, when made, occurred largely for nonacademic reasons. For some programs, adequate data were not yet available.

In February 1993 Phi Delta Kappa, the Institute for Educational Leadership, and the Educational Excellence Network collaborated to host a conference on education reform. The inspiration for the conference was a good and hopeful one: assemble the conservative and liberal reformers from around the country and let them haggle for a couple of days to find their common ground. Indeed, "Common Ground" was the name that two of the organizers, Michael Usdan and Harold Hodgkinson of the Institute for Educational Leadership, initially used to refer to the conference. While liberals and conservatives did show up, that was about all they did. The participants talked politely around the issues and seldom confronted an issue — or one another — head on.

The only sparks occurred when someone repeated the oft-made observation that Americans are generally satisfied with their schools. "That is scientific proof that ignorance is bliss," huffed Denis Doyle of the Hudson Institute.

Emeral Crosby, a Detroit high school principal, then admonished Doyle that the car makers in his city had gotten into trouble precisely because they had forgotten the consumer. But the issue died there. It seemed to me part of the problem was that too many of the participants — mostly heads of organizations or high-ranking members therein — had been away from the classroom too long. Crosby was the sole participant among about 65 who was actually working in a school building.

A fledgling Canadian organization, the Alliance for Educational Renewal, held a congress in June 1993 in Toronto to fight back at the "one-sidedness of the conversation" about the decline of education in Ontario. The Alliance has not been around long enough for me to hazard a guess about what it will accomplish, but to attend a meeting on education reform in Canada is to realize how badly the national discussion has degenerated in the U.S., where talk almost invariably turns on dreary instrumentality: the role of schools in preparing a labor force. Vocational considerations have led us to regard education as little more than training. The dread "technologically complex society" threatens our workers. Not so in Canada. Perhaps it was the presence of Lloyd Dennis, co-author of the 1968 report *Living and Learning,* but much of the discussion reflected not only that document, which deigned to consider education as the pursuit of truth, but also Israel Scheffler's definition of education as

> the formation of habits of judgment and the development of character, the elevation of standards, the facilitation of understanding, the development of taste and discrimination, the stimulation of curiosity and wondering, the fostering of

style and a sense of beauty, the growth of a thirst for new ideas and visions of the yet unknown.[35]

The extent to which we accept Scheffler's definition is the extent to which we must realize that, for all the test scores and graduation statistics presented here and elsewhere, we really do not have the appropriate indices of how the system functions or doesn't. The tests we do have — virtually all of them decontextualized collections of multiple-choice questions — do not measure the traits, qualities, values, and habits that we cherish most. It is to be hoped that the new interest in various kinds of performance assessment will carry us toward measurement of these valued outcomes.

In May 1993 the National Academy of Sciences hosted a three-day conference titled "Re-Inventing Schools: The Technology Is Now." The conference was a mixture of politics, show-and-tell, and crass commercialism (a speaker for the violence-saturated Sega games had the chutzpah to speak of their "moral dimension" with a straight face). Yet the displays and demonstrations probably heightened people's awareness of the power of technology, which, as Arthur C. Clarke reminded everyone, is no substitute for people. Beamed in live from Sri Lanka, Clarke observed that "information is not knowledge, knowledge is not wisdom, and wisdom is not foresight."

In terms of publishing events, the long-suppressed Sandia Report, referenced often in the First Bracey Report, finally made it into print. In addition, Joe Schneider and Paul Houston compiled data from the first two Bracey Reports and from the Sandia Report — and much, much more — into an angry but thoughtful book.[36]

The Cities, Again

The Second Bracey Report accentuated the raging needs of city schools and the even more intractable problems of the largely invisible rural poor. The ensuing year provided additional evidence — as if any were needed — that our cities are in dire straits. It was interesting and telling that during the year, especially during the Presidential campaign, as critics and commentators weighed in on the subject of education, they all spoke of the problems of "American schools" but drew their concrete, horrible examples from the cities — usually New York, Chicago, or Washington, D.C.

The *Washington Post,* usually the most neglectful major newspaper on matters educational, redeemed itself in part with a series called simply "Condition Critical: The State of America's Cities." In her segment, *Post* education writer Mary Jordan observed that the city of Atlanta was 67% black, while the Atlanta public schools were 92% black.[37] Nationally, she found only one in four public school students in the 47 largest cities to be white. These statistics, of course, mask the real problem, because they present the situation in terms of race. But race and ethnicity are proxy variables for the real problem: class. Said Jordan, "To a large degree the black middle and upper classes also have abandoned urban schools. . . . In Atlanta, like the District [of Columbia], the majority of black students in the metropolitan area now live in the suburbs."

Logically, one would expect that, as the city schools acquire a higher and higher percentage of poor children with the kinds of difficult problems that demand pupil-teacher ratios of 4 to 1 rather than 25 to l, these schools would receive more funds to help solve their predicament. But it doesn't work that way. Newark did indeed spend more than $9,000 per student in 1992 and was still taken over by the state as educationally bankrupt. But Newark's bountiful level of spending is the exception. According to Michael Casserly of the Council of the Great City Schools, cities average $900 per student per year *less* than their nonurban counterparts.[38]

Iris Rotberg drove the point home dramatically in a contribution to the *Washington Post* op-ed page. She observed that funding inequities exist in the U.S. that are reversed in some other countries.

> In Sweden, per-pupil expenditures in low-income schools are two to three times higher than in affluent schools. These ratios are quite common in the United States — only here, rich children are the winners. . . . The 100 poorest districts in Texas spend an average of just under $3,000 per student. The 100 wealthiest districts, however, spend about $7,200

per student. In Illinois, school districts spend between roughly $2,400 and $8,300 per student. A judge in a school finance case put it this way: "If money is inadequate to improve education, the residents of poor districts should at least have an opportunity to be disappointed by its failure."[39]

As for the uselessness of "throwing money" at the problem, Rotberg commented that "this is true only if one assumes that offering poor children the opportunities routinely available to their more affluent peers is the same as throwing money at a problem. Teacher expertise and experience, class sizes, better science laboratories, and decent facilities do matter. If they don't, rich school districts haven't heard the message."

The neglect of cities has pernicious, insidious, and pervasive effects. A study by George Madaus and his colleagues at Boston College, sponsored by the National Science Foundation, found that schools with more than 65% minority enrollment were much more likely to put pressure on teachers to raise test scores than were schools with a minority enrollment of less than 10%.[40] Such pressure would be acceptable if the tests were worth teaching to — that is, if they measured knowledge and skills that people deemed truly valuable. But Madaus' team conducted an item-by-item examination of commercial achievement tests and tests that accompany textbook series and concluded that only a tiny proportion of items covered high-quality content or evoked higher-order thinking. "[The tests] are extremely well constructed instruments that don't measure anything of particular consequence," said Madaus. Thus students who are already behind and need acceleration receive more drill-and-practice on the "basic" skills that tests measure — and so fall ever farther behind.

No doubt such conditions are behind such frightful results as the relative placement of different ethnic groups on proficiency levels established by the NAEP. The Congressional Budget Office calculated that the differences between black, white, and Hispanic students had been generally declining but that huge differences remained. In the 1990 assessment, about 22% of white fourth-, eighth-, and 12th-graders attained "proficiency." Only about 7%

of Hispanics reached the proficient level, and a meager 2% of blacks did so.[41]

Minority students may be drilled a lot more on standardized tests, but they do not do well on them — not even those who get good grades in school. A study by Abt Associates for the U.S. Department of Education examined this question. It found that students in high-poverty schools (defined as schools in which at least 75% of the students are eligible for free or reduced-price lunches) were much less likely to get the best grades than those in low-poverty schools (those with poverty rates between 6% and 20%).[42] In high-poverty schools, the highest grades (defined as at least half A's and half B's) were awarded to anywhere from 15% to 32% of the children. In low-poverty schools, the range was 35% to 47%.

However, when the researchers examined the performance of the students on standardized tests, enormous differences appeared. For example, seventh-graders receiving A's in low-poverty schools had an average score on a standardized test at the 81st percentile in reading and at the 87th percentile in mathematics. In high-poverty schools, students receiving A's scored at the 36th and 35th percentiles respectively. Students receiving A's in high-poverty schools scored *lower* than students receiving C's in low-poverty schools. Students receiving C's and D's in high-poverty schools got only into the low teens. No one has suggested that these students might be posting such low scores because they are learning complex skills that are not measured by the standardized tests. Only a sophist would try. It might not be too harsh to call the "education" of these students a hoax.

Similar results show up on more difficult tests. For example, in Washington, D.C., only 60% of the students graduate, and only about 25% of them take the SAT. In 1992 the District students who took the SAT averaged 336 on the verbal section and 369 on the mathematics section.[43] This means that they got approximately 33% of the verbal items correct and approximately 25% of the mathematics items correct. The chance level for pure guessing is 20% correct. At the lowest-scoring D.C. high schools, SAT scores are actually below chance, hovering around 300.

If one assumes that the 25% of D.C. students who take the SAT are the most academically able and motivated students, then the average student in this "best group" barely qualifies to play freshman varsity sports in college. Proposition 48 of the National Collegiate Athletic Association requires a combined SAT score of 700 for freshman eligibility.

Although reformers and media alike target the District schools for much criticism, no one has ever suggested that they are the *worst* city schools in the nation. One can only wonder what achievement test scores and international comparisons would look like if scored separately for urban and nonurban areas.

One can also wonder what kind of a Dickensian novel might move American policy makers and politicians to take appropriate action. *Savage Inequalities*[44] is quoted everywhere — but, apparently, to no effect. On the same day that Mary Jordan's story appeared on page 1 of the *Post,* a story in the Metro section noted that the population of jail inmates in Maryland had increased by 250% since 1980. "You can't build your way out" of the problem of crowded prisons, said the head of public safety for Maryland, observing that the prisons contained almost double the number of inmates they were built to hold.[45] He recommended parole and early release, with electronic tracking for burglars, car thieves, minor drug users, and other nonviolent prisoners. But even if all such nonviolent criminals were released, the state's prisons would still contain more prisoners than they were designed to hold and would still contain almost twice as many prisoners as in 1980. Although the two stories appeared in separate sections of the paper, they are, no doubt, intimately related in reality.

After examining these data and reflecting on the conditions from which they derive, I can only echo Robert Coles in the second volume of *Children of Crisis.* Describing the horrid lives of migrants, sharecroppers, and poor mountain people, Coles wrote, "There are moments, and I believe this is one of them, when, whoever we are, observers or no, we have to throw up our hands in heaviness of heart and dismay and disgust and say, in desperation: God save them, those children, and for allowing such a state of affairs to continue, God save us too."[46]

The New Administration

Although he garnered only 43% of the popular vote, Bill Clinton rode into Washington on a wave of good will and hope unlike any I have seen in the 40 years I have watched Presidential elections. Not everyone bought the transformation from Slick Willie to William the Conqueror. But, except for those absolutely phobic about the federal government (George Will most prominent among them), after 12 years of minimal attention to domestic affairs, people wanted Clinton to succeed and hoped that he would.

The unrealistically high expectations meant that Clinton could fall farther faster than most officials, and by May the press was awash with stories of nepotism and trivia. "Hairport" and "Travelgate" led some columnists to suggest that the Clintons' behavior evoked images more reminiscent of Ron and Nancy than of Franklin and Eleanor. Mary McGrory, writing like a strict doyenne to an incipiently delinquent grandson, felt obliged to remind Clinton that he was not Louis XIV.[47]

After the pounding public schools had taken under Secretaries Bennett, Cavazos, and Alexander, hopes were perhaps highest and faded fastest among educators. I thought the expectations for big changes were misinformed from the beginning. Clinton was, after all, the president of the National Governors' Association when it and President Bush came up with the national education goals. Any change would have to be evolutionary, not revolutionary. When Richard Riley, the newly designated secretary of education, gave a short speech about national standards and assessments at an inauguration night party, I figured he must have them seriously on his mind.

During the campaign, Clinton had not talked much about education, nor had he risen to defend schools. In the Richmond, Virginia, debate, Ross Perot stated flatly that the U.S. "has the worst educational system in the developed world." Certainly no one was surprised that break-the-mold Bush let this comment pass, but Clinton ignored it as well.

What was noticeable about the few comments on education from Clinton and Riley, however, was that they were notably devoid of references to failing schools. National standards were necessary, they said, but they associated that need with what the future demanded of workers, not with our present, "dismal" schools.

Clinton emphasized from the start the long-term benefits of early childhood education, often making the observation that society gets back three dollars for every dollar it invests in such programs. Numerous commentators, including myself, pointed out that this figure came from one unique study, the Perry Preschool Project, which involved a high-quality program and intensive and extensive efforts of program staff and parents.[48] It was not likely that the many low-quality, custodial daycare programs that are more the norm could replicate those outcomes. Edward Zigler, the father of Head Start, was cited as saying that 30% of Head Start programs were so poor they should be shut down.

The message apparently got through, because talk of early childhood programs died out. The college-for-service idea took its place when education was spoken of at all, which, by the end of July 1993, was seldom. The service idea was attacked by conservatives as too costly and unnecessary because, with 58% of high school seniors already attending college, college is easily accessible. In addition, the payoff from education is sufficiently high that students can recover their costs quickly. As Denis Doyle put it, "The widening gap between the educated and the uneducated is not an accident; well-educated people command greater incomes because they produce more. Put simply, education pays. And it pays handsomely. There is no longer a compelling need to subsidize it through national service or subsidized loans."[49] In the Second Bracey Report I observed that we already had more of a problem with *over*education than under, with 26% of college graduates working at jobs that did not require college. Nearly nine months later, Tait Trussell put the figure at 30%.[50]

Although Clinton stopped talking about early childhood, an article by Steven Barnett of Rutgers University suggested that he shouldn't have.[51] Barnett, who conducted the initial cost-benefit analysis for the Perry Preschool Project, reviewed 22 studies of the long-term effects of preschool programs. He found that, while I.Q. gains did fade after a few years, many of the programs had beneficial effects in terms of grade retention, special education placement, and graduation rates. Barnett found that some studies usually cited as not finding sustained effects, including the Westinghouse evaluation of Head Start, suffered methodological flaws that obscured the gains. For example, because those in the comparison groups who do not attend preschool are more likely to be retained, over time the comparison groups filter out the lowest-scoring students.

Barnett estimated that $14 billion could provide a national pre-school system with the kind of quality found in the Perry Pre-school Project. Zigler has also called for full funding of Head Start because it produces benefits other than increased test scores.[52] Such funding would be welcome, but it would leave one enormous problem unsolved: For many children, Head Start comes after five years of Bad Start.

Education, Productivity, and Economic Well-Being

Many of the calls for break-the-mold schools originated in the widely held myth that our "dismal" public schools had produced a poorly functioning workforce, which, in turn, caused problems for U.S. industry, diminished the nation's economic competitiveness, and augured ill for our national future in a technologically sophisticated world. The Second Bracey Report challenged this myth, and that challenge need not be repeated. It has now become abundantly clear that the relationship between education and national economic well-being simply isn't there (although for the economic prosperity of individuals, education is more important than ever). The recession and high unemployment rates in Europe are the most direct evidence that elementary and secondary school performance, as ordinarily measured, does not drive an industrialized nation's fortunes.

BMW is building a plant in South Carolina that "could become the birthplace of the next revolution in automobile manufacturing.

. . . . BMW has come to the United States because it is cheaper —
it offers well-trained workers at comparatively low wages . . .
about 60% lower than in Germany."[53] The plant will require that
American workers become even more skilled because they will be
building a variety of automobiles on a single assembly line. Today,
when demand slows for specific models, especially in the U.S.,
workers are laid off. When this happens at the new BMW plant,
workers will simply make a different model.

A year after the Second Bracey Report's challenge, though,
something else is equally clear: The schools may not be a threat to
the emerging economic situation, but the emerging economic situation may be a threat to the schools. Some argue that our changing economic climate is a threat to democracy as well. Call it the
"South America Syndrome" because South American metaphors
are invoked so often. But it is a concern that arcs across the
American political spectrum.

Lester Thurow of MIT, examining America's elite as it compares to those in Japan and South America, notes that advantaged
Japanese evince concern for the whole society and understand that
their children's success depends on the success of the nation as a
whole. "America's elite, on the other hand, more and more resembles the oligarchy of Latin American countries where a small
handful of immensely privileged people have it very good and
don't care at all about the fact that the rest of the country is doing
poorly."[54] Similarly, Robert Reich, now secretary of labor, wrote
that members of the elite are "quietly seceding from the large and
diverse publics of America into homogeneous enclaves within
which their earnings need not be redistributed to people less for-
tunate than themselves."[55]

The past year was one in which company after company —
IBM, Sears, GM, American Express, Westinghouse — faltered. I
found it telling that in all of the exposition about these companies'
travails that I read in the national news weeklies, in the *Wall Street
Journal,* in *Business Week,* in the *New York Times,* and in the
Washington Post, the quality of the work force was not mentioned
once as a cause of their woes. Story after story described how

management action or inaction had brought a company to grief. Said Helmut Panke, president of BMW's North American operations, "[In the 1980s] everybody tried to make a fast buck, breaking up companies and diversifying. Everyone concentrated on shareholder value in the short term."[56]

Surveying all the damage, Robert Samuelson proclaimed "The Death of Management":

> By management, I mean the peculiarly American idea (still taught at many business schools) that a "good manager" should be able to manage any enterprise, anywhere, any time. Through incisive analysis and decisive action, our supermanagers supposedly could make any company productive and profitable. The idea has collapsed with failures at companies that once symbolized U.S. management prowess. . . . With hindsight we can see the absurdity. We don't imagine a winning football coach switching to basketball, nor a concert pianist becoming a symphony violinist. . . . What seems astonishing is how such a bad idea survived so long. . . .
>
> Roger Smith, GM's chairman between 1981 and 1990, exemplified this sort of know-nothing executive. When asked by Fortune to explain what went wrong, he answered: "I don't know. It's a mysterious thing." To fathom what went wrong, Smith truly had to understand how automobiles are designed and made; he apparently never did, despite a career at GM. As a society we have spent the past decade paying for mistakes like Smith's.[57]

When stories of improved productivity appeared, the American worker was an integral part of the improvement. One such report told of a manufacturer of speakers that used to produce 520 units a day with 10 workers. But "after a few inexpensive changes, including rearranging the assembly line and training workers to perform multiple tasks, eight people produce 816 units a day — doubling each worker's output."[58] (Note that retraining the work force is viewed as an inexpensive change.) No doubt the owners of this manufacturing enterprise are elated. One wonders, however, about the ultimate social good of such improvement when a doubling of productivity for some is purchased at the loss of employment for 20% of the work force. I know of no model of social well-being that takes this factor into account. For their part, American workers continued to be the most productive in the world. The McKinsey Global Institute reported as follows:

> In 1990, the aggregated OECD [Organisation for Economic Cooperation and Development] data show that GDP (Gross Domestic Product) per capita in the United States was 16% greater than in West Germany, 22% greater than in Japan, 23% greater than in France, and 37% greater than in the U.K. when measured in units of equal purchasing power. These are surprising facts, and not only because they contradict the commonly held view that the U.S. has fallen behind. In a world where technology and capital are fully mobile among advanced market economies, and where workers are equally healthy and well educated, we would have expected to find that full convergence has occurred. Certainly in 1945 the U.S. GDP per capita was very much higher than in Europe and Japan. However, 47 years is a long time and rebuilding and matching best practice is easier than pushing out the frontier.[59]

Per-capita GDP is not the only measure available, though. If one looks at the "per-worker" data, the differences between the U.S. and Germany and France become much smaller, while the differences between the U.S. and Japan become even larger. Since this report is based on 1990 data, it does not take into account the 2.2% productivity increase that occurred in the U.S. in 1992, an enormous increase that surprised and stunned everyone.

While the workers were doing their part for the economy, the economy was not doing its part for them. "The economy is failing nearly every American," said Lawrence Mishel of the Economic Policy Institute.[60] Mishel estimated that even persons earning over $80,000 a year were losing ground to inflation. College graduates were more and more likely to take jobs that require no college or to return to community colleges to learn a practical skill.

Said Secretary of Labor Reich, "The average wages of America's production workers, adjusted for inflation, are the lowest they've been since 1967. Eighteen percent of full-time workers don't earn enough to keep a family of four out of poverty; this level is up from 12% in 1979."[61] While graduates were having a harder time finding jobs that paid well, those without skills were having even tougher times, and the jobs they landed tended to be the lowest paying. Reich asked, "Must we choose between more jobs or better jobs?" He provided no answer. "No country has yet found the formula," he said.[62]

Scott Scanlon, who publishes a newsletter for out-of-work executives, told a *New York Times* reporter that America will not find it either.[63] "When people talk about economic recovery, people think that means more jobs. There's not going to be a recovery in jobs," Scanlon said. Others quoted in the same article echoed Scanlon's discouraging news.

One still hears the argument that lousy schools that produce lousy workers are decreasing our competitiveness — but less often. However, one still hears frequently the argument that our workers must be "more skilled" in the future if they are to compete in both a global economy and a technologically complex society. The U.S. is often compared unfavorably to Europe in this regard. This is the "high skills or low wages" argument, and it is true that we cannot continue to create low-paying jobs in service industries and to lose high-paying jobs in manufacturing. This appears to have nothing to do with the schools, though, and those countries that have made work "smarter" have paid for it dearly: unemployment rates in Europe are currently running at an average of 10%. According to various news reports, the terrible economic climate in Europe threatens to scuttle not only a unified currency system, but also the whole notion of the much-ballyhooed "United States of Europe," as the nations turn inward and self-interest dominates.

Conclusion

I repeat, as I have in earlier reports, that American schools face many challenges, some of them horrific. In this report I have detailed problems in the cities and alluded to the even more intractable problems in impoverished rural areas. Schools in poor districts need resources that they are neither getting now nor are likely to get soon. I am certain that in the U.S. there are unspecified numbers of incompetent teachers, corrupt administrators, and inept board members. Why should education be different from other institutions?

In addition, our perceptions of school success are conditioned largely by our expectations. And those expectations have changed enormously, if irrationally. A system that formerly satisfied expectations by functioning as a sorting machine is now asked to optimize the learning of all students. The dominant element in this system remains "25-kids-in-a-box," hardly a means of optimization. We know much more from cognitive psychology about how people learn, and we should use what we know much more often and much more wisely than we do. We should abandon what I have elsewhere called a "pathology of envy" that inhibits the spread of good practice.[64]

Beyond that, however, I think that we should examine our data afresh. I think David Berliner was onto something when he responded to Harold Stevenson, "I accept your data but challenge your interpretations." We need to look at the interpretation of the data afresh, freed from the chronic perception that schools have failed.

Consider a mild example of this in Merseth's *Kappan* article mentioned above. (Hers is, in many respects, a reasonable piece, and I use it with no intent to embarrass her or to hold it up as a horrible example. It is, rather, a typical example — and that is the problem.) Early in her essay, Merseth asks us to consider this problem:

> There are 125 sheep and 5 dogs in a flock. How old is the shepherd?

Merseth says that researchers report that "three out of four schoolchildren will produce a numerical answer to this problem." I would ask, "And why not?" We teach our children that adults in general and teachers in particular are not out to trick them with absurd, unsolvable problems.

95

More important for our fresh look at the situation is to note that Merseth poses this result as a problem for America: "America has produced a generation of students who engage in problem solving without regard for common sense or the context of the problem."[65] Perhaps, but I wonder. The children in this research were Swiss. After all, what American test-maker or researcher would construct a problem whose actors are shepherds, dogs, and a flock of sheep? Perhaps Swiss kids trust adults more than American kids. From everything I have read about the press for conformity in Japanese and Chinese schools, I would expect the number of students who would give numerical answers in those countries to approach 100%. Merseth offers no comparative data.

Similarly, she cites *The Underachieving Curriculum* as finding that 40% of American eighth- and 12th-graders agree that mathematics is a set of rules.[66] Again, she presents these proportions as a problem, an American problem, and she contrasts this belief in rules with the "zigzag path" that mathematicians follow when they "do" mathematics or discourse about it. But if 40% hold such a belief, this leaves fully 60% who don't.

And mathematicians were once schoolchildren, too. Were a Martian to read Merseth's essay or the many current critiques of mathematics education, surely it would conclude that mathematics education absolutely precludes the existence of mathematicians. How do some people break out of this awful instruction to become the people who engage in the kinds of mathematics investigations that are nowhere to be found in school? It is, at the very least, an intriguing problem in etiology.

Again, no comparative data are presented about how many children in other countries hold similar beliefs about mathematics. If such data were presented, maybe we'd look bad, maybe not. In the absence of such data, people are simply assuming that the situation here is awful relative to that in the other countries that get higher test scores. This approach is not very becoming to researchers who like to think of themselves as objective, analytic, and rational.

And while we try to shake off our cultural cobwebs and act a little more like anthropologists and a little less like stern aunts, we might want to keep the following incident in mind. In the 1960s "The G.E. College Bowl" matched teams of undergraduates in a kind of academic Rose Bowl every Sunday evening. The all-time champions, the Brandeis team of 1968, were dubbed "The Waltham Wonders," a team so unbeatable that they were forced to retire in order to give someone else a chance. As the class of '68 was about to gather for its 25th reunion, one of the Wonders suggested a contest between his team and a team composed of the class of 1993. Agreed.

"Fantasy is that you come back 25 years later and beat the pants off them," said one Wonder. But then he said, "This is real life." The class of '93 won in a walk, 280 to 180. Hardly the definitive test of intergenerational academic achievements, but, as another of the Wonders said, "You sort of feel that in a good world the next generation is better than the previous one, and that's what happened here."[67]

Notes

1. Gerald W. Bracey, "The Second Bracey Report on the Condition of Public Education," *Phi Delta Kappan,* October 1992, pp. 104-17.
2. Gerald W. Bracey, "Why Can't They Be Like We Were?" *Phi Delta Kappan,* October 1991, pp. 104-17.
3. William Kristol and Jay P. Lefkowitz, "Our Students, Still at Risk," *New York Times,* 3 May 1993, p. A-23.
4. Edward Lederman, "Two Modest Proposals for Public Education," *Rocky Mountain News,* 2 April 1993, p. 65-A.
5. "Still at Risk," *Washington Post,* 22 April 1993, p. A-21.
6. Edward A. Fiske, "The Report That Shook Up Schools," *Washington Post,* 25 April 1993, p. C-7.
7. Robert J. Samuelson, "Hollow School Reform," *Washington Post,* 28 April 1993, p. A-19.
8. "Special Education Report," *USA Today,* 17 March 1993, pp. 5-D - 8-D.
9. Harold Stevenson, "Learning from Asian Schools," *Scientific American,* December 1992, pp. 70-76.
10. Albert Shanker, "Competing for Customers," *New York Times,* 27 June 1993, Sect. 4, p. 7.

11. Albert Shanker, "World Class Standards," *New York Times,* 4 July 1993, Sect. 4, p. 7.

12. Albert Shanker, "The Wrong Message," *New York Times,* 11 July 1993, Sect. 4, p. 7.

13. Katherine K. Merseth, "How Old Is the Shepherd? An Essay About Mathematics Education," *Phi Delta Kappan,* March 1993, p. 549.

14. Harold Stevenson, Shin-Ying Lee, and James W. Stigler, "Mathematics Achievement of Chinese, Japanese, and American Children," *Science,* February 1985, pp. 693-99.

15. "From Risk to Renewal: Charting a Course for Reform: The Next 10 Years," *Education Week,* Special Report, 10 February 1993, p. 4.

16. *Profiles of College-Bound Seniors, 1982* (New York: College Board, 1982); and *Profiles of College-Bound Seniors, 1992* (New York: College Board, 1992).

17. Jessica Mathews, "Lessons from Asian Schools," *Washington Post,* 30 November 1992, p. A-23.

18. Archie E. Lapointe, Nancy A. Mead, and Janice M. Askew, *Learning Mathematics* (Princeton, N.J.: Educational Testing Service, Report No. 22-CAEP-01, February 1992); and Archie E. Lapointe, Janice M. Askew, and Nancy A. Mead, *Learning Science* (Princeton, N.J.: Educational Testing Service, Report No. 22-CAEP-02, February 1992).

19. Pat Wingert and Melinda Beck, "The Young and the Gifted: Are Our Schools Nurturing Talented Kids?" *Newsweek,* 28 June 1993, pp. 52-53.

20. Claudio Sanchez, interview with Gerald Bracey, "Morning Edition," National Public Radio, 2 November 1992.

21. Gerald W. Bracey, "The Media's Myth of School Failure," *Inter Ed,* Summer 1993, p. 1.

22. George Kaplan, *Images of Education: The Mass Media's Version of America's Schools* (Washington, D.C.: Institute for Educational Leadership, 1992).

23. Warwick B. Elley, *How in the World Do Students Read?* (Hamburg: International Association for the Evaluation of Educational Achievement, July 1992).

24. Robert Rothman, "U.S. Ranks High in International Study of Reading," *Education Week,* 30 September 1992, p. 1.

25. Anita Manning, "U.S. Kids Near Top of Class in Reading," *USA Today,* 29 September 1992, p. 1. (Although the *USA Today* article is

dated prior to the *Education Week* article, it was actually a reaction to that piece. In the D.C. area, *Education Week* typically arrives two days prior to its official publication date.)

26. German Research Service, *Special Science Reports, Vol. VIII,* November 1992, pp. 12-14.

27. *NAEP 1992 Mathematics Report Card for the Nation and the States* (Washington, D.C.: National Center for Education Statistics, Report No. 23ST02, April 1993).

28. Robert A. Forsyth, "Do NAEP Scales Yield Valid Criterion-Referenced Interpretations?" *Educational Measurement: Issues and Practice,* Fall 1991, pp. 3-9.

29. *Educational Achievement Standards: NAGB's Approach Yields Misleading Interpretations* (Washington, D.C.: General Accounting Office, GAO/PEMD-93-12, June 1993), p. 3.

30. David P. Baker, "Compared to Japan, the U.S. Is a Low Achiever . . . Really," *Educational Researcher,* April 1993, pp. 18-20; and Ian Westbury, "American and Japanese Achievement . . . Again," *Educational Researcher,* April 1993, pp. 21-25.

31. Lena H. Sun, "China's 'Schools for Aristocrats'," *Washington Post,* 20 March 1993, p. A-1.

32. Lena H. Sun, "Chinese Swaddled, Not Coddled," *Washington Post,* 1 June 1993, p. A-l.

33. David E. Sanger, "Student's Killing Displays Dark Side of Japan Schools," *New York Times,* 3 April 1993, p. 1.

34. Peter Boylan, personal communication, 30 April 1993.

35. Israel Scheffler, quoted in John Goodlad, "Toward Educative Communities and Tomorrow's Teachers," No. 1 in a Works in Progress Series, University of Washington, Seattle, November 1992.

36. C. C. Carson, R. M. Huelskamp, and T. D. Woodall, "Perspectives on Education in America," *Journal of Educational Research,* May/June 1993, pp. 259-310; and Joe Schneider and Paul Houston, *Exploding the Myths: Another Round in the Education Debate* (Rosslyn, Va.: American Association of Educational Service Agencies, 1993).

37. Mary Jordan, "In Cities Like Atlanta, Whites Are Passing on Public Schools," *Washington Post,* 24 May 1993, p. A-l.

38. Michael Casserly, statement made at a press conference on the release of baseline data on the National Urban Goals, September 1992.

39. Iris Rotberg, "Sure-Fire School Reform," *Washington Post*, 11 June 1993, p. A-21.

40. George Madaus, *The Influence of Testing on Teaching Math and Science in Grades 4-12* (Chestnut Hill: Center for the Study of Testing, Evaluation, and Educational Policy, Boston College, October 1992).

41. *The Federal Role in Improving Elementary and Secondary Education* (Washington, D.C.: Congressional Budget Office, May 1993).

42. *Prospects: The Congressionally Mandated Study of Educational Growth and Opportunity, Interim Report* (Washington, D.C.: U.S. Department of Education, Planning and Evaluation Service, May 1993).

43. Courtland Milloy, "Teaching Failure by Example," *Washington Post*, 17 March 1993, p. D-1.

44. Jonathan Kozol, *Savage Inequalities* (New York: Crown, 1991).

45. Paul W. Valentine, "'You Can't Build Your Way Out,' Maryland Prison Official Says," *Washington Post*, 24 May 1993, p. B-1.

46. Robert Coles, *Children of Crisis, Vol. 2* (Boston: Little, Brown, 1971), p. 116.

47. Mary McGrory, "A Week of Clintonian Lapses," *Washington Post*, 25 May 1993, p. A-2.

48. John R. Berrueta-Clement et al., *Changed Lives: The Effects of the Perry Preschool Program on Youths Through Age 19* (Ypsilanti, Mich.: High/Scope Press, 1984).

49. Denis P. Doyle, "Service Costs, Education Pays," *Washington Post*, 13 May 1993, p. A-27.

50. Tait Trussell, "National-Service Deceptions," *Education Week*, 16 June 1993, p. 29.

51. W. Steven Barnett, "Benefits of Compensatory Preschool Education," *Journal of Human Resources*, Spring 1992, pp. 279-312.

52. Edward Zigler, "Head Start, the Whole Story," *New York Times*, 24 July 1993, p. A-17.

53. Frank Swoboda and Warren Brown, "Cutting Edge, Cutting Costs," *Washington Post*, 18 July 1993, p. H-1.

54. Cited in Schneider and Houston, p. 37.

55. Ibid.

56. Swoboda and Brown, op. cit.

57. Robert J. Samuelson, "The Death of Management," *Newsweek*, 10 May 1993, pp. 55, 59.

58. Steven Pearlstein, "Industry's Productivity-Led Recovery Shows Promise," *Washington Post*, 5 July 1993, p. A-1.

59. *Service Sector Productivity* (Washington, D.C.: McKinsey Global Institute, October 1992), p. 1.

60. Quoted in Louis Uchitelle, "America Isn't Creating Enough Jobs and No One Seems to Know Why," *New York Times*, 4 September 1992, Sect. 4, p. 1.

61. Robert B. Reich, "Workers of the World, Get Smart," *New York Times*, 20 July 1993, p. A-19.

62. Ibid.

63. Bob Herbert, "Looking for Work," *New York Times*, 1 August 1993, Sect. 4, p. 15.

64. Gerald W. Bracey, "Filet of School Reform, Sauce Diable," *Education Week*, 16 June 1993, p. 28.

65. Merseth, p. 549.

66. Curtis McKnight et al., *The Underachieving Curriculum* (Champaign, Ill.: Stipes, 1987).

67. "The 60's Versus the 90's in a Quiz Show Reprise," *New York Times*, 26 May 1993, p. B-7.

THE
FOURTH
BRACEY REPORT ON
THE CONDITION
OF PUBLIC EDUCATION

October 1994

The first three Bracey Reports presented a great deal of data that demolished two myths. The first myth was that a Golden Era of American education once existed, from which state of grace we have since fallen and to which state of grace we must struggle to return. The second was that the performance of American students is dreadfully low, both in comparison to Asian and European students and in comparison to the performance of American students in years past.

Of Hoaxes and Myths

This report continues the demolition work. But first I must take note of an even more pervasive hoax. It is one that I fell victim to, as did most of the nation. By itself, the hoax is not so important, but as a symbol it reveals how readily people believe any terrible thing about schools.

In 1986, when I took up residence in the administration building of the school district in Cherry Creek, Colorado, I noticed a sheet of green paper on the bulletin board outside my office. It listed the most pervasive school problems of the 1940s, followed by those of the 1980s. The catalogue of horrors for the 1940s included, in order, talking, chewing gum, making noise, running in the halls, getting out of place in line, wearing improper clothing, and not putting paper in wastebaskets. The list for the 1980s was dramatically different: drug abuse, alcohol abuse, pregnancy, suicide, rape, robbery, and assault. The paper gave as its source the police department in Fullerton, California. That attribution made me wonder. I had spent five years as a police dispatcher and had consulted for the police department in New York City. And surveys of this sort just didn't seem to be the typical police department activity. But who knew? Maybe police work in California was closer to social science than was the case in New York.

In any case, my puzzlement led no further. Too bad. Had I but thought about it for a moment, I would have noticed that the 1980s list did not apply to the schools in Cherry Creek, a district that sends about 85% of its students on to higher education. Nor did it seem to apply in the neighboring suburban districts, nor in the approximately 150 small-town and rural districts in Colorado. Even in Denver, Colorado's only large city, the list would seem far-fetched. Moreover, there hadn't been much talk of these horrific problems during the decade I had spent in the state department of education in Virginia.

When the lists turned up on a bulletin board at Yale University, they sparked more dissonance in the mind of Professor Barry O'Neill than they had in mine. O'Neill found the 1940s list too trivial, and he was skeptical of the 1980s list. So he decided to seek the source.[1]

After collecting 250 versions of these lists, with various attributions, O'Neill found the lists to be a fabrication of one T. Cullen Davis of Fort Worth. Davis, acquitted of murdering his estranged wife's lover, had taken a hammer to his million-dollar collection of jade and ivory statues, smashing them as idols of false religion. He became a born-again Christian. And he used the lists to attack public schools. Cullen revealed to O'Neill his method of con-

104

structing the lists: "How did I know what the offenses in the schools were in 1940? I was there. How do I know what they are now? I read the paper."

But by the time O'Neill elicited this admission, virtually everyone in the nation had adopted the lists as gospel. On the political Right, William Bennett, Rush Limbaugh, Phyllis Schlafly, Ross Perot, and George Will dutifully cited them. On the Left, Anna Quindlen, Herb Caen, and Carl Rowan trotted them out. They turned up in Time and on CBS television. They were variously attributed to CBS News, *CQ Researcher*, and the Heritage Foundation. In their migration from Texas to the rest of the nation, the lists did pass through the Fullerton Police Department, which, knowing of the public's anxiety over teenage drug use, moved drugs from their original position as sixth on the 1980s list to number one.

While the problems in schools are certainly more serious today than they were four or five decades ago, they are not the problems that appear on the 1980s list. A warning many researchers receive early in their training applies here: Don't trust secondary sources. Perhaps a popular bumper-sticker slogan from the 1960s applies as well: Question Authority.

Having unearthed the lists' source, O'Neill asked a more difficult question: What makes them so popular? He placed his answer in the tradition of the Puritan jeremiads. In these sermons, the preacher would remind the members of the congregation of their covenant with God, then attribute any current afflictions to God's just retribution for the broken covenant, and finally warn them to mend their ways and renew the covenant with God.

Said O'Neill, "Americans today regard their country as the richest, freest, and fairest, with the best social system, but cannot square this with the social problems of America's young. . . . The school lists are a collective moan of anxiety over the gap between ideals and reality. When Puritans or modern Americans enumerate their faults, they are declaring their dedication to their ideals, reassuring each other that at least their goals remain high."

Something similar occurs constantly in education. The state of education is never ideal, and drugs, violence, and pregnancy are problems in ways they never were 50 years ago. As with the lists, the political Right and Left agree on these problems. They part ways on how to solve them. In addition, the tradition of criticizing schools is a long one. From my forays into the history of education, it seems that in the last century such criticism has abated only during World Wars I and II and during the Great Depression, when people had more immediate and more intense things to worry about.

The hoax of the lists was not alone this year. Sam Ginn, chairman of Pacific Telesis, gave speeches declaring that his company had administered a seventh-grade reading test to 6,400 applicants for operator positions and that only 2,700 had passed with a score high enough for him to hire them. This showed, said Ginn, the need for education reform to develop "workers with skills that will allow us to be competitive in the next century."[2]

What Ginn did not say was that his jobs paid only $7 an hour. Based on a 40-hour week and a 50-week year, this works out to the princely annual income of $14,000, only about 60% of the average starting salary for teachers and a sum slightly below the official 1993 poverty level for a family of four. It's not an income likely to attract the nation's literati. Moreover, Ginn also failed to say that he had only 700 jobs to offer. His test had yielded nearly four times as many qualified applicants as he could use.

Similarly, in April 1994 a book titled *Reinventing Education* appeared.[3] The lead author was Louis Gerstner, Jr., CEO of IBM and former CEO of RJR Nabisco. The book charged that American high school students place last or next to last in international comparisons of math and science achievement; that SAT scores have fallen to historic lows; that we spend more money on education than any other nation; that, despite a decade of increasing expenditures, achievement test scores are static; and that the high school graduation rate is 72%. All of these statements are false, and below, under the heading "New Data," I will expose them for the hoaxes they are. Because high school completion is not discussed below, let me note that the First Bracey Report found the on-time completion rate to be 83%.

106

Benjamin Barber of Rutgers University had a different take on public education and its discontents.[4] Barber accepted the myth of school failure but proffered an alternative theory of how these miserable conditions came to be. It's not the kids, the teachers, or the administrators, he said.

> I am increasingly persuaded that the reason for the country's inaction [to rescue the schools] is that Americans do not really care about education — the country has grown comfortable with the game of "let's pretend we care." . . . The children are onto this game. They know that if we really valued schooling, we'd pay teachers what we pay stockbrokers; if we valued books, we'd spend a little something on the libraries so that adults could read, too; if we valued citizenship, we'd give national service and civic education more than pilot status; if we valued children, we wouldn't let them be abused, manipulated, impoverished, and killed in their beds by gang-war crossfire and stray bullets. Schools can and should lead, but when they confront a society that in every instance tells a story exactly opposite to the one they are supposed to be teaching, their job becomes impossible.

Barber cited the writings of E.D. Hirsch, Jr., of Chester Finn, Jr., of Diane Ravitch, and of the late Allan Bloom; then he hurled his accusation: "How this captious literature reeks of hypocrisy! How sanctimonious all the hand-wringing over still another 'education crisis' seems." Given the mass of data contained in the four Bracey Reports, I must disagree with Barber's assessment of the state of education — but not so much with his assessment of our national values.

New Data

Of the data that have surfaced since the Third Bracey Report was published last October, the most interesting surely were those contained in *Education in States and Nations*, a report from the National Center for Education Statistics.[5] This report compares the 19 developed nations of the Organisation for Economic Cooperation and Development (OECD) on a variety of participation, input, financial, and outcome variables.

107

One section contains results from the Second International Assessment of Educational Progress (IAEP-2), transformed into National Assessment of Educational Progress (NAEP) scales. While these results are interesting in themselves, the picture becomes even more intriguing when one combines these data with other NAEP reporting categories used in the 1992 NAEP mathematics assessment. By so doing, we obtain the following results:

Top Finishers

1. Asian students (U.S.)	287
2. Taiwan	285
3. Korea	283
4. Advantaged urban students (U.S.)	283
5. White students (U.S.)	277
6. Hungary	277

Thus the great majority of American students finish at or near the top of the most recent international comparison in mathematics, a subject in which our national performance is reputed to be dismal. Whites and Asians together make up over 70% of the K-12 population of U.S. schools.

At the 1993 meeting of the American Educational Research Association, Lauren Resnick — who in 1991 was beginning all of her speeches with the message, "We all know how terrible we are" — acknowledged, "We look pretty good in some areas."[6] Resnick had in mind reading and language arts, she said, but these new IAEP-2 data show many students looking good in mathematics, too.

Overall American rankings in IAEP-2 mathematics were low, though the scores were just below average. Many countries are tightly bunched together, and a small difference in scores makes a large difference in the rankings. But if most American students are near the top and the U.S. overall mean score is below the international average, this must mean that some groups are scoring low. And they are.

Bottom Scorers

Jordan	246
Mississippi	246
Hispanic students (U.S.)	245
Disadvantaged urban students (U.S.)	239
Black students (U.S.)	236

There is no NAEP category for "disadvantaged rural students," else there would doubtless be another entry in this list. Because ethnicity is a central fact of American life, we tend to overreport things in ethnic terms and underreport things in terms of class. But these low scores are largely a class-linked phenomenon. As Harold Hodgkinson has shown, while Asians usually score highest of all ethnic groups in mathematics, wealthy blacks outscore poor Asians.[7]

Paradoxically, another table in *Education in States and Nations* strongly suggests that comparing national and state school systems on the basis of average test scores is senseless. This chart shows the average scores and the range from the 5th to the 95th percentile of each country's or state's sample. As one goes from Mississippi's and Jordan's average at the bottom to Taiwan's at the top, one traverses 39 NAEP scale points. As one goes from the bottom of Taiwan's distribution (1st percentile) to the top (99th percentile), one traverses about 150 NAEP scale points.

Many states and nations show similarly large ranges. The within-country variance swamps the between-country variance. Given the enormous within-country variance, it doesn't even seem reasonable to speak of "American schools" or "Taiwanese schools" in reference to average scores. Such variability also raises an important practical question for standard-setting programs, such as the New Standards Project: Where can one place a standard that is credible as a "high" standard without failing a large proportion of students? More important than that, what happens to all the students who do fail? The answer is usually that they will be given more time to meet the standard. No one seems to have noticed that this solution may be very cruel, as well as ineffective.

While people have continued to write that test scores are falling, test scores have continued to rise. Since about 1990, scores in Iowa for all grades except 8 and 12 on the Iowa Tests of Basic Skills (ITBS) and Iowa Tests of Educational Development (ITED) have been at record highs.[8] As is the case with the SAT I, but not with other commercial achievement tests, new forms of the ITBS and ITED are equated to previous forms. This allows us to compare trends over time in the same way that we do for SAT scores.

Actually, trend data for the ITBS and ITED in Iowa are better than trend data for the SAT because the SAT average score depends on who takes the test, and the demographics of the test-taking pool have been and are still changing. Similarly, "then and now" studies of test scores, while they generally favor "now," are hard to interpret in most places because of changing demographics. Iowa, by contrast, is in some ways frozen in time. It has no large cities with their attendant problems. And it is still nearly 98% white.

Moreover, the statewide testing program in Iowa dates from the 1930s. It is a familiar aspect of schooling, not a recently imposed high-stakes endeavor. It is thus not subject to the charge that rising scores reflect curricular alignments, inappropriate administrative procedures, cheating, or other malignancies that are alleged in some quarters to have produced testing's "Lake Wobegon Effect." In sum, whatever the ITBS score represented in 1937, it probably represents much the same thing in 1994. In recent years Iowa has ranked first or second among the states in SAT scores, ACT (American College Testing) scores, and in scores on NAEP mathematics and reading tests. Such a combination of high scores would seem to confirm that they are real.

Still, some might have reservations about the generalizability of data drawn from a single state that is not really representative of the nation as a whole. It is telling, therefore, that the national norming studies for the ITBS track the Iowa data very closely. At some grade levels, national scores are actually *higher* than those in Iowa. As this article went to press, 1992 norms for the ITBS were not yet available for formal publication, but the director of the Iowa program assured me that they would be slightly higher than the 1985 norms. It is thus possible that ITBS scores are at all-time highs.

Such record-setting performance is not so much at variance with other results as one might think at first. In 1993 the proportion of students scoring above 650 on the SAT mathematics section climbed to what appears to be an all-time high of 11%. (I say "appears" because my data go back only to 1963.) And these scores were posted before the "recentering" of SAT scores recently announced by the College Board.

This might seem like a small proportion. Indeed, a note in *Education Week* suggested that the editors of that publication think so.[9] But recall that the standards for the SAT were set in 1941 and were based on the performance of 10,654 students. Ninety-eight percent of them were white, 60% were male, 40% had attended private high schools, and most lived in the North-east, where, by and large, they planned to attend private colleges and universities. The makers of the SAT imposed on the scores of this elite group a normal bell-shaped, or Gaussian, distribution. Thus we know from the statistical properties of the normal curve that only 6.68% of this elite group scored above 650. The current crop of SAT-takers is 30% minority and 52% female. Thirty-one percent of them report family incomes of under $30,000 annually. The test-taking pool for the SAT has been democratized, yet the proportion of high scorers is at its highest point — 65% above the mark obtained by the standard setters.[10]

Two factors other than general performance increases might account for this improvement at the top of the distribution: 1) an increase in the number of Asian students, who outperform all other groups and/or 2) an increase in the number of students from states where small proportions of the senior class take the SAT. If the latter were true, it would be possible that those states were adding very bright students to the test-taking pool.

Neither of these hypotheses holds up under scrutiny, however. First, while Asian students average 535 on the math portion of the SAT, they constitute only 8% of all test-takers, up from 4.5% a decade ago. This means that, of the more than 110,000 students scoring above 650, only about 14,000 are Asian Americans. Their performance exceeds that of all other groups, but the improved scores must be occurring in other groups as well. In 1993 some 10,000 more seniors took the SAT than in 1992, while 5,600 more seniors scored above 650. Moreover, even the SAT verbal scores showed an increase in the number of high scorers, with some 2,600 more seniors scoring above 650 in 1993 than in 1992.

State-by-state results reveal that the recent growth in the number of SAT test-takers has been largely in states where the test was already taken by more than 50% of the senior class. In those states whose populations are growing rapidly from immigration — e.g., Texas, Florida, and California — the proportion of the senior class taking the SAT has been stable and relatively high at 45%, 52%, and 47% respectively.

Average scores on the SAT held little interest for the media last year. They rose for the second year in a row. The *New York Times* carried the story deep in the interior of Section A.[11] The *Washington Post* buried it in the Metro section, playing it as a story of local interest.[12] The headline mentioned results for Metro Washington districts only. Not until the seventh paragraph of the piece did the story reveal national averages and trends. Of course, downturns have consistently found their way to the front pages of both papers.

Much of the information I've reported so far suggests that levels of performance on academic indicators may reflect demographic factors more strongly than they reflect the quality of the education system. Indeed, this is precisely the conclusion that Glen Robinson and David Brandon reached when they found that they could account for 89% of the variability in state-level NAEP mathematics scores by using only four variables: number of parents in the home, level of parental education, type of community, and state poverty rates for ages 5-17.[13] A rank-order correlation coefficient of actual state ranks versus predicted ranks using these same four variables was .995. Note that none of these four variables can be controlled by the school. Robinson and Brandon strongly suggest that state NAEP scores reflect not the *quality* of a state's schools, but the *difficulty* of the educational task different states face. (These findings were reported in detail in the Research column in the September 1994 *Kappan*.)

Education in States and Nations also carried information on how countries spend money for education — something that continues to be poorly reported in the U.S. As David Berliner pointed out, George Bush and virtually his whole Cabinet repeatedly pronounced some variant of "We spend more money on schools than any other country."[14] Gerstner made the same claim in the book mentioned above, as did Herbert Walberg of the University of Chicago in the *Chicago Sun-Times*.[15]

Walberg's allegation is particularly curious because he serves as a consultant to the Organisation for Economic Cooperation and Development, and it is OECD data that show that the United States is not a big spender. There are a variety of ways of calculating school spending, and they all have flaws with regard to their comparability across nations. Richard Jaeger reported several calculations indicating that the U.S. is average or below average in school spending.[16] Perhaps the fairest method is to express expenditures in terms of percentage of gross domestic product. Using this method, the U.S. ranks ninth among 19 nations in spending for K-12 education, according to *Education in States and Nations*.

Yet even this figure overestimates our spending on education, because a smaller slice of the pie goes to instruction in the U.S. than in many other countries. American schools provide many services that schools in other countries do not provide or provide in reduced amounts: transportation, food, medical care, counseling, and, especially, special education. In the U.S. in 1989-90, transportation alone cost more than $8 billion.[17] As the Sandia Report showed, costs for special education have soared for the last 20 years, while costs for regular instruction have risen virtually not at all.[18] And while costs were rising, so were special education enrollments. Between 1976 and 1990, special education enrollments increased by 39%, from 8.3% of the school population to 11.6%.[19]

Money matters loomed large in 1993. The American Legislative Exchange Council, described in the *Washington Post* as a conservative group of legislators, released a study conducted by former Secretary of Education William Bennett that purported to show that there is no relationship between spending and achievement.[20] This study used per-pupil expenditures as a measure of spending, while it used SAT scores for individual states as a measure of achievement. In a column headlined "Meaningless Money Factor," George Will commented that the top five SAT states — Iowa, North Dakota, South Dakota, Utah, and Minnesota — were all relatively low spenders, while New Jersey spent more money than any other state and finished only 39th.[21]

What neither Will nor Bennett bothered to point out, of course, is that in the high-scoring states virtually no one takes the SAT. For 1993 the percentages of high school seniors taking the SAT in the top five states were 5%, 6%, 6%, 4%, and 10% respectively. Most seniors in those states take the ACT. In New Jersey, on the other hand, fully 76% of the senior class filled in the bubbles on SAT answer sheets. A state that includes three-fourths of its student body in a tested population will not look good in comparison with a state whose tested population is made up of an academic elite seeking admission to selective colleges.

The notion that money makes a difference in education outcomes has been gaining ascendancy in recent years, and new data arrived in 1994. For a number of years, school critics have claimed that education's problems cannot be solved by "throwing money at the schools." The usual source cited by these skeptics is a review of the research conducted by Eric Hanushek.[22] Although Keith Baker demonstrated in the pages of the April 1991 *Kappan* that Hanushek's data did not substantiate Hanushek's claims, Baker's analysis of the data had little impact on those who believed Hanushek to be correct.

A recent reanalysis of Hanushek's set of studies, however, might lead us to place *more* emphasis than ever before on money as an important factor in achievement. (Recall that, in the Third Bracey Report, I suggested that, if money makes no difference, someone should inform the wealthy districts so that they'll stop spending so much more of it than other folks.) Indeed, in the new analysis, money seems to be most important when used directly in the service of instruction.[23]

For his part, Hanushek now claims that he never said money makes no difference. He asserts that the reason he found no strong or systematic relationship is that some school districts find effective ways of spending money, while others do not. What we need to know is what kinds of expenditures are effective and how they exert their effect. "The available evidence," Hanushek contends, "simply indicates that the natural proclivities of school systems do not systematically lead to effective use of resources." He does not define further these "natural proclivities" of school systems, but he gives as an example the proposal that we increase the salaries of teachers by 10%. This, says Hanushek, wouldn't increase the relationship between salary and student performance. Rather, it might "slow down turnover of teachers, so that policies designed to attract better people into teaching would be thwarted."[24]

In connection with teacher salaries, it is worth noting that the starting, mid-level, and maximum salaries of teachers do not compare well with the salaries of other white-collar professionals. Nor do they compare well against salaries for teachers in many other developed nations. The U.S. was seventh in a comparison of teacher pay in 13 developed nations.[25]

Money for education is important in ways many people don't usually think about. A headline in the *Washington Post* told the story: "Across U.S., Schools Are Falling Apart."[26] In *Education Week* a headline ran simply: "Schoolhouse Rot."[27] Actually, though these reports were highly relevant, they weren't news. A 1990 report from the Education Writers Association told the same story, as did a 1991 survey by the American Association of School Administrators.

In September of 1993, the Educational Testing Service released *Adult Literacy in America*, a study it conducted for the

U.S. Department of Education.[28] With rare exceptions, the report was seen as further proof of education's low state. "Dumber Than We Thought" screeched the headline of a *Newsweek* story on the report.[29] One had to read much of the story to learn that the headline was not *Newsweek*'s studied assessment, but a direct quote from former Secretary of Education William Bennett. Indeed, this study defined literacy in quite a complicated way, and, as Pauline Gough observed in an editorial in the *Kappan*, among those who scored low were significant numbers of the old, the foreign born, the visually impaired, or individuals who had "physical, mental, or health conditions that kept them from participating fully in work, school, housework, or other activities."[30]

Before leaving the topic of literacy, recall that the Third Bracey Report discussed an International Association for the Assessment of Educational Achievement study of reading in which American 9-year-olds finished second in the world among students from 31 nations, while U.S. 14-year-olds finished eighth and with scores as close to first place as those of the 9-year-olds. Such data are hard to square with the alarmist reactions to the adult literacy survey, unless we assume that the entire world faces a literacy crisis.

Judging from my mailbox, the U.S. Department of Education has increased the rate at which it reports statistics. I understand from officials at ED that they are striving to improve the quality as well. When ED strayed from the mere facts last year, the outcomes were less than successful. Two interpretive reports, *National Excellence: A Case for Developing America's Talent*[31] and *Prisoners of Time*,[32] left much to be desired. The former contained no new data and numerous factual errors; the latter was thin and repeated oft-made, mostly commonsensical recommendations. Given that *Prisoners of Time* was two years in production, one wonders how the researchers spent their time.

The George Will Affair

Nothing better captured the political Right's antipathy toward public education than its campaign for Proposition 174, a referendum in the 1993 California election that would have established a $2,600 credit for parents to use at the school of their choice. The referendum apparently (the wording was so vague that even the measure's authors couldn't answer questions about its impact) would have permitted anyone who could round up 25 children to open a school. Reports cited a coven of witches that planned to do so, since their beliefs were not included in the state's Curriculum Frameworks. Even California's Gov. Pete Wilson, generally a supporter of vouchers, came out against Proposition 174 because it would have devastating effects on the already devastated California economy. Wilson reportedly would have backed the measure if its creators had phased in the fiscal jolts over five years. But they refused, and Wilson felt obliged to oppose it.

Not so William Bennett, who stumped for it, and George Will, who dedicated several columns to it. In his column of 26 August 1992, Will wrote, "Nationally about half of urban public school teachers with school-age children send their children to private schools."[33] Three days later, Will pitched this statistic at Keith Geiger, president of the National Education Association (NEA), on "This Week with David Brinkley." Unfortunately, Geiger swung wildly and said, erroneously, "It's about 40%." Will shrugged, as if to say, "Thanks for proving my point." And a new urban legend was born.

Will's numbers looked spurious to me — almost as spurious as those two lists on the bulletin board in Cherry Creek. Will's office said that the figures came from "School Choice Cases," by Clint Bolick of the Institute for Justice. Bolick, in turn, sent me to David Boaz of the Cato Institute and to his *Liberating Schools: Education in the Inner City*. Boaz passed me on to Denis Doyle of the Hudson Institute. In 1986 Doyle and Terry Hartle, both then working for the American Enterprise Institute, had actually written a never-published paper on the topic.[34] Doyle's and Hartle's figures, which they considered to be "preliminary," in no way approached 50%. The usually cited figure of 46% (which Will interpreted as "about half" applied only to teachers in Chicago,

117

and 80% of those teachers sent their children to parochial schools. The numbers Doyle and Hartle actually used in their paper would yield an estimated figure more like 21% for urban public school teachers and 16% for all teachers — not much above the national average for all parents.

Readers can find a complete analysis of this affair in the September 29 issue of *Education Week*.[35] Here I wish only to note further that it is inappropriate to compare teachers with the general public. All teachers have a college education, and, because so many teachers are not the sole wage earners in their families, the average annual family income for teachers is more than $70,000. Moreover, a 1992 study by James Coleman put the average income of families with children in private schools at $70,000.[36] The proper comparison would match teachers with another group of similar socioeconomic status. When the American Federation of Teachers conducted such an analysis, it found a greater proportion of teachers using public schools than was true of comparable families with similar incomes.[37]

Various versions of my analysis were sent to various media outlets. One found its way to the *Washington Post*, where Will's columns originate. It was turned down by a form letter. Another went to the *Wall Street Journal*. Daniel Henninger, the editorial page editor, sent a letter neither accepting nor rejecting the piece, but thanking me for "the Third Bracey Report and the debunking of George Will's statistic." Imagine my surprise, then, at the long lead editorial that appeared in the *Journal* of October 25 in support of Proposition 174, headed by a segment of the transcript of the Will/Geiger exchange from "This Week with David Brinkley."[38] The editorial gave no indication that either figure was in error and went on to castigate public educators for opposing Proposition 174.

My investigations failed to impress Will himself. A letter from him read, in its entirety, "Your problems multiply. Mr. Geiger, head of the teachers union, concedes 'about 40%,' which strongly suggests that my apogee may be bang on." Enclosed with the letter was the transcript from the relevant part of the Brinkley show.

Responding to my article in a letter to *Education Week*, Doyle also accepted Geiger's figure. Surely Will's and Doyle's letters marked two historic moments. Both usually hold the NEA in the same high esteem as Jim Brady holds the National Rifle Association. Yet here they were, apparently accepting on faith with no questions asked a statistic mumbled by the president of the NEA off the top of his head. It was as if the head of the Tobacco Institute had said that nicotine was not addictive, and Garry Trudeau had agreed.

Yet another copy of my analysis went to *News & Views* of the Educational Excellence Network, a monthly compilation of articles and essays that had been initiated by Chester Finn, Jr., when he was at Vanderbilt University and that is now published by the Hudson Institute. I knew that the piece would not be published in the newsletter. My modest goal was only to preempt the reproduction of Will's essay. In a letter, Michael Heise, then director of *News & Views*, wrote, "I want to thank you for forwarding me a copy of the papers entitled 'George Will's Urban Legend' and 'The Third Bracey Report on the Condition of Public Education.' We will give them careful consideration for the next issue of *News & Views*." The next issue contained only Will's article.

I tried to enlist the aid of media watchers in debunking this statistic. The *Washington Post* ombudsman, Joann Byrd, had been unresponsive to earlier entreaties, so I approached the *Post's* designated media watcher, Howard Kurtz. He wrote a short and accurate summary of the episode.[39] No one could account for the transformation of a statistic for Chicago into one for the nation. Kurtz quoted the Cato Institute's Boaz as saying, "All I did was repeat the findings of Doyle and Hartle." Kurtz concluded with a quote from Henninger of the *Wall Street Journal*: "The precise figures are less important than 'that public school teachers send their children to private school at a rate higher than the general population'." This certainly was in line with the earlier editorial. In the body of that editorial, the editors had cited the figures for California public school teachers as 18%. But rather than draw attention to the distance between 18% and 50%, the *Wall Street*

119

Journal commented only that this rate was higher than for the general public.

As I noted above, the comparison between teachers and the general public is not even the proper comparison, and the proper comparison finds the allegation false. As Shanker had said, "When teachers are compared with other college graduates, it becomes clear that they send their kids to private schools less often than other people of comparable socioeconomic status."[40]

How the figure of "nearly half" got generalized from Chicago to the nation remains a mystery. Six months earlier, Will had cited it correctly. He closed his 7 March 1993 column in support of vouchers for Chicago with "About half the Chicago public school teachers with school-age children send them to private schools."[41] Queries to Will's office to explain how half of Chicago teachers in March became half of the nation's urban teachers in August went unanswered.

Education and the Economy

The First Bracey Report raised questions about the link between schools and the performance of the economy. The Second Bracey Report expressed those doubts more vehemently and presented some evidence that schools were not responsible for the economic malaise. By the Third Bracey Report, this evidence had grown to mountain size. Conditions now allow us to lay to rest, once and for all, the misbegotten notion that schools are dragging our economy down — or, for that matter, pushing it up.

It's not that people aren't still trying to make that connection. In May of this year, IBM's Gerstner took to the op-ed page of the *New York Times* to declare that "Our Schools Are Failing" and to talk about the threat posed by that dismal prospect.[42] The usually reasonable and moderate David Broder declared in the *Washington Post*, "Once again, Americans are being asked to take a gut-check on how serious we are about our children's future. If we're serious, almost everyone agrees, we have to lift the performance of the youngsters coming out of high school, so they have the skills required in the new economy."[43]

In other words, the schools haven't gotten any better, and we are still "a nation at risk." As *A Nation at Risk* had said in 1983, "If only to keep and improve on the slim competitive edge we still retain in world markets, we must dedicate ourselves to the reform of our educational system." It would seem that the economy depends on it.

Fortunately, the economy wasn't listening. It roared off to heights that — if Gerstner and Broder and *A Nation at Risk* were right — ought to be impossible. A lead article by Sylvia Nasar in the business section of the *New York Times* trumpeted this success in the headline, "The American Economy, Back on Top." The *Times* waxed ecstatic:

> A three percent economic growth rate, a gain of two million jobs in the past year, and an inflation rate reminiscent of the 1960s make America the envy of the industrialized world. The amount the average American worker can produce, already the highest in the world, is growing faster than in other wealthy countries, including Japan. The United States has become the world's low-cost provider of many sophisticated products and services, from plastics to software to financial services.
>
> For the most part, these advantages will continue even after countries like Japan and Germany snap out of their recessions. It is the United States, not Japan, that is the master of the next generation of commercially important computer and communications technologies and also of leading-edge services from medicine to movie making.[44]

The *Times* article gushed on in this fashion for 2,500 euphoric words. And it was scarcely a lone voice. T. R. Reid, *Washington Post* foreign correspondent, filed a report from Tokyo, noting that Japanese business was learning from America once again.[45] The *Post* article followed an earlier *New York Times* article headlined "Now It's Japan's Turn to Play Catch-Up."[46] That article carried the subhead, "From PC's to Cable TV, Tokyo Finds Itself Far Behind in the Next Electronics Revolution." And *U.S. News & World Report* carried a long feature article titled "America Cranks

It Up."[47] Even *Fortune* was forced to concede, "For all the criticism of U.S. education, youngsters enter the work force far better equipped than today's mature workers."[48]

That last comment was as close as the schools came to getting any credit for the recovery. None of the other articles cited, nor myriad similar pieces published elsewhere, even mentioned the schools.

Only a couple of years ago, Marc Tucker, Lester Thurow, and Robert Reich, to name but a few, were decrying the state of our schools and our Taylorized production lines. "Japan makes television sets; we watch them," declared the Hudson Institute's Denis Doyle in 1992.[49] We might ask ourselves the question, If the schools are still awful, how on earth did the economy manage such a miraculous turnaround? According to all the articles, the new successes derived from "reengineering" — industry's equivalent of education's "restructuring" — and the application of new technologies. Companies downsized to become lean and mean. Management savvy saved the day. The schools were, at best, invisible in the process. In fact, John McClain of the Associated Press reported a survey confirming that the economy is booming but also pointing out that pervasive weaknesses in elementary and secondary education still threatened its health.[50]

Stanford University's Larry Cuban was among those to notice the asymmetry between blame for the bad economic times and credit for the good ones. "Why is it that now with a bustling economy, rising productivity, and shrinking unemployment American public schools are not receiving credit for the turnaround?" Cuban wondered.[51] Citing some of the evidence disclosed earlier in this report, he continued his questioning: "Now that America outstrips Japan and Germany in labor productivity, economic growth, and share of world merchandising exports, why haven't public schools received the equivalent of the Oscars?"

Cuban knew that his questions were rhetorical. "Not even a cheaply framed certificate of merit is in the offing for public schools. For the myth of better schools as the engine for a leaner, stronger economy was a scam from the very beginning," he concluded. Just so. In the First Bracey Report, I called *A Nation at Risk* a "xenophobic screed." These days, I simply call it a lie: much of the evidence backing its claims is highly selective; some of it doesn't even exist.

This particular economic boom comes with a most unusual downside. While Nasar's *New York Times* piece, cited earlier, spoke of the creation of two million jobs, it didn't say how many of them are good jobs. The reality is that damn few are good. In recent years, people have been indoctrinated with the argument that the fastest growing fields all require highly skilled people. This is true. But according to the Bureau of Labor Statistics, these fields account for very few jobs overall: 3,162,000 by the year 2005. On the other hand, the single largest occupation, retail sales, by itself accounts for 4,500,000. The 10 occupations with the highest numbers of workers are largely unskilled, and these account for 30,100,000 jobs — almost 10 times more than the fastest growing fields.[52] As manufacturing lost 255,000 jobs in 1992, the restaurant industry alone added 249,000 jobs. Not many called for executive chefs.[53]

Who is taking all these new jobs? In addition to the usual new graduates and immigrants, the answer is people who already have jobs. The Labor Department reported that seven million people hold 15 million jobs, and for the first time it documented the existence of a phenomenon heretofore known mostly through anecdote: the three- and four-job couples. Some of these multi-job workers, it is true, are people trying to break into new fields; but the largest group consists of those just trying to pay their bills.[54]

Ironically, the creation of some jobs dooms others. Patte Barth, the editor of *Basic Education*, once declared in the pages of that journal that advanced algebra would soon be a basic skill, and by way of example she wrote of a restaurant that was run by only two people.[55] Barth concentrated on the breadth and depth of the skills those people would have to have and on what that implied for education. I am more impressed by the fact that there are only two of them on the premises.

123

Meanwhile, Richard Barnet of the Institute for Policy Studies pointed out that, "between 1979 and 1992, the Fortune 500 companies presented 4.4 million of their employees with pink slips."[56] Barnet saw two forces operating to kill jobs. One was moving the job to another locale — maybe within the U.S., maybe not. "More and more of us, from wastebasket emptiers to CEOs of multinational corporations, are waking up to the fact that we are swimming in a global labor pool," he wrote. The movement has particularly pernicious effects in the countries of Asia, Africa, and Latin America — because in those areas large numbers of women are entering the workforce, and those nations have traditionally paid women much less than men.

The other force is technology. In the past year, article after article announced layoffs of a few hundred to many thousand workers, even as other articles (sometimes the very same ones) displayed curves of rising productivity. The relationship is causal: as people become more productive, fewer of them are needed in the workforce. Barnet had this to say: "I have visited a variety of highly automated factories in the United States and Europe, including automobile, electronics, and printing plants. The scarcity of human beings in these places is spooky."

In 1979 Christopher Evans predicted that the microchip would end work as we know it.[57] Evans foresaw pervasive affluence and the possibility of a 25-hour work week. To date, the scenario has been more like that described 15 years earlier by Kurt Vonnegut in *God Bless You, Mr. Rosewater*, wherein one character mused, "The problem is, how to love people who have no use." As Barnet observed, "In the end, the job crisis raises the most fundamental question of human existence: What are we doing here?"

Given all of this, it is not surprising that Frank Swoboda, *Washington Post* business writer, found workers asking "one of the most fundamental questions facing the nation today: Can a worker acquire enough skills to achieve job security in a world of global competition?" Swoboda found the short-term answer to be "no." He didn't have a long-term answer.[58]

While education is at best tenuously linked to the well-being of the nation, it is becoming even more important to the well-being of the individual. That is, education is related to the likelihood of getting a job in the first place or of finding another job when you lose the one you had. Still, as Swoboda reported, it is not a guarantee. It is a necessary, but not a sufficient, condition for well-paying employment. The number of college-educated door-to-door salesmen grew from 57,000 in 1983 to 75,000 in 1990, while the number of bus drivers with bachelor's degrees increased from 99,000 to 166,000. Ross Perot wondered why all the hotel people who carried his luggage had bachelor's degrees, giving rise to the phrase "B.A. Bellhops," while in a *Washington Post* piece titled "Take This Job and Love It," a recent college graduate was quoted as saying, "We're getting jobs chimps could do."[59]

That last article described college graduates working as file clerks and photocopy makers. Compared to high school graduates, though, they had it good. "For hundreds of thousands of people graduating from high school this spring, the diploma is a one-way ticket to low-paying, part-time jobs at best," wrote Peter Kilborn.[60] The lucky ones might get full-time jobs doing what they did as part-time employees after school and on weekends.

Some companies, including large ones such as Federal Express, are taking advantage of the situation by offering only part-time work that comes without benefits. "There is a myth in this country that, if you want to be something, you can be it," said economist Richard Rothstein. "This generation is finding out it isn't true with a vengeance. And we wonder why they're cynical."[61]

In fact, high school graduates now face a new source of competition for jobs: college graduates. "Industry is shedding layers of middle-management jobs held by college graduates," wrote Kilborn, "creating an additional challenge for high school graduates: People with college degrees have invaded their blue-collar turf." Of 1993 high school graduates who tried to enter the labor market, 24% were still unemployed as of October, almost four times the national average for all workers.[62]

For those who do find jobs, whether they be college or high school graduates, wages are down. Entry-level wages fell in real dollars from just above $12 an hour for college graduates in 1973 to $11 an hour in 1991. For those with only a high school diploma, the drop was from just above $8 an hour to just above $6 an hour.[63] Alan Wurtzel, chairman of the board at Circuit City, an electronics discount chain on the East Coast, wrote that "Circuit City is a large national company that seldom hires people right out of high school. . . . In hiring new employees for our stores, warehouses, and offices, Circuit City is looking for people who are able to provide very high levels of customer service, who are honest, and who have a positive, enthusiastic, achievement-oriented work ethic."[64] These are characteristics that our high school graduates lack, Wurtzel claimed. He somehow failed to mention that Circuit City warehouse employees start at $4.25 an hour, while salespeople are paid no salary at all and work strictly on commission.

Still, education pays. The U.S. Census Bureau reported the following lifetime earnings for various levels of education:[65]

Not a high school graduate	$609,000
High school diploma	$821,000
Some college	$993,000
Associate's degree	$1,062,000
Bachelor's degree	$1,421,000
Master's degree	$1,619,000
Doctorate	$2,142,000
Professional (doctor, lawyer)	$3,013,000

Despite the turnaround in the U.S. economy since 1992, the Census Bureau also reported that the number of poor Americans continued to grow, reaching 14.7%. For children, the figure was 20%, and for African Americans and Hispanics it reached nearly 50%. These statistics seem to verify the charge that economic success in America continues to be polarized along class lines. They are all the more horrific when one considers that the threshold of poverty for a family of four is a scandalously low $14,335, according to the Census Bureau — a figure less than half of $30,786, the median American household income for a family of four. As discussed in the Third Bracey Report, children of poverty do not perform well in school.

Indeed, other studies of poverty in America suggest that we are moving away from rather than toward our first national goal: that all children begin school ready to learn. The proportion of low-income children in preschool programs is far smaller than that for upper-income children. And daycare programs that serve low-income families are more likely to be custodial than are programs serving upper-income families, which are likely to be developmental.

School Choice

School choice as a one-stop solution to education's problems might have crested with California's Proposition 174, a 1993 referendum that would have created a voucher system with public funds available for use in private schools. Interest now seems to be on the wane, perhaps because interest in charter schools is waxing. While John Chubb continued to tout free-market choice,[66] while Terry Moe showed up at California's "Education Summit" in February to promise another choice referendum, and while Gerstner and his co-authors plumped for choice in their book, most other writers urged caution. So did the data.

Harold Howe II exposed choice as no more than the latest episode of what he termed "millennialist thinking" — thinking that embodies the hope that a single social reform might bring the millennium.[67] Certainly, in their book Chubb and Moe sang a most ardent paean to the free market as a panacea for most anything, especially the ills of schools:

> The eighth wonder of the world is the capitalist system of economic organization. It has brought more good to more people than any other large-scale social invention. Therefore its basic assumptions are to be treasured and transferred to all possible realms of human activity. . . . The wonderful power of competition to produce quality will solve all the messy little problems like how to pay for schools, find and prepare good teachers, and motivate children to learn.[68]

This passage leaves Howe all but mute. He can declare only, "If this isn't millennial thinking, I can't imagine what is." Such gushiness coming from supposedly serious scholars certainly is bewildering.

In two similar books, sociologist Peter Cookson, Jr., of Adelphi University and political scientist Jeffrey Henig of George Washington University independently demolished the central premises of market-driven school choice. Both reviewed the history of choice as an idea and the data from choice experiments. The claims for choice are strong; the evidence, weak. Henig found most success stories to be casual claims without real substance, studies with inadequate measures to demonstrate the claims, or studies so lacking in controls as to render them impossible to interpret.[69] Both Henig and Cookson are particularly dismissive of Chubb and Moe's analysis, which turned tiny test score gains into a scale they claimed showed years of growth. Chubb and Moe, says Cookson, "have so magnified their results by altering the unit of analysis . . . that they have lost sight of their own finding, which indicates that there are very few achievement gains between the sophomore and senior years of high school."[70]

In fact, Henig stands the market metaphor on its head. Examining the evidence, he concludes that, when choice works, it works not because it unshackles pent-up market demands, which often can't even be found. It works because of the much-maligned bureaucrats and government agencies:

> The expanded use of choice . . . is better understood as having arisen from collective negotiation, public leadership, and authoritative government, rather than from an unleashing of individual interests and market forces. . . . Whether reactive or activist, in all cases the process of experimentation [with choice] has been public and political — mediated through collective institutions and made to work through the application of authoritative government action.[71]

Both Henig and Cookson warn that market-based choice systems would hide this collective and public discussion and would deprive schools of one of their most important qualities, their openness to public scrutiny and debate.

Henig and Cookson both favor choice, but they see it as one tool among many to improve education, not as a solution to education's problems. Henig conjectures that there might even be choice situations in which public funds would be appropriately spent in private schools.

Joe Nathan, a leading advocate of public school choice, also urged moderation. "Those who promote school choice as a 'panacea' are ignorant and/or foolish," Nathan charged. "Chubb and Moe have done more to harm the choice movement than anyone else."[72] Nathan reasons that we need school choice because there is no one best system for all children; because choice is central to teacher empowerment; because without government-sponsored choice, only the affluent can have it; and because competition stimulates improvement.

For these and other reasons, choice advocates have closely watched Milwaukee's experiment with choice, which provides public money for tuition at private schools. The data from the third year of this program are decidedly mixed. The program has never recruited as many students as it has places for, and the attrition rate is high. It might be no higher than that for low-income children elsewhere in Milwaukee, but — if people are picking schools they want — we ought to expect those schools to have stronger holding power.

Test results are mixed, too.[73] Scores have bounced around and shown no sizable increases, even when the results are statistically significant. (That tests of statistical significance are inappropriate for such program evaluations was a topic treated in the *Kappan* Research column in September 1992.)

The parents in the Milwaukee choice program are better educated, make more money, and are more involved with schools than those who are not. They were angry at their neighborhood schools and had better attitudes about the choice programs. But this finding, too, is an equivocal outcome, as the authors of the report point out: "While they look like just the kinds of parents that choice programs were designed to serve, they might have provided an even greater social good by staying behind to work to improve the neighborhood school."[74]

Poverty

Under the heading "New Data," above, we have already seen that poverty depresses school performance. Poverty wreaks its havoc not only through home and community conditions that are antithetical to academic success, but through the underfunding of the schools themselves. Most schools are still funded largely through property taxes, thus ensuring the existence of inequities. Indeed, reports from the South, especially Mississippi, reveal the growth of "rural ghettos," communities of largely black people with little or no industrial base that are ignored by the larger white culture.[75]

There is growing interest in removing these savage inequalities. While the supreme court in Minnesota decided that that state's constitution did not require it to provide equal funds to all districts, more and more state supreme courts have found that inequitable school financing is a violation of state constitutions. One of the most recent is New Jersey, where in ordering changes the court was clearly concerned with equity in outcomes, not merely inputs. New Jersey had already made considerable progress since a similar decision in 1990. While the wealthiest districts in many states spend two or three times as much money as the poorest districts, the poorest districts in New Jersey currently receive 84% of the funding that wealthy districts receive.

Still, in interpreting New Jersey's constitutional provision for a "thorough and efficient" education, the state supreme court strongly implied that, since poor children are disadvantaged in all other aspects of their lives, the schools must attempt to compensate for such disadvantage: "Success cannot be expected to be realized unless the department and the commission identify and implement the special supplemental programs and services that the children in these [poor] districts require." Some programs and

130

services in poor districts will be "unique to those students, not required in wealthier districts."[76]

Although the arguments are typically cast in economic, not educational terms, the focus on poverty and welfare reform also drew attention to illegitimacy. Daniel Patrick Moynihan showed that out-of-wedlock births held at a flat 4% from 1940 to 1956, then began an accelerating upturn. Currently, 30% of all births are out-of-wedlock births, as are 80% of those to teenage mothers.[77]

Charles Murray observed that women with family incomes of more than $75,000 account for just 1% of illegitimate babies, while women with family incomes under $20,000 account for 69%.[78] The annual cost to taxpayers of illegitimate births to the poor is estimated at $34 billion. According to Murray, "Throughout human history, a single woman with a small child has not been a viable [economic] unit." Murray claims that we have been able to tolerate the demise of the black family, as horrible as that has been, because it involves only a small minority of the population. Significantly, he titles his essay "The Coming White Underclass."

Murray has performed a public service by recommending a policy of eliminating all economic support for single mothers. Few agree with this move, including me; but by framing the issue in this stark, draconian light, Murray has forced others to consider more moderate welfare reforms.

The Media

This report has already cited numerous examples of the media's misreading or misreporting the situation in education. For the most part, media attacks on schools continued as in previous years. However, there did seem to be an increase in what I have termed "gratuitous media violence" visited on the schools this year. Gratuitous violence occurs when schools are criticized in an article whose subject is something other than education.

A few examples should suffice. *Conde Nast Traveler* carries periodic contests called "Where Are You?" It provides clues, and

131

the reader must determine his or her precise location. In the June 1994 edition, one of the clues begins, "In a nation of rampant illiteracy (no, it's not the United States). . . . " By the same token, the June 9 edition of the cartoon strip "Kudzu" contains a discussion of Generation X in which one character thinks that young adults are called that because they can't write their names. In an article about border collies, Charles Krauthammer declared that "we have gotten used to falling SAT scores, coming in dead last in international math comparisons, [and] high schoolers who cannot locate the Civil War to the nearest half-century."[79] And so on. For the record, in none of the nine comparisons contained in the Second International Mathematics Study and in the Second International Assessment of Educational Progress does America finish "dead last." U.S. scores are, in fact, close to the international averages.

The media's indifference to good news about schools earned it a collective jibe from Project Censored, which annually names the top 10 censored stories of the year. In 1993 it gave the number-three ranking to the Sandia Report and applauded the *Kappan* for publishing an article summarizing the report. Wrote the people at Project Censored, "This report was suppressed by the Bush administration and virtually ignored by the mainstream media because it challenged the widespread view that public schools are self-destructing."[80]

The *Utne Reader*, a bimonthly collection of articles that bills itself as "the best of the alternative press," reprinted Project Censored's report,[81] but it must be said that editor Eric Utne's hands are not entirely clean in this matter either. I had sent a copy of the Sandia Report to the *Utne Reader*, and each year I also dispatched a copy of the Bracey Report. A cover letter urged the publication to give as much attention to these kinds of reports as it had to critical articles. But no response ever came from the *Utne Reader*.

In the Third Bracey Report, I noted that people tend to like their local schools and quoted Denis Doyle as saying, "That is scientific evidence that ignorance is bliss." It now looks as if another aphorism more accurately describes the situation: "Seeing is believing." Polling data from the American Association of School Administrators indicate that people get most of their information about the nation's schools from television, followed by newspapers.[82] Given the uniformly negative coverage provided by both media, a less than grim view would be hard to come by.

Television and newspapers play a major role in providing information about local schools, too, but so do friends, neighbors, children, local school officials, local school newsletters, and school visits. A lesson for school people might be to include information about the national education scene as well as local information in the materials that go home to parents.

Of course, education is not the only subject that is misreported. (Indeed, that's something I worry about when citing journalists on, say, the economy.) Richard Harwood, former *Washington Post* ombudsman who is now retired, writes often about the general decline in journalism. He cites David Broder's comment that "citizens now perceive the press as part of the insider's world. . . . We have, through the elevation of salaries, prestige, education, and so on among reporters, distanced ourselves to a remarkable degree from the people we are writing for and have become much, much closer to the people [experts and politicians] we are writing about."[83]

In a similar vein Harwood quotes another journalist, Tom Koch, who commented, "For twenty years content analysis studies have shown that between 70 and 90 percent of our content is at heart the voice of officials and their experts, translated by reporters into supposedly 'objective' news. People don't trust us anymore . . . because the way we quote and attribute and build factoids as if they were truth is a lie. And folks are catching on."[84] I had an inkling of this in a conversation with Broder shortly after he wrote a favorable column about *Prisoners of Time*. Although the Bracey Reports contain much more data than that slim volume — some 200 references in the first three Bracey Reports — Broder told me that he would require "more than a single voice" to be convinced of my position. Does an official government report, one commissioned by a former secretary of education who wishes to privatize public schools, constitute a chorus?

On the rare occasion when a major publication did include something good about U.S. schools, no one else seemed to notice. In December 1993, William Celis III wrote a front-page story in the *New York Times* titled "International Report Card Shows U.S. Schools Work."[85] Many statistics from the OECD study that Celis included in his story have either appeared in the Third Bracey Report or show up in this one. He found American students only slightly below international averages in math and science and almost at the top in reading. He found that more Americans get a college education than is true of citizens in any other nation. He found that a great deal of money from American school budgets goes for noninstructional programs (e.g., transportation, food), which is not the case in other nations. And no other major media outlet carried Celis' story.

One story of American educational success did appear in the *Washington Post,* but it was played only for its local angle. The American team finished first in the 1994 International Mathematics Olympiad, and one team member was from Bethesda, Maryland, just over the Maryland state line from the District of Columbia. The story was filed by the *Post*'s Montgomery County, Maryland, desk and discussed the Bethesda student's achievements in more detail than those of the team.[86]

That the U.S. did well was not exactly news. Our worst finish in the Olympiad was sixth place in 1993. To finish first, the U.S. team had to outscore teams from 68 other nations. But in addition to taking first, the U.S. team truly aced the test: all six team members posted perfect scores, a first-ever occurrence for any team and something that astonished program organizers.

That small triumph aside, it is likely that only in America could a movie about a simple man who accidentally participates in events that shape the nation and achieves fortune and happiness set off a national debate about education. Many moviegoers saw *Forrest Gump* as delightful entertainment with, perhaps, another Academy Award in the offing for Tom Hanks. Many others saw it as avowing that it's good to be dumb. These people also saw its popularity as proof that Americans celebrate stupidity and passivity, that we derogate brains and hard work.[87] It's certainly true that a brainy person risks being called geek, dork, and nerd, and the celebration of our Olympiad math champions was brief. Still, the proportion of high scorers on the math section of the SAT continues to grow, more kids show up each year for and show well on the Advanced Placement tests, and as a nation we come close to the gold medal in reading. Somebody, somehow, must have been encouraging these kids.

Notes

1. Barry O'Neill, "Anatomy of a Hoax," *New York Times Magazine*, 6 March 1994, pp. 46-49.
2. Richard Rothstein, "The Myth of Public School Failure," *The American Prospect*, Spring 1993, pp. 20-34.
3. Louis V. Gerstner, Jr., et al., *Reinventing Education* (New York: Dutton Books, 1994).
4. Benjamin R. Barber, "America Skips School," *Harper's Magazine*, November 1993, pp. 39-46.
5. *Education in States and Nations* (Washington, D.C.: National Center for Education Statistics, Report No. 93-237, 1993).
6. Lauren Resnick, "New Standards: What to Measure," symposium at the annual meeting of the American Educational Research Association, New Orleans, April 1994.
7. Harold Hodgkinson, "A Demographic Look at Tomorrow," Institute for Educational Leadership, Washington, D.C., 1992.
8. H. D. Hoover, director of the Iowa Testing Program, personal communication, July 1994.
9. Ronald A. Wolk, "Editor's Note," *Education Week*, 10 March 1993, p. 29.
10. These and other SAT-related data are from the College Board's annual publication, *Profiles of College-Bound Seniors*.
11. Karen De Witt, "Scores Improve for 2d Consecutive Year," *New York Times*, 19 August 1993, p. A-19.
12. Lisa Leff, "SAT Scores Rise in Fairfax, D.C., Drop in Alexandria, Pr. George's," *Washington Post*, 19 August 1993.

13. Glen E. Robinson and David P. Brandon, *NAEP Test Scores: Should They Be Used to Compare and Rank State Educational Quality?* (Arlington, Va.: Educational Research Service, 1994).

14. David C. Berliner, "The Author Responds," Backtalk letter, *Phi Delta Kappan*, October 1993, p. 193.

15. Herbert C. Walberg, "Are Proposed Educational Reforms Effective?" *Chicago Sun-Times*, 5 February 1994, p. 16.

16. Richard M. Jaeger, "World Class Standards, Choice, and Privatization: Weak Measurement Serving Presumptive Policy," *Phi Delta Kappan*, October 1992, pp. 118-28.

17. National Center for Education Statistics, *Digest of Education Statistics 1993* (Washington, D.C.: U.S. Department of Education, 1993), Table 161, p. 159.

18. C. C. Carson, R. M. Huelskamp, and T. D. Woodall, "Perspectives on Education in America," *Journal of Educational Research*, May/June 1993, pp. 260-310.

19. *Digest of Education Statistics 1993*, Table 51, p. 65.

20. American Legislative Exchange Council, "Report Card on American Education 1993," Washington, D.C., 1993.

21. George F. Will, "Meaningless Money Factor," *Washington Post*, 26 August 1993, p. C-7.

22. Eric A. Hanushek, "The Impact of Differential Expenditures on School Performance," *Educational Researcher*, May 1989, pp. 45-65.

23. Larry V. Hedges, Richard D. Laine, and Rob Greenwald, "Does Money Matter? A Meta-Analysis of Studies of the Effects of Differential Inputs on Student Outcomes," *Educational Researcher*, April 1994, pp. 5-14.

24. Eric A. Hanushek, "Money Might Matter Somewhere: A Reply to Hedges, Laine, and Greenwald," *Educational Researcher*, May 1994, pp. 5-8.

25. William Celis III, "Teachers in U.S. Trail Those Elsewhere in Pay," *New York Times*, 18 August 1993, p. A-17.

26. Mary Jordan and Tracy Thompson, "Across U.S., Schools Are Falling Apart," *Washington Post*, 22 November 1993, p. A-1.

27. Drew Lindsay, "Schoolhouse Rot," *Education Week*, 13 July 1994, pp. 27-33.

28. *Adult Literacy in America* (Washington, D.C.: National Center for Education Statistics, U.S. Department of Education, 1993).

29. David A. Kaplan, Pat Wingert, and Farai Chideta, "Dumber Than We Thought," *Newsweek*, 20 September 1993, pp. 44-45.

30. Pauline B. Gough, "Shame on the Press," *Phi Delta Kappan*, January 1994, p. 355.

31. *National Excellence: A Case for Developing America's Talent* (Washington, D.C.: Office of Educational Research and Improvement, U.S. Department of Education, October 1993).

32. *Prisoners of Time* (Washington, D.C.: Office of Educational Research and Improvement, U.S. Department of Education, April 1994).

33. George F. Will, "Taking Back Education," *Washington Post*, 26 August 1993, p. A-27.

34. Denis Doyle and Terry Hartle, "Where Public School Teachers Send Their Children to School: A Preliminary Analysis," unpublished paper, Spring 1986.

35. Gerald W. Bracey, "George Will's Urban Legend," *Education Week*, 29 September 1993, p. 29.

36. James Coleman, "Choice in Education: Some Effects," paper presented at a conference on "Choice: What Role in American Schools?" sponsored by the Economic Policy Institute, Washington, D.C., 1 October 1992.

37. Albert Shanker, "Urban Legend," *New York Times*, 31 October 1993, p. E-7.

38. "Teacher Knows Best," *Wall Street Journal*, 25 October 1993, p. 20.

39. Howard Kurtz, "Will's Way," *Washington Post*, 6 November 1993, p. C-1.

40. Shanker, op. cit.

41. George F. Will, "When the State Fails Its Citizens," *Washington Post*, 7 March 1993, p. C-7.

42. Louis V. Gerstner, Jr., "Our Schools Are Failing: Do We Care?" *New York Times*, 27 May 1994, p. A-27.

43. David Broder, "How Serious Are We About Education?" *Washington Post*, 11 May 1994, p. A-21.

44. Sylvia Nasar, "The American Economy, Back on Top," *New York Times*, 27 February 1994, Sect. 3, p. 1.

45. T. R. Reid, "Rising Sun Meets Rising Sam," *Washington Post*, 10 February 1994, p. A-1.

46. Andrew Pollack, "Now It's Japan's Turn to Play Catch-Up," *New York Times*, 21 November 1993, Sect. 3, p. 1.
47. Sara Collins, "America Cranks It Up," *U.S. News & World Report*, 28 March 1994, pp. 57-60.
48. Louis S. Richman, "The New Work Force Builds Itself," *Fortune*, June 1994, p. 70.
49. Denis Doyle, presentation at a Junior Achievement Workshop, Colorado Springs, June 1992.
50. Cited in Craig Bowman, "What Makes for Success in School?" *Denver Post*, 14 July 1994, p. 7-B.
51. Larry Cuban, "The Great School Scam," *Education Week*, 15 June 1994, p. 44.
52. *Monthly Labor Review*, November 1991, p. 81.
53. Steven Pearlstein, "Unemployment Holds at 6.7%; Shift from Factory Jobs Continues," *Washington Post*, 9 October 1993, p. A-8.
54. Louis Uichitelle, "Moonlighting Plus: 3-Job Families on the Rise," *New York Times*, 15 August, 1994, p. A-1.
55. Patte Barth, "When Good Is Good Enough," *Basic Education*, December 1991, p. 1.
56. Richard J. Barnet, "The End of Jobs," *Harper's Magazine*, September 1993, pp. 47-52.
57. Christopher Evans, *The Micro Millennium* (New York: Viking, 1979).
58. Frank Swoboda, "At GM, Skills and Anxiety Run High," *Washington Post*, 6 July 1994, p. F-1.
59. Susan Gregory Thomas, "Take This Job and Love It," *Washington Post*, 7 December 1993, p. C-5.
60. Peter T. Kilborn, "For High School Graduates, a Job Market of Dead Ends," *New York Times*, 30 May 1994, p. A-1.
61. Richard Rothstein, presentation to the President's Professional Development Symposium, American Association of School Administrators, Arlington, Va., June 1994.
62. Kilborn, op. cit.
63. Tamar Lewin, "Low Pay and Closed Doors Greet Young in Job Market," *New York Times*, 10 March 1994, p. A-1.
64. Alan Wurtzel, "Getting from School to Work," *Washington Post*, 7 December 1993, p. A-25.
65. Melissa Lee, "When It Comes to Salary, It's Academic," *Washington Post*, 22 July 1994, p. D-1.

66. John E. Chubb, "Vouchers, Public Policy, and Educational Reformation," paper presented at the annual meeting of the American Educational Research Association, New Orleans, April 1994.

67. Harold Howe II, *Thinking About Our Kids* (New York: Free Press, 1993), p. 79.

68. Quoted in ibid., p. 79.

69. Jeffrey R. Henig, *Rethinking School Choice: Limits of the Market Metaphor* (Princeton, N.J.: Princeton University Press, 1994).

70. Peter W. Cookson, Jr., *School Choice: The Struggle for the Soul of American Education* (New Haven, Conn.: Yale University Press, 1994), p. 85.

71. Henig, p. 150.

72. Joe Nathan, "A Few Observations About School Choice," paper presented at the annual meeting of the American Educational Research Association, New Orleans, April 1994.

73. John F. Witte, Andrea B. Bailey, and Christopher A. Thorn, "Third-Year Report: Milwaukee Parental Choice Program," unpublished paper, University of Wisconsin, Madison, December 1993.

74. Ibid.

75. Peter Applebome, "Deep South and Down Home, But It's a Ghetto All the Same," *New York Times*, 21 August 1993, p. A-1.

76. Kimberly J. McLarin, "At Issue: What Is Adequate for the Poor?" *New York Times*, 13 July 1994, p. B-6.

77. David S. Broder, "Illegitimacy: An Unprecedented Catastrophe," *Washington Post*, 22 June 1994, p. A-21.

78. Charles Murray, "The Coming White Underclass," *Wall Street Journal*, 29 October 1993, p. A-14.

79. Charles Krauthammer, "Save the Border Collie," *Washington Post*, 15 July 1994, p. A-21.

80. Press release, 29 March 1994, Project Censored, Public Information Office, Sonoma State University, Rohnert Park, Calif.

81. "The Top Censored Stories of 1993," *Utne Reader*, May/June 1994, pp. 42-47.

82. Bruce Hunter, "The Public's Attitudes Toward Public Education," paper presented to the Willard Fox Seminar, Appalachian State University, Boone, N.C., June 1994.

83. Richard Harwood, "Reporting On, By, and For an Elite," *Washington Post*, 28 May 1994, p. A-21.

84. Ibid.

85. William Celis III, "International Report Card Shows U.S. Schools Work," *New York Times*, 9 December 1993, p. A-1.

86. Chastity Pratt, "U.S. Math Team: Perfect," *Washington Post*, 20 July 1994, p. A-1.

87. Sarah Lyall, "It's 'Forrest Gump' vs. Harrumph," *New York Times*, 31 July 1994, Sect. 4, p. 2.

THE
FIFTH
BRACEY REPORT ON
THE CONDITION
OF PUBLIC EDUCATION

October 1995

The past year was a relatively quiet one in terms of the emergence of new data. Alas, rhetoric rushed in to fill the vacuum created by the absence of facts. I began the last report in this series by debunking myths and hoaxes. This one continues the tradition.

Rhetoric Versus Data

Let me briefly recap a situation before offering an update. In the summer of 1993, when conservatives nationwide were laboring ardently on behalf of Proposition 174, a California school voucher referendum, George Will penned a column in which he claimed that "nationally, about half of urban public school teachers with school-age children send their children to private schools." A few days later, on the TV show "This Week with David Brinkley," Will hurled the statistic at Keith Geiger, president of the National Education Association, who unfortunately bobbled the ball and said it was "only" about 40%. "What do teachers know that we ought to?" Will wondered.

On seeing Will's column and the TV program, I called Will, who referred me to Clint Bolick at the Institute for Justice, who referred me to David Boaz at the Cato Institute, who referred me to Denis Doyle at the Hudson Institute. Doyle, along with Terry Hartle, had actually written a paper on the subject in 1986, when both resided at the American Enterprise Institute. He sent me a copy.

That paper led me to publish my own, "George Will's Urban Legend," in *Education Week* (29 September 1993), because Doyle's numbers showed that the figure was nowhere near half. In response, Will sent me the segment of the TV transcript where Geiger uttered his apparently immortal but erroneous statistic. For his part, Doyle fired off a letter to the editor and also cited Geiger's gaffe. I had also sent a copy of "George Will's Urban Legend" to the *Wall Street Journal* and received a reply from Daniel Henninger, editorial page editor, thanking me for "debunking Will's statistic." I was thus surprised when, on 25 October 1993, the *Journal* ran a long editorial, "Teacher Knows Best," that began by citing the TV transcript. (A more detailed account of the chronicle up to this point appeared in the Fourth Bracey Report in the October 1994 *Kappan*.)

Meanwhile, in his latest analysis of where teachers send their children to school, Doyle continues to cite the Will-Geiger figure as if it were true. The title of Doyle's new work — which bears a May 1995 date and the imprimatur of the Center for Education Reform — certainly makes it sound like public school teachers are up to no public good when it comes to their children's education: "Where Connoisseurs Send Their Children to School: An Analysis of 1990 Census Data to Determine Where School Teachers Send Their Children to School."

Ominous-sounding comments pervade the text. "Not to make too fine a point, teachers, public and private, white and black, Hispanic and non-Hispanic, low income, middle income, and high income, know how to address the nation's education crisis: they vote with their feet and their pocketbooks. They choose private schools for their children when they think it serves their interest best" (p. 7). "If private schools are good enough for public school teachers, why aren't they good enough for poor children? Why indeed" (p. 28). "With teachers choosing private schools, the truth is self-evident: while they work in public schools they choose private schools for their own children because they believe they are better. They are connoisseurs. And no one in our society is better qualified to make that judgment than teachers" (p. 29). These comments are not taken out of context, as those who seek out Doyle's paper will discover.

The conflict between rhetoric and data, noted in the heading of this section, can be seen in the clash between Doyle's statements and Doyle's own numbers. It must have been this dissonance that led him to make at least one error: "Nationally, teachers — public and private — are 50% more likely than the public at large to choose private schools (17.1% to 13.1%)." Actually, the difference is only 30%.

But the fact that really doesn't resonate with the rhetoric quoted above comes in Doyle's next statement: "Yet public school teachers as a group choose private schools less often than the public at large, by a one-point margin, 12.1% to 13.1%." That public school teachers are less likely than the public to choose private schools is quite remarkable. Other studies have found that the use of private schools increases with income and level of education. All teachers have college educations (compared to less than 25% of parents in the general population), and almost all teachers have above-average family incomes. The national average salary for teachers is about $35,000, but most teachers are not the sole wage earners in their families.

It is also striking that only about one-third of private school teachers (32.7%) send their children to private schools. Doyle takes the use of private schools by a smaller minority of public school teachers as an indictment of public schools. It would be equally absurd for me to take the failure of some 67% of private school teachers to send their children to private schools as an indictment of private schools. But doesn't it at least suggest that acceptance of public schools is widespread?

What is even more remarkable is that, as income increases, the difference between teachers and the rest of the nation also increases. Some 8.4% of families with incomes under $35,000 a year use private schools, while 9.8% of public school teachers in that income bracket do so. For those earning between $35,000 and $70,000, 15.2% of all families use private schools, while only 11.6% of public school teachers do. Above $70,000, it's 24.2% of all families versus 15.2% of public school teachers.

Doyle contends that "we are left, then, with a striking spectacle. By and large it is the poor and dispossessed, particularly in large, troubled urban areas, who are forced into the public schools" (p. 29). Poor and dispossessed? Forced? Hardly. In addition to finding that two-thirds of the children of private school teachers are in public schools, Doyle's own data show that 76% of children whose family incomes exceed $70,000 per year also attend public schools.

Given Doyle's negative spin on the data, it is surprising that his paper didn't receive more attention. Only a surprisingly uncritical *Education Week* and the *Washington Times* reported the study straight as Doyle delivered it to them.[1] The reporter who wrote the latter story is also editor of a monthly compendium, the conservative and highly selective *Educational Excellence Network News & Views*. She reprinted her *Times* article in that compendium.

Rhetoric Versus Reason

During the year, another bit of apparent misinformation appeared that has not yet achieved mythic status but shows the potential to do so. In December 1994 William Raspberry, a nationally syndicated columnist for the *Washington Post*, reported a study in which researchers apparently found that 10- to 12-year-olds could read VCR manuals better than 18-year-olds and that high school dropouts could read the manuals better than high school graduates.[2] Given a VCR, a manual, and a 10-minute time limit, the younger students were better able to connect the VCR to a TV, set the clock, and program the machine to record a movie the following day. The reason given was as remarkable as the finding itself: In high school, students read literature, not technical material.

The results and the reasoning seemed implausible, to say the least. I consulted the experts — cognitive psychologists such as Robert Calfee of Stanford University and Lauren Resnick of the University of Pittsburgh and reading specialists such as Richard Venezky of the University of Delaware, Alan Purves of the State University of New York at Albany, and John Guthrie of the University of Maryland. None of them had ever heard of the study, but some reached an immediate (if somewhat facetious) conclusion: We should encourage more students to drop out and earlier.

Raspberry's source was one Willard Daggett, a consultant based in Schenectady, New York. Seeking more information, I phoned Daggett's office and was told that the study was an "old example" that he no longer used. I wrote, asking for a source. In his reply, Daggett indicated that he had made casual use of the research in a speech four years ago. He wrote that he had "made reference to the research [in a speech] because I had read it the previous day in the *New York Times*." He did claim to have received "other summaries of the research from a variety of groups" and promised "more detailed references" when he returned from a speaking tour. No such references were ever forthcoming.

Given Daggett's description of the study as a casual addition to a speech, I was surprised when I later viewed a Daggett videotape. The research hardly figured as marginal. Rather, it served as the keynote, the linchpin of the presentation, occupying six minutes of the tape. Moreover, it was fully integrated into what preceded and what followed. (A second tape of a different presentation contains a virtually identical performance, including the same jokes.)

According to Daggett, a research entity — not specified beyond "Carnegie" — "was commissioned to go out across the nation and find the groups that had the greatest capability of using consumer-friendly technology." In a 1994 article, Daggett claims the studies were done with 14 "consumer-friendly" tools and that "the results were the same for all 14 products in all 50 states."[3] On the tape he reports only on the results for VCRs, but he claims that the results are the same for all tools.

According to Daggett, in all 50 states (repeatedly emphasized) and for both genders, 10- to 12-year-olds were more successful than 18-year-olds in setting up and programming a VCR, and 18-year-old school dropouts read manuals better than high school graduates. These graduates, in turn, read better than college graduates, who, in turn, read better than people with master's degrees. On another tape, Daggett claims that the dropout-to-graduate results hold up at ages 30, 40, and 50.

How can we explain this result? Simple, says Daggett. In elementary school we "read short passages and respond," while in high school we read literature. Research by the "National Reading Teachers Association" (no such association exists) has shown that reading a novel is a right-brained process while reading technical material is a left-brained process. Daggett concludes, "If we develop one at the expense of the other, you, indeed, retard the development of the other."

Daggett says that "Carnegie" then went to six countries and conducted the same research, only to find that, in these other nations, the more education youngsters have, the better their performance on the VCR task. (On the second tape, "Carnegie" is joined by "Ford," and the number of countries visited rises to 12.) Why do young people with more education do better in other nations? Because these nations, Daggett claims, require "the equivalent of four years of technical reading" in high school. In addition, 19 of 21 developed nations require a year of applied physics; only Canada and the U.S. do not. Seventeen of these countries require two years of applied physics, and four require three years. By 1996 Germany and Japan will require five years, Daggett claims. He makes all of these and many other claims without citing any study that would be available to public scrutiny and without showing any actual data.

After viewing the videotape, I wrote him again to ask for citations and sources. I received no list of citations. But I did receive a letter from his lawyer (!?) stating that, "As I am sure you know, Dr. Daggett is vitally interested in research in educational issues. However, his international schedule prevents him from consideration of matters outside the scope of his projects." Hardly a response that meets minimal professional standards of someone "vitally interested in research."

I invite readers to imagine the research described above, conducted with 14 devices, five age groups, two genders, four educational levels, in all 50 states, and, later, six or 12 countries. Also, consider the logistical complexities of rounding up equivalent groups of 40- and 50-year-old high school dropouts in all 50 states. If we assume that there were only 25 students per condition, this means a total participation by some 50,000 people in this country alone. If different groups were used for each of the 14 devices, the number climbs to 700,000. To obtain results that were reliable at the state level, of course, many more students would need to be tested — enough, probably, to bankrupt both "Ford" and "Carnegie."

If there is anything to these findings at all, it might well have to do with familiarity, not reading skill. The study was apparently reported in 1991, meaning that the 10-year-olds had never known a world without VCRs. Recall, too, the comparative difficulty that many adults have learning computer technology and the ease with which many children do so. But this has nothing to do with the failure of high schools to teach "technical reading." In any case, a search of the *New York Times Index* from 1988 to 1993 failed to locate any articles on the topic.

School-Bashing as Leisure-Time Fun

Futurists advise young workers that they can look forward to 10 or more occupations in their lifetimes. On the supposition that even people of my age should take this prediction to heart, I think that I will not audition for the role of prophet. In the Second Bracey Report (October 1992 *Kappan*) I wrote, "In the course of a year, those who were disparaging the schools have come to acknowledge that schools are performing as well as or better than ever, and we can hope that the days of school-bashing are over." As they used to say in *Mad* magazine, in reference to monumental mistakes, hoo boy.

As the spring of 1995 arrived, the latest cease-fire in Bosnia ended, and a variety of domestic warriors launched their own versions of blitzkrieg against the schools, including Diane Sawyer on ABC, Louis Rukeyser on PBS, and Albert Shanker in his weekly paid advertorial in the *New York Times*. For sheer outrageousness, though, no one matched the editors of *Family Circle*, who turned their op-ed page over to that noted educator, Rush Limbaugh.[4] Limbaugh repeated the usual litany about school failure and called for school choice.

If *Family Circle* wins the 1995 prize for least credible op-ed page, *Business Week* garners the intensity-of-loathing award. Its April 17 cover asked, "Will Our Schools Ever Get Better?" The lead paragraph of the story was typical of this spring's showers of school-bashing verbiage:

> Americans are fed up with their public schools. Businesses complain that too many job applicants can't read, write, or do simple arithmetic. Parents fear that the schools have become violent cesspools where gangs run amok and that teachers are more concerned with their pensions than their classrooms. Economists fret that a weak school system is hurting the ability of the U.S. to compete in the global economy. And despite modest improvements in test scores, U.S. students still rank far behind most of their international peers in science and math.[5]

Not one statement in this litany is true, of course, but all are widely held as gospel.

Unfortunately, many school critics do not seem to care whether what they say can be backed up with data. In early 1994, reading a book by Louis Gerstner, Jr., CEO of IBM, I came across this statement: "During the decade of the Eighties, spending on education increased by 34% (in real dollars), but the only outcome measures, test scores, were, by and large, static."[6] I found this statement at least mildly surprising, for it was identical in content and syntax to one uttered by one of Gerstner's co-authors, Denis Doyle, in a debate with me two years earlier. At the time, I showed Doyle charts that revealed a test score decline that began in the mid-1960s and ended in the mid-1970s. By about 1990 test scores were indeed "flat," but they were flat at all-time highs. I thought that was the end of it, but I was dealing in fact-based thinking. I hadn't reckoned with the strength of ideology.

In late 1994, Eric Hanushek of the University of Rochester and Chester Finn, Jr., a former assistant secretary of education, also claimed that the nation was throwing more money at the schools while test scores adamantly refused to rise. At a Brookings Institution luncheon to fete the publication of Hanushek's new book, they claimed that, in the last 20 years, money spent on schools had doubled, while test scores were "flat." I showed them the same data that I had shared with Doyle. But this scarcely deterred them, failed to alter their presentation, and, indeed, caused no more than a momentary pause.

The Hanushek-Finn encounter, among others, inspired me to write an essay for *Education Week*, titled "Education's Data-Proof Ideologues" (25 January 1995). It recounted episodes in which inconvenient data had been either ignored or selected in such a way as to fit an idcology apparently impervious to evidence.

If my essay made any of the ideologues I named therein more respectful of the facts, the change was scarcely noticeable. In February 1995 Albert Shanker, president of the American Federation of Teachers (AFT), who has drifted of late into the camp of the ideologues, spoke at another Brookings Institution luncheon. Shanker referred to a study that apparently showed that only 4% of American students can perform as well as 40% of English students. It sounded like a new international comparison, and, because I was unfamiliar with its source, I wrote Shanker asking for a citation. None was forthcoming, even after three written requests.

It appears that Shanker may have been partly misinterpreting and partly misremembering a study conducted jointly by the AFT and the National Center for Improving Science Education.[7] This investigation reviewed tests in various areas of science taken by advanced high school students in various countries. The review included the British A-level examinations; the German Abitur; the French Baccalauréat; college entrance tests from Sweden, Israel, and Japan; and the College Board's Advanced Placement (AP) tests.

The review found that 31% of an age cohort in England and Wales take the A-level biology test and that some 25% of the total age cohort pass it. This was apparently the source of Shanker's misremembered "40%." This figure compares with 7% of U.S. high schoolers who take the AP biology examination, with 4% "passing" — that is, earning a score of three or better on the test's five-point scale. A score of three is sufficient to garner college credit at many institutions of higher education.

Of course, these foreign high school examinations differ in many ways from the AP tests. The most immediately noticeable difference is their function. In other countries, students must pass these tests to gain admission to college, while AP examinations are strictly voluntary and can earn college credits for students. Doing well on these tests for college entrance in other nations is no small matter; in many nations the colleges are free. If such conditions attached themselves to AP exams, I suspect that many more U.S. students would take them and do well.

In some of the countries, as students prepare for the admissions tests, they drastically reduce the number of courses they take. Therefore, they have more time available to study the topics to be tested. In addition, students who fail a test will often spend a year preparing to retake it.

There are other differences. The review by the National Center found that the exams in other countries present a very traditional picture of the subject tested. Said the review of the math tests, "Reformers in mathematics internationally would be quite unhappy with the view of mathematics communicated to the students."[8] The tests depict mathematics solely as the manipulation of symbols. In biology, the National Center found that the topics of ecology, evolution, and genetic engineering receive little attention. However, these topics are given substantial coverage on the AP biology test. It is not stretching too much to say that students in other countries are struggling to learn subjects considered obsolete by many professionals in the fields of study.

The National Center also found that there is surprisingly little information on how the tests in other nations are created or scored or on how much they cost. Thus to compare "passing rates," as Shanker — and the report — did, is to engage in an essentially meaningless process.

Still, in talking with many people about the comparability of the tests, I found a general sense that the tests are functionally equivalent in that they all ask the student to render a performance of college-level caliber. Thus it seems that anywhere from 25% to 36% of high school students in other countries are doing some quantity of college-level work, at least in biology (the only topic reported so far). Is this a problem that needs attention in the U.S.? It is impossible to provide a decisive answer. People I have spoken with, however, seem to feel that there is a common expectation in some other countries that advanced students at the end of their secondary education should accomplish what we expect of students in the first year of college.

Certainly many students could learn more and perform at higher levels than they are asked to perform in U.S. high schools. Since 1978 the number of students taking AP tests has grown from 98,000 to 448,000. This growth has occurred during a period when the number of high school students decreased in most years. But the 448,000 AP test-takers are probably still a small proportion of the number of students who could perform at such a level. When my own children started college, both of them saw their grade-point averages tumble in the first semester. Realizing that the rules of the game had changed, they both then ratcheted up their performance and achieved better in college than in high school. And their experience is hardly unique. There is no good reason for such a high school/college performance gap to exist. We could increase the intellectual challenge of many high school courses without inducing the kind of burnout seen in Japanese students once they get through the "exam hell" of high school.

In spring of 1995 I spoke to the Educational Press Association, inundating the audience with as many statistics as an hour could hold. Shanker, on taking the stage, declared that my view was contradicted by his own and others' "personal experiences," which he found "more compelling than all the numbers Jerry just put up there [on the screen]." Of course, it is the unreliability of those personal experiences that led to the invention of science and research in the first place.

Daggett and Shanker might have overstated their findings, but they were hardly alone. In January 1995 Eric Hanushek addressed the American Economic Association on his long-standing concern about the relationship between money and achievement. The talk was later published as Working Paper No. 397 of the Center for Economic Research at the University of Rochester, with Steven Rivkin and Lori Taylor as co-authors with Hanushek.[9] In the second paragraph of this document, Hanushek writes, "Between 1940 and 1990 the average pupil/teacher ratio in the United States public schools has fallen from 28 to 16." Given such a statement in a formal, technical research paper, one would certainly anticipate a reference. Yet no citation for the claim is made, no warrant for the assertion is given. Surely Hanushek knows that this is precisely the kind of bald generalization that politicians and/or ideologues love to jump on and cite repeatedly. Yet he provides no means by which anyone might verify the accuracy of this claim.

When I have mentioned the 16-to-1 figure to teachers and other educators, their reaction has been, essentially, "In his dreams!" This response reflects a very common confusion. People unfamiliar with the U.S. Department of Education's rather peculiar calculation system will naturally assume that pupil/teacher ratio is the same thing as average class size. But to the feds, it isn't. It's a different animal altogether. The *Digest of Education Statistics* gives the 1991 average class size as 24 for elementary schools and 26 for secondary schools, figures much more in line with what most people think of when they think of pupil/teacher ratio. For Hanushek to use such a statistic without explaining its meaning or at least providing a citation where the statistic might be found is misleading, to say the least.

The naked claims of ideologues are, unfortunately, abetted by the many in the university community who have invested heavily

152

in the idea of school failure, staking their reputations and their grant applications on a condition of crisis. Shortly after my first report appeared, I received a letter from David Clark of the University of North Carolina. He said, in part, "The American common school is an endangered species; the wimps in education will not defend it. They are afraid of losing their money or access to the corridors of power." Clark had in mind his fellow professors. At the time I was skeptical of Clark's contentions, but the four years since he wrote that letter have affirmed them.

Recall that Gunnar Myrdal some 30 years ago had observed that U.S. professors were not supporting public education.[10] This lack of support was evident in the heated rhetoric of *A Nation at Risk*, a document that not only warned of "a rising tide of mediocrity," but also claimed that "if an unfriendly foreign power had attempted to impose on America the mediocre educational performance that exists today, we might well have viewed it as an act of war." Although criticism of public schools has abounded since their founding, these and similar statements in *A Nation at Risk* unleashed an unprecedented flood of school-bashing documents. And how did the members of the National Commission on Excellence in Education, who wrote the infamous report, arrive at their conclusions? They held hearings and commissioned papers. And who wrote those papers? Thirty-six of the 41 commissioned papers were written by people who worked in universities; most of the rest were by people who worked in think tanks. Only one was written by a person who worked in a school system, and that was a critique that lambasted one of the hearings from a practitioner's point of view.

International Data

On the international front, no new studies were released in the past year. The Third International Mathematics Study (TIMS) is in progress, but reports have begun to surface that the study is having difficulty obtaining an American sample. Having been beaten over the heads with previous international data, school districts are refusing to abet the collection of more. How odd. Unrepresentative data have been a problem in a number of other countries in international studies. Perhaps the same problem will also afflict the U.S. data for TIMS.

One earlier international study did find an echo in 1995. Because the installers of my new TV had omitted a couple of cables (no doubt another failure of American public education?), I found myself channel-surfing rather than watching a movie on the evening of 10 June 1995. When the changer arrived at C-SPAN, it found Speaker of the House Newt Gingrich speaking in Nashua, New Hampshire. At one point, Gingrich said, "Three out of four of our children are not learning to read."

This seemed at odds with the 1992 study *How in the World Do Children Read?* That study found American 9-year-olds second only to Finnish youngsters in a comparison involving 31 nations. American 14-year-olds finished eighth. A later analysis by the National Center for Education Statistics (NCES) found that, statistically speaking, only Finnish 14-year-olds were ahead of the U.S. This same study also found that there were no significant differences between the countries that ranked second through 11th: the scores are so tightly bunched that the various high-scoring nations were indistinguishable.

A similar clustering of nations holds in other areas as well. For instance, American 13-year-olds finished 13th among 15 nations in science in the Second International Assessment of Educational Progress (IAEP-2). Had they scored 72 instead of 67, they would have ranked fifth. On the same assessment, American 9-year-olds finished third in the world. Had they scored 60 instead of their actual 65, they would have ranked 11th. It is astonishing that anyone would be willing to draw strong conclusions about entire national systems of education from such tiny differences. Even in the IAEP-2 comparison that left the U.S. the farthest from first place, 9% more correct answers would have landed our 13-year-olds in sixth place.

In the *Condition of Education 1994*, the U.S. Department of Education's analysis of the reading data finds that the 90th, 95th, and 99th percentiles of U.S. 9-year-olds are actually ahead of Finland. At the low end of the spectrum of scores, the scores of U.S. 9-year-olds at the fifth and 10th percentiles leave them in second place among the nations, although they are farther behind Finland than American 9-year-olds at the average score. At the first percentile, French 9-year-olds move ahead of those in the U.S., leaving the worst readers in America in third place among the worst readers in 31 nations.

Similar differences are shown for 14-year-olds: the 90th, 95th, and 99th percentiles of American students give them first place among the 31 nations. At the low end, the U.S. first percentile places it 10th among 31 countries, while at the fifth percentile the U.S. ties for 12th place — and, at the 10th percentile, for 15th place. Overall, the best teenage readers in the world are Americans, while the worst American readers are no worse than their counterparts in the other countries in the study. It is possible, of course, that even more than three out of four children in other countries are not learning to read. It is possible, I suppose, that what we have here is a global literacy crisis. But I doubt it. In any case, Gingrich's office has yet to respond to my several requests for a citation.

While the data are not yet in for TIMS, information surfaced that impugns the representativeness of at least the Japanese sample in the Second International Mathematics Study (SIMS), in which Japan finished first in the world. Kazuo Ishizaka, chief of the Curriculum Division of the Japanese National Institute for Educational Research, declares, "In the Second International Mathematics Study, Japanese samples were chosen from those students' who were intending to enter the science and engineering field."[11] Could this be why Japan finished first, with the highest average score? In some schools, Ishizaka declares, the average score on a national test of mathematics can be as high as 98% or 99%. In his own school, on the other hand, he states that the average is 5%. He wonders why his school is never chosen to participate in the international comparisons. He recounts how he took some visitors to what he claims is a typical Japanese school, and they were repelled by what they saw and wondered why he guided them there. Their reaction was so strong because visitors are typically guided only to good schools, he says.

Ishizaka also repudiates the work of Harold Stevenson and Merry White. White, cited by Ishizaka, asserted that "the curriculum — the courses taken and the material covered — is so rich that a high school diploma in Japan can be said to be the equivalent of a college degree in the U.S." Ishizaka is incredulous that Americans would believe this. He observes that the *intended* curriculum is, indeed, rich and difficult. However, he also notes that there is a large gap between the intended curriculum and the *attained* curriculum. His views seem to corroborate the common stories one hears that, by the time Japanese students reach high school, as many as 80% of them don't know what is going on.

Ishizaka also bemusedly quotes White as saying, "At the beginning of a classroom day, Japanese children rise and bow, saying 'Please do us the favor of teaching us.'" Says Ishizaka, "I have been teaching 10 years, and none of my students ever said 'Please do us the favor of teaching us'." He reports that his fellow teachers have never heard this comment either. Ishizaka is equally incredulous at Stevenson's work, at least partly because his own children attended school in Illinois (where Stevenson conducted some of his studies), and Ishizaka found schools there "excellent."

Ishizaka is even skeptical of the accomplishments of Japanese elementary schools, usually portrayed as warm places for children. In first grade, for instance, the national curriculum requires teachers to teach 80 kanjis, Chinese characters still used in the Japanese language. Some students arrive at school already knowing the 80 *kanjis*, and some can learn them in a few weeks. However, some children will need the entire year to master them. As a consequence of these individual differences, the teachers never teach beyond the 80 kanjis, leaving many members of the class bored. Ishizaka writes:

> It is very tiring, so many of the Japanese kids bring small toys and hide them in their desk and are playing almost always. So if you happen to go to a Japanese class, ask to

visit the regular school, not the schools that the government recommends. Those recommended schools are very good. Students [in the recommended schools] are very attentive even though they already know what they are studying — they have perseverance and endurance.

When I lived in Hong Kong in 1965 and 1966, I occasionally taught advanced undergraduates majoring in psychology at Hong Kong University. On my first such foray, I prepared some material to give to the students, and I also asked "leading" questions that seemed (at least, to me) to be thought-provoking. None of my questions were ever answered. (And my tolerance for "wait time" is considerable.) After the class was over, I asked the regular professor why the students sat like stones. "They were probably embarrassed for you because you didn't know the answers," he replied. Questions on the part of the professor were taken as admissions of ignorance, not as stimuli for reasoning. I dropped such questions from subsequent instruction.

Recently, I came upon a letter to Stevenson from a William Lew, a professor of education at National Chengchi University in Taiwan. Lew challenged Stevenson's conclusions about the superiority of Taiwanese schools and suggested that Stevenson "do a comparative study of Chinese and American students at college and graduate school in terms of their academic achievement and personality development. Such a study will probably disclose the real quality of education in our two cultures." Lew implied that American students would win in a walk. Early in the letter he had described the damage done by the Taiwanese system of education to students' physical, social, moral, and emotional development. I wondered if Stevenson had ever responded and wrote Lew to ask. In his reply, Lew said that "Stevenson did answer my letter, but he did not admit his misconceptions about Chinese education."

In addition to wondering about the place of thinking in Asian schools these days, I asked Lew about the variability of Taiwan's scores in the IAEP-2. Critics of U.S. schools often portray schools in other nations as monolithically excellent, but IAEP-2 had revealed enormous variability in scores.

For instance, Taiwan had the highest average score, but its 95th percentile was relatively even higher. Its fifth percentile, however, was much lower than countries or U.S. states with average scores similar to Taiwan's. As one progressed from the fifth percentile of Taiwan's scores to the 95th, one traversed 125 NAEP (National Assessment of Educational Progress) scale-score points. In contrast, as one progressed from the lowest average scores (those of Mississippi and Jordan) to the highest average score (Taiwan), one traversed only 39 NAEP points. Lew responded that the variability could be "attributed to the fact that Taiwan's education emphasizes the teaching of elite (high-achieving) students while neglecting low-achieving students."

As for my earlier experiences, Lew commented that "Chinese education in Hong Kong and Taiwan has not changed much since you lived in Hong Kong 30 years ago. Thought is still discouraged throughout the system. 'Students' stony silence' is common when they are asked 'thought-provoking' questions." Is this a system to emulate?

Domestic Data

It was a slow year for new data on the domestic front as well. Some of the few facts that did appear had a positive cast to them. They were largely ignored by the media. Actually, in the past year the media did not even pay a lot of attention to data that could be given a negative spin. For instance, the 1994 NAEP reading data appeared in the spring of 1995, showing a decline for 12th-graders and stability at grades 4 and 8.[12] The *Washington Times* did manage to misreport these results under the headline, "U.S. Pupils Continue Slide in Reading."[13] Actually, this was the first time in eight NAEP assessments of reading that scores for older pupils had ever declined. Previously, the scores had inched upward since the first assessment in 1971.

Given this first-ever nature of the fall, it is impossible to tell whether this is a trend or a one-time dip. And it is very difficult to determine if the decline means anything in practical terms. This

158

did not stop Chester Finn, Jr., and Diane Ravitch from penning an "ain't-it-awful" editorial in the May issue of their newsletter, *Educational Excellence Network News & Views*, calling the decline "significant."[14] Actually, the "significance" is only statistical and comes from an analysis in which such significance is easy to find. Recall that tests of statistical significance were designed for small groups, and recall that as the groups being compared become larger, smaller differences between groups become statistically significant. There are almost 20,000 students in the NAEP analysis, which means that tiny differences will be statistically significant.

The RAND study titled *Student Achievement and the Changing American Family* was also overlooked by the print media and by television, although David Grissmer, the senior researcher on the project, told me that he spoke on a number of regional radio talk shows.[15] The *New York Times* seems to be alone among major papers in carrying the story, but even then it was run only as an AP wire story and was buried deep inside Section B. The *Times* editorial page did spring to life as a result of this dispatch, though, with an editorial titled simply "The Schools Are Getting Better." It stated, "This startling evaluation deserves careful examination by politicians and Washington officials before they indiscriminately dismantle social programs that may actually have worked."[16]

The study that evoked this comment from the *Times* was a cleverly constructed one that not only ran counter to conventional wisdom about schools, but also ran against the widely accepted wisdom that the American family is in decline. Perhaps two assertions in one report that run counter to conventional wisdom were too much for most of the media.

Using data from the National Longitudinal Survey of Youth and from the National Educational Longitudinal Study (NELS), Grissmer and his colleagues analyzed changes both in family conditions and in school achievement between 1970 and 1990. They first undertook to establish which family variables were related to school achievement. These variables included family income, family structure (proportion of single-parent families), parental education, age of mother at a child's birth, mother's participation in the labor force, and ethnicity. Once the relationships of these variables to achievement had been established for 1970, the researchers were able to construct equations that predicted test scores in 1990.

Somewhat surprisingly, applying these equations led to predictions of increased test scores. A large part of that outcome has to do with the fact that families of all ethnicities had more education in 1990 than in 1970. This led the researchers to warn against policy or program changes that might impair the educational attainments of minorities. Smaller family size is also associated with higher test scores, and family size decreased over the 20-year span. Mothers did tend to be younger at the birth of a child in 1990, and this was negatively associated with test scores. Part of the change in age of mothers had to do with their age at the birth of the first child, but it also had to do with the fact that smaller families meant that fewer older women were giving birth. In other words, mothers stopped bearing children when they had reached what they perceived to be the ideal family size.

Whether or not a family was headed by a single parent had little influence on test scores except through its association with income: Single-parent families tended to have much lower incomes. Family income was highly associated with test scores, but income in real dollars had changed little in the 20-year period. (The researchers offer one significant caveat to their claims for improvements in family status from 1970 to 1990: Their research used children between the ages of 15 and 18. Thus any recent changes in family conditions that affect young children would not show up in the data; those who were 18 years old in 1990 would have passed their most formative years before 1980. On the other hand, it may be that the image of schools as "violent cesspools" is yet another media excess.)

As noted earlier, this constellation of associations permitted the researchers to predict from 1970 data what scores would look like in 1990. Because all children were living in better-educated families (and because of changes in some other variables as well), scores were predicted to rise. When the researchers compared their predicted test scores to actual test scores, they found the actual test scores to be higher than predicted — at least for blacks and Hispanics. The actual gains for whites, while positive, were slightly smaller than predicted. The researchers hypothesize that the larger-than-expected gains for blacks and Hispanics are both policy- and program-related:

> The most likely explanation for the gains made by black and Hispanic students over and above those predicted by family effects is the changes in public policies and the very large increases in public investment in social and educational programs aimed at minorities and lower-achieving students. Further research is needed to better identify those programs and policies that were effective.[17]

They conjecture that these increases in investment in minorities and low-achieving students carried an implicit tradeoff that led to the lower-than-expected gains for white students.

In the fall of 1994, Hanushek wrote a piece for the *Brookings Review* in which he claimed that, "for every study that finds that increases in basic school resources promote higher achievement, another study shows just the opposite."[18] This, of course, is directly contradicted by the collection of research studies that Hanushek himself assembled, as Keith Baker showed in the pages of the April 1991 *Kappan*, and as Larry Hedges and his colleagues have demonstrated more recently in *Educational Researcher*. Hanushek also claimed that "econometric and experimental evidence shows vividly that across-the-board reductions in class size are unlikely to yield discernible gains in overall student achievement." Yet the data from Tennessee's Project STAR (Student/Teacher Achievement Ratio) show that such reductions in class size not only yield "discernible gains" in all subjects, but that these gains are maintained over time. Class size was reduced for some students in grades 1, 2, and 3, and the gains that resulted have been sustained at least through eighth grade. (Data on Project STAR were reported in detail in last month's *Kappan* Research column.)

Meanwhile, Chester Finn, Jr., pounced on one statistic released by NCES.[19] "More money is spent in districts with the highest percentages of minority students compared to districts with the lowest percentages of minority students ($4,514 versus $3,920)," said Finn. "We can think of a lot of education groups that would like that fact not to become widely known."[20] Actually, those numbers have yet to achieve the status of "fact."

The categories NCES used for the spending amounts are not useful, and this is true of many other groupings as well. For instance, the districts with the lowest percentages of minority students are 5% minority or less, while those with the largest percentages are 50% minority or more. "Fifty percent or more" is a silly category when it comes to categorizing minorities, since many cities are more than 75% minority. Similarly, the NCES study lumped together all districts with average household incomes of $35,000 or more and all districts with median housing values of $85,000 or more. Even in 1990, when these numbers were collected, this procedure lumped many disparate districts together. The same can be said of the categories for poverty percentages. There are four: less than 5%, 5%-15%, 15%-25%, and 25% or more. But about half of all black children and more than 40% of Hispanic children live in poverty. NCES reports that only 21% of the households in the data set had incomes of $35,000 a year or more. That number seems small and conflicts with the $35,000 median reported by Doyle for the same database (the 1990 U.S. Census).

In addition, the figures on minorities and spending are contradicted by other figures in the report. For instance, communities with the lowest rates of poverty spent $6,565 per child per year, while those in districts with the highest poverty rates spent $5,173. This difference of almost $1,400 is much larger than the differences between districts with different percentages of minorities. Similarly, districts with more valued housing spend much more — about $1,800 more — than districts with less valued housing, even though any house worth more than $85,000 gets lumped into the highest category. Of course, such categorizing greatly blunts the differential wealth of different districts.

Finally, if one turns from money to pupil/teacher ratios, one finds that, as the percentage of minorities increases in districts, so does the class size. Taken alone, this would suggest that high-minority districts spend less than low-minority districts. Thus, if those districts are spending more, they are not spending it on hiring teachers. Or it might be that high-minority districts spend much more on special education, which isn't figured into the ratio. This would be an important set of facts to know, but it is not possible to glean them from the data as NCES has categorized them.

NCES should be encouraged to pursue this kind of analysis, but the agency should also be encouraged to devise more useful reporting categories. Frankly, the ones in this report are so gross and confusing that, had not the report received some commentary from Finn and others, I wouldn't have bothered to refer to it here.

Education and the Economy

While I was in Vermont to conduct a workshop last spring, I taped a television program and was told by the host that Louis Gerstner had passed that way recently and had announced that, if America's schools didn't shape up soon, our economy would quickly degenerate to the level of a Third World nation. This came as something of a surprise: The previous September, the Geneva-based World Economic Forum had released its 14th annual "World Competitive Report" and announced that, for the first time, the United States had the most competitive economy in the world.[21] Japan was third; Germany, fifth.

Since the economy has now slowed a bit, some commentators might have experienced an urge to criticize the schools even more, as they did during the recession of the early 1990s. Most of them seemed to realize, though, that the slowdown had more to do with the Federal Reserve Board's raising interest rates seven times in one year than with the failure of the schools. And the troubles American automobile and parts makers were having in Japan were not cast in terms of the schools' churning out doltish workers. Only David Broder (reporting on a Gerstner speech) appeared to be still propounding the myth that, "in a competitive world, the quality of the education America's youngsters receive is the prime determinant of the nation's future well-being."[22] Broder's words, ostensibly written in support of Goals 2000, served mostly as an excuse for him to plump for Presidential candidate Lamar Alexander.

In some areas, schools at various levels are supplying more skilled workers than the economy can absorb. In an article titled "No Ph.D.s Need Apply," *Newsweek* reported that more than 12% of new Ph.D.s in math had no jobs, the highest rate ever for that profession.[23] While the unemployment rate for scientists with doctorates was much lower, that rate alone obscures a problem: Undergraduates are going to graduate school because they can't find work, newly minted Ph.D.s are taking postdocs for the same reason, and many holders of advanced degrees are finding work as permanent temps. One postdoc in chemistry reported that he had applied for 60 jobs, gotten one interview, and received no offers.

Beyond the problems posed by unemployable holders of doctorates, ominous clouds loom on the economic horizon. They could be seen forming a year ago in the Fourth Bracey Report, which conveyed Richard Barnet's gloomy conclusions.[24] Barnet's article has now been expanded to a book-length treatise, *The End of Work*, by Jeremy Rifkin.[25] Evidence also exists outside of Rifkin's tome: So far this year, as the Labor Department has cheerily reported on the number of jobs created each month, it has had to concede that the high-paying manufacturing sector has been pink-slipping about 100,000 people every 30 days. The situation described by Rifkin in nauseating detail was captured well in a Jeff MacNelly cartoon. It depicted an after-dinner speaker telling the audience, "The current recovery has produced 7.8 million new jobs," while a busboy clearing tables near the speaker thinks to himself, "And I have three of them."

While Daggett claimed on his tape that soon 85% of all jobs will require high skills and that half of all new jobs are for "technicians or technician repair," the Bureau of Labor Statistics painted a very different picture with its projections from 1990 to 2005.[26] Fully 13 of the fastest-growing occupations are concerned with medicine; these include home health aides, physical therapists, licensed practical nurses, and the like. No doubt this is related to the graying of

164

America. However, the fastest-growing occupations account for very few jobs overall. For instance, the occupation accounting for the largest number of jobs — retail sales — accounts for one-third more jobs than the top 10 fastest-growing jobs combined. Virtually none of the jobs in either the fastest-growing list or the largest-number list concern technicians. As for "technician repair," the category does not make the fastest-growing list at all and appears only in 17th place in the list of occupations accounting for the most jobs.

Not only is technology taking away jobs, as predicted by many people some 40 years ago, but soon many new foreign workers will be looking for something to do. In this country, farmers account for less than 3% of all workers. Globally, they account for half. But other nations will soon undergo the revolution in farming efficiency that we have experienced, and billions of workers will be dumped into the global labor market. What will they do?

At the very moment that MacNelly's cartoon appeared, *Time* carried a long story, "Working Harder, Getting Nowhere."[27] The subhead of the article read: "Millions of American families hold two or three jobs but still can't afford necessities and see little relief in sight."

The evidence *Time* offered corroborated Rifkin. Rifkin not only describes the takeover of skilled work by machines, but he also saves his most dire prediction for the unskilled areas. He contends that, for the first time ever, intelligent technology is cutting into the service sector. The service sector has traditionally served as the buffer to soften the shocks from lost jobs in other segments of the economy. But now, the ATM is making bank tellers an endangered species, voice recognition technology has cut legions of operators from the ranks of the employed, and the electronic office is eliminating insurance agents. Middle management for service industries may soon come to be an oxymoron. The onset of automation in fast-food restaurants threatens to terminate between half and two-thirds of the human hamburger flippers. The earlier report from the National Center on Education and the Economy might soon be appropriately retitled "America's Choice: High Skills and *No* Wages."

Rifkin ultimately waxes optimistic. While he worries about the tensions produced by the ever-growing chasm between haves and have-nots, he believes that the idle and leisure hours made possible by the end of work can be turned to social improvement. In recent years, volunteerism has become something to be shunned. During the Reagan and Bush Administrations, calls for a renewal of volunteerism were seen as either facile speechifying or cynical politics. Recall the scorn heaped on Bush's "thousand points of light." Historically, though, the tendency of Americans to join organizations dedicated to social good is among our most defining characteristics. Rifkin cites observers ranging from Alexis de Tocqueville to Margaret Mead who have noticed this crucial aspect of the American character.

I hope Rifkin is right, but I worry that, like most social commentators, he is better at describing a problem than at proposing a solution. As I write this, Head Start, Healthy Start, and Title I are all coming in for cuts, and the Pentagon is getting funds it says it doesn't want. And nowhere in the Contract With America does one find anything like the government-guaranteed income that Rifkin proposes in return for community improvement work.

Perhaps because so many people are having to take low-paying jobs, the proportion of children living in poverty crested at a 30-year high. Naturally, this poverty is not evenly distributed. While 17.8% of white children live in poverty, 40.9% of Hispanic children and 46.4% of black children do so. And recall that the definition of "poverty" has never been a generous one. Currently, the poverty line is just over $14,000 for a family of four. Naturally, poverty has an enormous influence on achievement in school.[28]

The distribution of wealth, in general, seemed to be shifting in unhealthy ways. "America's Tide: Lifting the Yachts, Swamping the Rowboats" was the title of an article that appeared last summer in the *Washington Post*.[29] It elaborated on an earlier report showing that the U.S. has the greatest gap between rich and poor of any nation in the West. The top 20% of U.S. households control more than 80% of the wealth. The wealthiest 1% in this nation control nearly 40% of the wealth. In the United Kingdom, by contrast, the amount controlled by the top 1% has fallen from 59% in the 1920s to 18% currently. In this country, the top 20% garner 55% of the after-tax income, while the bottom 20% earn only 5.7% of the after-tax income.[30]

In 1973 the top 20% of wealthy households had incomes of about $77,500 (in 1990 dollars), while the lowest 20% had incomes of $10,400. By 1992 the top 20% were earning $98,800 (in 1990 dollars), while the bottom 20% were earning only $9,700. Some have argued that this state of affairs is good because it motivates people to work to change their condition. All of those who make such arguments have good jobs.

Schools Are Falling Down

The answer is $112 billion dollars. The question? How much money will it take to make our schools fit for human habitation? That's the figure that the General Accounting Office (GAO) arrived at in the latest of a series of reports on the crumbling of American schools.[31] That sum works out to about $3,000 per student. The GAO estimates that about one-third of American students — some 14 million children — attend "inadequate" schools. And in the GAO's lexicon, "adequate" is not synonymous with "trouble-free."

Indeed, school systems face a Catch-22 of sorts. Because of shortages of funds, they forgo needed repairs. But postponing repairs accelerates the deterioration of buildings and results in even higher costs later.

Even when schools are "adequate," there are new problems stemming from what the GAO in another report calls the "technology infrastructure":

> Data, voice, and video systems cannot operate without the supporting building or system infrastructure. Building infrastructure consists of what needs to be built into the facility to make any technology operate effectively in the school: the conduits/raceways through which the computer and computer network cables are laid in the school, the

167

cables and electrical wiring for computers and other communications technology, and the electrical power and related building features such as electric outlets. Although designing a new building with this infrastructure is relatively easy and inexpensive, installing it in existing school buildings can be expensive and disruptive.[32]

The GAO concludes that the infrastructure of schools is not ready for the 21st century. Indeed, the report may underestimate the lack of readiness. The report finds that about three-fourths of the schools surveyed indicated that they have sufficient numbers of computers and TVs. About two-thirds indicated that they have sufficient numbers of printers, laserdisc players, and cable TV hookups. But other reports have repeatedly found that instruction assisted by information technology remains tangential for most students. For instance, *Computers in American Schools 1992* reports that one-fourth of American students said that they did not use computers in any subject area and another one-fourth indicated that they used them in one curriculum area only.[33]

Sometimes this lack of use can be attributed to the infrastructure — one school reported that circuit breakers tripped any time more than four computers were in operation at the same time — but it is more likely attributable to the fact that teachers and administrators do not yet view computers as central to instruction. The GAO reports of "sufficient" may well reflect tunnel vision.

First Things First

In researching a new book on education reform, I looked into the history of school-bashing and found it to have been a favorite pastime almost from the beginning of the public schools. The criticism really hit its stride just after World War II. Historian Diane Ravitch traces the flood of diatribes back to 1949 and notes that it rose to a crest in 1953, the year in which Arthur Bestor's influential book *Educational Wastelands: The Retreat from Learning in Our Public Schools* was published.

The crest has never really receded. Baby boomers have never heard anything except that the schools are failing. In such a climate it came as no surprise that a survey by Public Agenda found that the public was not in step with the current efforts at reform.[34] I am not convinced that Public Agenda's main conclusion is correct — that the public is principally concerned with "safety, order, and the basics." Or, if Americans are focused on these things, I suspect that they are overly influenced by such misleading myths as that of the now infamous two lists that purport to compare the schools' biggest problems in the 1940s and 1980s. Still, I would concur that we haven't done a good job of explaining to the public what reforms we have proposed, and I see why "people don't understand why the reforms are considered better, and people haven't been all that impressed with the teaching reforms they have seen in the past."

One of the interesting aspects of the survey is that the general public perceives the schools to be in more trouble than white parents as a group do and in less trouble than African Americans do. For instance, 72% of the public thinks that drugs and violence are a serious or somewhat serious problem, while 58% of white parents and 80% of African-American parents have such perceptions. The one question that ran counter to this trend concerned money: A smaller percentage of the general public (58%) sees lack of money as a problem than do white parents (67%) or black parents (77%).

Look Back in Anger

One thing you have to admit about the 1960s: Americans possessed a fine sense of outrage. Today, some commentators, such as George Will, like to blame all of our current social problems on that decade, but our indignation then stood us in good stead. Had the Bosnian crisis erupted then, we would have taken to the streets in a flash to demand that the U.S. and Europe do something. On a much smaller scale, the suppression of a government-funded report by that same government would have elicited howls of protest on editorial pages all over the nation. But today it's different. When the Sandia Report was suppressed by the Bush Administra-

169

tion for almost three years, there was nary a peep nationally, save for a lone and inconclusive article in *Education Week*.

One can recapture a sense of anger in a recent book by David Berliner and Bruce Biddle, *The Manufactured Crisis: Myths, Fraud, and the Attack on America's Public Schools*.[35] This is not a tome for those disposed to high blood pressure because it was clearly written in anger — the authors use the word "outrage" to describe their feelings. But this is not to say that the book's chapters are not solidly researched. Moreover, it should make readers angry too. It is a tough-minded, well-written exposé; before the phrase became a cliché, it would have been called "hard-hitting."

In their opening sections, Berliner and Biddle cover data that have been presented in previous Bracey Reports and in the Sandia Report, but they also offer much additional material. They begin with a list of scarifying headlines about the terrible things that go on in schools; then they note that all of these headlines are from stories that appeared in the Japanese media and referred to Japanese schools. Why do we believe the Japanese have such a wonderful education system when the Japanese media present it as fully as awful a system as our own?

Berliner and Biddle are not conducting an exercise in sophistry when they wonder about the Japanese system. In 1985 the Japanese National Council on Educational Reform pointed out that Japanese education was thoroughly at odds with changes in Japanese society and that, because of this, it was the cause of much deviant behavior in both schools and the society at large. It declared that the system was in a "grave state of desolation" and called for reforms that would "establish the principles of dignity of individuals, respect for the individual, freedom and self-discipline, and self-responsibility — in other words, the principle of putting emphasis on individuality."[36] These are centuries-old issues here, but they are revolutionary stuff in a group-dominated society such as Japan's.

Berliner and Biddle do not attempt to determine if, like their American counterparts, the Japanese media have gotten the story wrong, but they do devote much attention to destroying the myths

170

and revealing the fraudulence of many charges leveled against American education by the media and by reformers. Of course, if the analyses are loopy to begin with, then the reform proposals are likely to be off-base, too. And they devote one chapter, "Poor Ideas for Reform," to describing why some ideas either didn't work or won't work.

Having dispatched the myths and inappropriate reform proposals, they then present what they see as the true problems facing American education. These have received less attention in the Bracey Reports and got none at all from the Sandia engineers, and that makes these chapters fresh.

Having analyzed the real problems of schooling in America, the authors then logically go on to present not solutions, but suggestions. Berliner and Biddle are not what Harold Howe likes to call "millennialist thinkers" — people who believe a single social reform can bring the millennium. They are educators who know that progress is slow, that change is hard, and that some problems border on the intractable. Their suggestions won't "solve" our educational problems, but they will help. While their book is generally positive about our accomplishments in education, it is not a paean to educators. Indeed, the authors launch some slings and arrows at educators for practices of racial discrimination in spite of apparent integration.

A chapter titled "Why Now?" offers reasons why the educational events of the 1980s happened as they did. Although the starting point in this chapter is the 1960s and the history is fairly cursory, it is sufficient to the authors' purpose. For readers who want a better — or at least longer — view of such history, I just happen to have a forthcoming book that chronicles a century of criticism of education and of education reform. It is titled *Final Exam* and should be available from the Agency for Instructional Technology about the time that you read this.

Hopeful Signs

Not everyone was critical of schools last year. On August 26, the *Washington Post* looked at the data in the U.S. Department of

Education's newest *Condition of Education* and gave the schools a "B+" (p. A-12). And just about the time that the Fourth Bracey Report hit the streets, so did a survey of public and private schools in *Money* magazine. *Money* editors looked at the survey and declared themselves "shocked." In suburbs of some affluence, public schools seemed to be doing as well as private schools, better in some areas. *Money* offered this advice on living in a suburb and using a private school: "Here's the bottom line: You are probably wasting your hard-earned money."[37]

In stark contrast to all the bombast in *Business Week*, in Gerstner's speeches, and elsewhere, *Money* summarized the situation as follows:

> The best news to come out of *Money*'s survey of public and private schools across America was that, by and large, public schools are not lacking in experienced topnotch teachers, challenging courses or an environment that is conducive to learning. What many public schools are lacking is a student body brimming with kids eager to take advantage of what the school has to offer. But just because other kids disdain getting a good education doesn't mean your kid has to. Most teachers are dying for young, motivated minds to nurture. If they find an industrious student who is eager to learn, more often than not they will give him or her all of the personal attention that private tuition money could buy.[38]

I couldn't have said it better myself.

Notes

1. Ann Bradley, "Where Teachers Enroll Own Children Tracked," *Education Week*, 7 June 1995, p. 6; and Carol Innerst, "Blackboard Jungle? Not for My Children," *Washington Times*, 1 June 1995, p. 1.
2. William Raspberry, "The Secret of How-to Know How," *Washington Post*, 19 December 1994, p. A-27.
3. Willard Daggett, "Today's Kids, Yesterday's Schooling," *Executive Educator*, June 1994, pp. 18-21.
4. Rush Limbaugh, "Our Schools Are Failing," *Family Circle*, 16 May 1995, p. 146.

5. Michael J. Mandel, "Will Schools Ever Get Better?" *U.S. News & World Report*, 17 April 1995, pp. 64-68.

6. Louis V. Gerstner, Jr., et al., *Reinventing Education* (New York: Dutton, 1994), p. 229.

7. *What College-Bound Students Abroad Are Expected to Know About Biology: Exams from England and Wales, France, Germany, and Japan* (Washington, D.C.: National Center for Improving Science Education, 1994).

8. Edward Britton, presentation at the Annual Assessment Conference of the Council of Chief State School Officers, Phoenix, 19 July 1995.

9. Eric Hanushek, Steven G. Rivkin, and Lori L. Taylor, "Aggregation and the Estimated Effects of School Resources," Working Paper No. 397, Center for Economic Research, University of Rochester, February 1995.

10. Gunnar Myrdal, *Objectivity in Social Research* (New York: Pantheon Books, 1969), p. 53.

11. Kazuo Ishizaka, "Japanese Education — The Myths and the Realities," in *Different Visions of the Future of Education* (Ottawa, Ont.: Canadian Teachers Federation, 1994).

12. Paul L. Williams et al., *1994 NAEP Reading: A First Look* (Washington, D.C.: Office of Educational Research and Improvement, U.S. Department of Education, 1995).

13. Carol Innerst, "U.S. Pupils Continue Slide in Reading," *Washington Times*, 28 April 1995, p. 3.

14. Chester E. Finn, Jr., and Diane Ravitch, Editorial, *Educational Excellence Network News & Views*, May 1995, first page.

15. David W. Grissmer et al., *Student Achievement and the Changing American Family* (Washington, D.C.: RAND Corporation, 1994).

16. "The Schools Are Getting Better," *New York Times*, 2 January 1995, p. A-24.

17. Grissmer et al., p. 107.

18. Eric Hanushek, "Making America's Schools Work," *Brookings Review*, Fall 1990, pp. 10-13.

19. Thomas B. Parrish, Christine S. Matsumoto, and William J. Fowler, *Disparities in Public School District Spending, 1989-1990* (Washington, D.C.: National Center for Education Statistics, U.S. Department of Education, 1995).

20. Chester E. Finn, Jr., "Network Notes," *Educational Excellence Network News & Views*, April 1995, p. i.
21. Peter Behr, "Study: U.S. Economy Is Most Competitive," *Washington Post*, 7 September 1994, p. F-1.
22. David Broder, "Just Plain Dumb," *Washington Post*, 2 August 1995, p. A-25.
23. Sharon Begley, "No Ph.D.s Need Apply," *Newsweek*, 6 December 1994, pp. 62-63.
24. Richard Barnet, "The End of Jobs," *Harper's Magazine*, September 1993, pp. 47-52.
25. Jeremy Rifkin, *The End of Work* (New York: Putnam, 1995).
26. Bureau of Labor Statistics, *Monthly Labor Review*, November 1991, p. 81.
27. Nancy Gibbs, "Working Harder, Getting Nowhere," *Time*, 3 July 1995, pp. 17-20.
28. Patricia Edmonds and Margaret L. Usdansky, "Children Get Poorer; Nation Gets Richer," *USA Today*, 24 November 1994, p. 1; and Carol Jouzatis, "Working Poor Seen Getting Poorer," *Atlanta Constitution*, 11 July 1994, p. A-4.
29. Gary Burtless and Timothy Smeeding, "America's Tide: Lifting the Yachts, Swamping the Rowboats," *Washington Post*, 25 June 1995, p. C-3.
30. "The Rich Get Richer Faster," *New York Times*, 18 April 1995, p. A-24; and Keith Bradsher, "Gap in Wealth in U.S. Called Widest in West," *New York Times*, 17 April 1995, p. A-1.
31. *School Facilities: Condition of America's Schools* (Washington, D.C.: General Accounting Office, Report No. GAO-HEHS-95-61, February 1995).
32. *School Facilities: America's Schools Not Designed or Equipped for the 21st Century* (Washington, D.C.: General Accounting Office, Report No. GAO-HEHS-95-95, April 1995), p. 5.
33. Ronald E. Anderson, *Computers in American Schools 1992* (Minneapolis: Department of Sociology, University of Minnesota, 1993).
34. Jean Johnson and John Immerwahr, *First Things First: What Americans Expect from the Public Schools* (New York: Public Agenda, 1994).
35. David C. Berliner and Bruce J. Biddle, *The Manufactured Crisis: Myth, Fraud, and the Attack on America's Public Schools* (New York: Addison-Wesley, 1995).

36. Quoted in Nobuo K. Shimahara, "Japanese Education: Miracle Re-Examined," in John J. Lane, ed., *Ferment in Education: A Look Abroad* (Chicago: University of Chicago Press, 1995), p. 63.
37. Denise M. Topolnicki, "Why Private Schools Are Rarely Worth the Money," *Money*, October 1994, pp. 98-112.
38. Ibid., p. 112.

Postscript:
The SAT: As Scores Rise, Media Interest Wanes

As this issue was in production, the College Board, in what has become an end-of-summer ritual, released this year's SAT scores. The good news is that the national average verbal score is up five points and the national average math score is up three points. But don't uncork the champagne just yet. In this month's Research column (page 185), I accuse the SAT of irrelevance: it tells colleges virtually nothing that they don't already know from students' high school grades and class rank; it adds little to the equation predicting first-year college grades; it tells even less about success beyond the first year of college. If SAT scores don't mean much when they're down, they don't mean much when they're up.

Moreover, the College Board and the Educational Testing Service have long contended that the SAT does not measure the quality of schools, and the state-level data are meaningless because the proportion of high school seniors who take the test varies from 4% in Utah to 81% in Connecticut. Such variation accounts for virtually all of the state-by-state differences.

Ever since the 1970s, when the College Board sponsored a study of the decline in SAT scores, the minuscule annual score changes have been front-page, prime-time news. At least, that's true when the scores go down. For the last three years, scores have been edging upward, with the 1995 gains the largest in a decade. When the scores were in decline, the *New York Times* and the *Washington Post* positioned the results on page 1. In 1993 and 1994, the *New York Times* buried news of the upticks in scores deep in Section A, while the *Post* relegated the outcome to the Metro Section, which contains news of local interest. This year, the *Post* continued its policy of placing the SAT results in the Metro Section, while on the morning of the release the *New York Times* ignored the story altogether. The *Washington Times* did put the story on page 1 but implied that the gains occurred because the new SAT is easier. — GWB

THE SIXTH BRACEY REPORT ON THE CONDITION OF PUBLIC EDUCATION

October 1996

Last year, the Fifth Bracey Report awarded *Family Circle* a "Least Credible Article" prize for its school-bashing op-ed piece by Rush Limbaugh. Unfortunately, Al Franken's exposé, *Rush Limbaugh Is a Big Fat Idiot*, was not yet available to use as a trophy. An "Intensity of Loathing" award went to *Business Week* for its "Will Schools Ever Get Better?" cover and accompanying article. This year, we have all new prize winners and more of them.

The Envelope, Please

The "Most Unethical Advertisement" award is won jointly by the National Alliance of Business, the National Governors' Association, the Business Roundtable, the American Federation of Teachers, and, most incredibly, the U.S. Department of Education. These august groups earned this accolade for sponsoring a full-page ad in the *New York Times* on Sunday, January 31, that lamented the state of education in this nation. On the left half of the page, 15 countries were listed by number. The United States was number 14, and the words "United States" were boldly circled. On the right, the text read, "If this were a ranking in Olympic hockey, we would be outraged." (This ad led me to coin the phrase "Worst Possible Spin Syndrome," a label that, unfortunately, must often be applied to reports about educational data.)

The number 14 is the rank of American 13-year-olds in math in the Second International Assessment of Educational Progress. Within the squishy boundaries of propaganda, the ad is accurate. American 13-year-olds did rank 14th among 15 nations. But ranks tell you nothing about performance. In the 200-meter dash at the Atlanta Olympics, Michael Marsh of Houston ranked third in his semifinal heat and finished dead last in the finals, although his performance in the two races differed by a mere .22 of a second. A 7% improvement in his performance in the finals would have given Michael Marsh — not Michael Johnson — first place and a world record.

If one looks at the performances — the actual scores on the math test — one finds that the American 13-year-olds averaged 55% correct. And the international average of all nations? Fifty-eight percent. For a nation obsessed with being number one, as America is, this sort of average performance is not acceptable. But it presents a very different picture from the gloomy one suggested by the ranks. Students from Korea, the top-ranked country, got 73% correct. This 18% difference between American and Korean students was the biggest gap between the two nations in the study; the smallest difference was just 3%. As we shall see below, this is not much of a reward for the price Korean youngsters pay to be number one.

The "Longest-Running Goofy Speech" award goes to Louis Gerstner, Jr., the CEO of IBM. Gerstner began his "the-system-is-broken" speech several years ago and continued it through the March summit with the nation's governors and business leaders. Along the way, he has maintained that, if we don't shape up our schools, we will soon be a Third World economy. Of course, this is ludicrous. In 1994 and 1995, the World Economic Forum declared the U.S. economy the most competitive in the world. In

178

1996 the Forum changed its formula, and the U.S. *fell* all the way to fourth place among 25 industrialized nations. The International Institute for Management retained a formula similar to the old one used by the Forum, and the U.S. maintained its top ranking.

The "Most Unethical Means of Publicizing a 'Study'" award is shared by Paul Peterson and Jiang Tao Du of Harvard and Jay Greene of the University of Houston. The basis for this award is discussed in the section on choice.

The "Most Ludicrous Fact Pulled from Thin Air" award goes to Speaker of the House Newt Gingrich (R-Ga.). This should be the speaker's second award in a row in this category; only an oversight kept me from handing out the prize last year for his comment, recorded in the Fifth Bracey Report, "Three out of four of our students are not learning to read." This year, addressing the National PTA Legislative Congress, Gingrich declared that "55% to 60% of our seniors don't know enough about our culture to sustain it." One wonders what Gingrich might have said a century ago, when the high school graduation rate was 3%.

The 'Failed Miracle'

This heading is the title of a 1996 feature article about Japan.[1] A heretofore adoring U.S. press is at long last showing some appropriate journalistic skepticism about Asian schools. Asian students still score higher on tests than American students, no question. But it is clear now from the *Time* article and from other essays that appeared over the past year that American students can beat the socks off their Asian counterparts if we are willing to take only four simple steps.

1. Convince American parents that, when their children come home from public school, they should feed them and then ship them off to a private school or tutor until 10 p.m.; most youngsters, both elementary and secondary, will need to go all day on Sunday, too.

2. Convince American parents to spend 20% to 30% of their income on these after-school schools.

179

3. Convince American parents that, when their children turn 4, they should take them on their knees and tell them, "You are big boys and girls now, so you need to start practicing for college entrance examinations."

4. Convince American students that, if they sleep four hours a night, they will get into college, but if they sleep five hours a night, they won't; they must study instead.

For more on these four steps, read on.

My Research column in the May 1996 *Kappan* contained a strong indictment of Japanese high schools that drew extensively on Paul George's monograph, *The Japanese Secondary School: A Closer Look*.[2] That volume chronicles a year George spent in a Japanese school, observing a group of students he had earlier observed for a year when they were seventh-graders. He reports that he and his son, who attended the school both years, took to exchanging glances to register their surprise and shock at what they were seeing.

And what they were seeing was a group of students so obsessed with the upcoming college entrance examinations that they could not pay attention and often acted in uncivil ways — when they were not actually sleeping in class. The students were sleep-deprived from keeping late hours at *jukus* (cram schools). Since their juku instructors tell them not to pay attention to what their regular teachers say, they use the school day to catch up on their Z's.

Here's what *Time* had to say about the Japanese high school:

> The most forceful indication that parents are disappointed in the public schools is the intense competition to get into private ones, from kindergarten through high school. The key to success is the juku, an evening and weekend cram school where children from the age of four prepare for entrance examinations. Nearly 60% of junior high school students take juku classes, which cost their parents as much as $400 a month. They usually study material at least a year ahead of the public school curriculum and endure rigorous schedules that leave no time for the playground.

Akiko Tsutsui, a 10-year-old fifth-grader, gets out of school at 3:30 p.m. and goes straight home to have a snack and do her homework. Three afternoons a week she leaves again at 4:45 for a juku session that lasts from 5:10 to 10:00. For almost the entire class, Akiko will listen to tutors explain how to answer test questions and will practice taking them herself. She sometimes attends all day on Sunday for extra help. The classes give Akiko a better chance of getting into a local private junior high school.

Competition in Japan has always been fierce, and the schools have always demanded conformity and intense rote learning. But the system has become an extreme, decadent version of what it used to be. And not only do children suffer on account of the schools and cram courses, but they may not be learning what they ought to.

Have a nice childhood, Akiko.

Recall that Susan Goya, an American who has taught in Japanese schools for 20 years, made similar comments in the October 1993 issue of the *Kappan*. She cited the juku as critical to the success of Japanese students because "the quality of education in Japanese public schools is poor."[3]

The observations of George and Goya were further corroborated by Susan Elbert, an American teaching English in a rural part of Japan. Even there, Elbert reports, 70% of the students attend *juku* and often do not get to sleep before 1 a.m. "I have talked to many teachers and students," Elbert reports, "and they all seem convinced that a student cannot get into a prestigious high school or college with only the knowledge acquired in public school. I was shocked. The exams are really difficult. You need special training and attention to pass them, and you can't get it at a public school."[4]

Elbert also confirms the comments of earlier authors that *ijime* — bullying — occurs when the object of the bullying is perceived as somehow "different." Elbert rejects the word *ijime*, though, saying that kurushime — torturing — is more accurate. "Looking deeper than the mentally damaging words, threats, demands, and beatings, these troubled students seem victims of what Japanese society institutionalizes as ideal, namely 'sameness.' Two tormentors said of their classmate after he hanged himself last fall, 'We have no regrets. He was weak, and his character was poor.'"

Elbert's and George's depictions of the uptight, hyperanxious Japanese students make Mary Jordan's comments on Korean youngsters even more telling and poignant. Jordan, a former education reporter for the *Washington Post*, now with that newspaper's foreign service in Tokyo, writes that "today's South Korean students make the famously intense Japanese students look easygoing." Her article on the topic opens with the following story:

> It was 11 p.m. and fourth-grader Moon Sae Bom was solving math problems and double-checking her social studies maps. For the past two hours, her mother had sat beside her, checking her answers, making sure the 10-year-old didn't fall asleep.
>
> This is a regular night at the Moon house and in millions of homes throughout South Korea, where mothers spend hours a day studying with their elementary and secondary school children, even plying them with caffeine to keep them awake and learning. There is a huge new industry of private tutors for women who need to relearn algebra, world history, and other subjects so they can help with homework.
>
> Across this academically hyperachieving country, students file out of public and private high schools not at 3 p.m. but at 10 p.m. Every weeknight they study in their classrooms from dinner until late into the evening.
>
> Sae Bom's mother not only helps check answers, she spends more than $30,000 a year for private tutors. Many Koreans, says Jordan, now spend 20 to 30 percent of their income this way.[5]

Korean youths appear to be even more sleep-deprived than the Japanese. Jordan cites one girl who says she studies 80 hours a week. She studies in school until 11 p.m., puts in another hour at home, and then is back on the subway to school at 7:40 the next morning. Nothing in Jordan's description suggests that this girl is an exception.

As in Japan, Korean schools pay no attention to individuality or creativity. All teachers teach the same thing, and the students memorize it. About the girl who studies 80 hours a week, Jordan writes, "She has heard about American high school students hanging out at malls, joining activities like the track team or the yearbook, and even dating, but there is little time here for that."

Anyone still want to be number one in the world in math and science? Are American parents willing to eliminate their children's childhood for a few measly percentage points on a math test and even less on a science test? Sae Bom, incidentally, is lucky. Her mother plans to send her to high school in Britain, where, she has been told, children can be children.

Given that they spend all this time grinding the books, one can wonder why the Korean students are not even farther ahead of our TV-drenched couch potatoes, who, according to a recent report, seldom spend even an hour a day on homework on school nights (and forget weekends).[6] In the Second International Assessment of Educational Progress, where U.S. students ranked 14th of 15 nations in mathematics and 13th in science, Korean 13-year-olds finished first, but they got only 18% more items correct in mathematics and only 11% more correct in science. A paltry 18% for all that effort and angst and a childhood forgone? I don't think so. Although Jordan contends that Korean children start worrying about college when they are 4, at age 9 they got exactly one more item right (out of 58) than American 9-year-olds. If we were to control statistically for hours of study, no doubt we'd find American youngsters ahead of the Korean children.

Choice, Charters, and Contracts: New Wines or Trojan Horses?

The grand proposals for choice have diminished since the biggest advocates at the national level — George Bush and Lamar Alexander — left office. But choice as a political movement is far

183

from dead. It has just moved from the White House to the state-house and "morphed" into newer forms: contracting for services, private vouchers, and, especially, charter schools. Not much is happening with the first two, but the charter school scene is hot. If Judy Garland and Mickey Rooney were around today, they'd probably shout, "Hey, gang, let's start a charter school!" Education's one consistency is its proneness to fads, but seldom have so many waxed so enthusiastic over an innovation yet to prove its effectiveness.

The arguments for charter schools were presented in the September *Kappan*. Here, I want to note some reservations. It is clear that many people are interested not in the impact of the first round of charter schools but in what are being called "second-order effects." For some, these second-order effects are the improvement of public education. For others, they are the destruction of public education.

Charter schools promise to improve the performance of students, and, in exchange for that promise, they are granted a "charter" relieving them of some regulations and entanglements with central office bureaucracy. Although they are supposed to supply data in order to obtain renewals of their charters, it is not clear that they will. The need to show that they are improving education will certainly provide an incentive to cook the books, as happened with the failed privatization experiment of the 1970s, performance contracting. At the moment, though, "Charter schools' ability to improve student achievement has yet to be proven."[7]

Whether charter schools will ever improve achievement is a question that might never be answered. Even right-wing enthusiasts Chester Finn, Jr., Louann Bierlein, and Bruno Manno lamented that they "have yet to see a single state with a thoughtful and well-formed plan for evaluating its charter school program. Perhaps this is not surprising given the sorry condition of most state standards-assessment-accountability-evaluation systems generally. The problem, however, is apt to be particularly acute for charter schools, where the whole point is to deliver better results in return for greater freedom."[8]

Jeffrey Henig, perhaps the most disinterested and careful observer on the choice front, agrees with Finn and his colleagues. He finds that charter schools "show few signs of interest in systematic empirical research that is ultimately needed if we are going to be able to separate bold claim from proven performance. Premature claims of success, reliance on anecdotal and unreliable evidence are still the rule of the day."[9]

Alex Molnar predicts that such unreliable anecdotes will prevail.

> Charter schools will fail, fraud will be uncovered, and tax dollars will be wasted. But just as certainly, glowing testimony will be paid to the dedication and sacrifice of the selfless teachers and administrators at some "Chartermetoo" school who transformed the lives of their students and proved the success of charter school reform.
>
> Free-market zealots will either claim vindication or argue that their revolutionary ideas need more time to work. Supporters of public education will call the experiment a costly failure and marvel at the willingness to spend large sums on unproven alternatives while cutting resources for the public system that serves most children. With an absence of any uniform standards, the war of educational anecdotes and misleading statistics will remain "subject to interpretation." And all the while, the desperation of America's poorest children and their families will grow.[10]

And these words were written before the disaster for children called "welfare reform" was passed.

Molnar observes that charter schools create a rather peculiar free-market setting. When the Edutrain charter school in California failed because of fiscal mismanagement, free-market fans cited it as a case of the market imposing its discipline. But in a true free-market setting, those punished are those who invested in the enterprise. Those punished by Edutrain's failure, though, were the children who attended the school and had their lives and education disrupted, along with the taxpayers of Los Angeles who funded the enterprise. "The charter school market feeds on

185

the revenue provided by taxpayers even in failure. It is a market in which the financial risks are socialized, and the financial gains are privatized," says Molnar. "The struggle is not, at its root, between market-based reforms and the educational status quo. Rather it is a battle over whether the democratic ideal of the common good can survive the onslaught of a market mentality that threatens to turn every human relationship, inside and outside the classroom, into a commercial transaction" (p. 167).

For the moment, though, charter schools are thriving. As Henig says, "Legislators and citizens who balk at full-fledged choice proposals seem to find charter schools less threatening, perhaps because they retain a clear role for governmental oversight; proponents of more extensive choice proposals seem to find charters an acceptable step in the right direction."

Elsewhere on the choice front, the results continue to be mixed at best. The only project that has received something close to an adequate evaluation is Milwaukee's choice programs, wherein up to 1.5% of the city's children are eligible to receive vouchers to attend private schools. John Witte and his colleagues at the University of Wisconsin have evaluated this program each year for five years, under contract from the Wisconsin Department of Public Instruction. They conclude that, while the attrition rate from the program remains puzzlingly high, "the majority remain and applaud the program." Witte's comments scarcely constitute a ringing endorsement of the program:

> Outcomes after five years of the Choice Program remain mixed. Achievement change scores have varied considerably in the first five years of the program. Choice students' reading scores increased the first year, fell substantially in the second year, and have remained approximately the same in the next three years. In math, choice students were essentially the same in the first two years, recorded a significant increase in the third year, and then significantly declined this last year.
>
> Regression results, using a wide range of modeling approaches, including yearly models and a combined four-year

model, generally indicated that choice and public school students were not much different. If there was a difference, Milwaukee Public Schools children did somewhat better in reading.[11]

This is actually a remarkable outcome. The number of students participating in the choice program has never approached the legal limit and has never exceeded, on average, 70 students per school. Thus the private schools involved are not being overwhelmed by a flood of low-income students. One might think that such students are sufficiently few in number that they could receive more attention in the private schools than they might in their neighborhood schools and that their test scores would rise as a consequence. On the other hand, Peter Cookson, another researcher in the choice arena, concludes from his observations that private school teachers are less creative, more by-the-numbers teachers than public school teachers.[12]

In conversation, Witte again said that the public schools are doing a better job with their students than the choice schools, but his reasoning presents a good-news/bad-news scenario. Initially, both choice and public schools serve similar clienteles. As one moves up the grade ladder, though, the public school student body is increasingly drawn from lower-income and minority families, groups that post lower test scores. That the public schools are able to maintain parity with the private schools, then, constitutes quite an accomplishment. That they are not able to hang on to their middle-class clients does not.

In connection with the Milwaukee choice program, I should note that a "study" purporting to show that the program is effective just happened to be released on the opening day of the Republican National Convention. The study, with Jay Greene of the University of Houston as lead author and ardent school choice advocate Paul Peterson as another author, was prepared for a conference on August 30. (Peterson brought to the Brookings Institution the research that produced John Chubb and Terry Moe's notorious book on school choice.)

Almost three weeks prior to the conference, the study was handed to the media. A press release was given to the Associated Press, and a short version, titled "School Choice Data Rescued from Bad Science," turned up on the op-ed page of the *Wall Street Journal* on August 14. The rhetoric and tone of this op-ed article reveal that the purpose of the "study" is not to learn what actually happened in the Milwaukee program, but simply to persuade those who might influence choice legislation that something positive came of it.

The study has been hyped by former Secretaries of Education William Bennett and Lamar Alexander and by noted educator Rush Limbaugh. Surely, this is a historic moment. It must be the first time that any of the three have accepted at face value the conclusions of a study conducted at Harvard. (They must have accepted it at face value, because — aside from the "Executive Summary" and the conclusions — it is virtually impossible to understand.) Limbaugh congratulated the Annie E. Casey Foundation, which he frequently targets, for actually funding something worthwhile. Although the manuscript cites that organization, the foundation has denied that it funded the research.

It is difficult to refute the study, because it is virtually impossible to determine what Greene and his colleagues did. In the introduction, they refer to a "natural experiment" similar to medical studies wherein one group of people receives a treatment and a comparable group does not. However, during the course of the report, they refer to both analysis of covariance and regression analysis as ways of analyzing the data. In a "natural experiment," however, neither technique would be needed.

The principal claim is that the effects of choice show up only after three or four years of participation. This result is from a comparison of children in the program for that length of time with those who applied initially and were not selected. This comparison is problematic from the outset because the attrition rate of participants in the program is so high that very, very few of the children who started the program are still in it after four years (perhaps not such a great recommendation for the program itself). It is even more difficult to find the nonselected children, who might differ from the selected group on any number of variables. When Witte attempted to reconstruct the analysis, he discovered that of some 72 cells that would be needed, 23 contained no children at all, and another 20 contained three or fewer. How anything could be determined by such empty cells and small numbers is, well, a mystery.

An analysis by Witte indicates that, after four years, the two groups are not random samples either of those who joined the program or of those who applied and were turned down four years earlier. But no adjustment is made in the Greene study for their differences.

Actually, in the end, Greene and his colleagues acknowledge that it is not choice that has produced the results — if, indeed, there are any results after the methodological flaws are factored out. They write, "The disruption of switching schools and adjusting to new routines and expectations may hinder improvement in test scores in the first year or two of being in a choice school. Education benefits accumulate and multiply with the passage of time." Certainly, one cannot take issue with this statement. On the other hand, this statement means that attributing the results to "choice" is an ideological decision, not one based on the data. Many of the students who were not choice students had experienced "the disruption of switching schools" many times during the four years. To draw the conclusions that they did, Peterson and his colleagues would have needed another group of students demographically similar to the choice group but who had been in the same public school for four years.

Kathryn Stearns, a senior fellow at the Carnegie Foundation and a resident of London, penned one article that suggests that choice in England has had all the outcomes its detractors predicted.[13] The schools that people choose (which she says are not always the effective ones) do, indeed, thrive. But since these schools have limited opportunities to grow, they soon become overcrowded, and so they end up choosing the students that they think will give them the least trouble. Such stratification is a commonly predicted negative outcome of choice plans in this country.

Middle-class parents, much more than working-class parents, are using their choice options, but Stearns doesn't think it's because they are better educated or more interested in their children's education. She thinks that the reason the middle class exercises its options to a greater degree is that poor people are more likely to see the local school as central to their communities.

Contrary to what market theory would predict, none of the unpopular British schools have closed. They simply serve a clientele that is increasingly more difficult to educate, and they serve that clientele less well. Writes Stearns, "The gains for certain individuals have come at the expense of others and at the expense of the community as a whole. The legislation has led to increased social segregation, and this, in turn, is leading to greater inequality of attainment. . . . If the British experience is any guide — and I think it is — abandoning the urban schools to the whims of the marketplace won't improve the lot of most students or the administration of urban education." Exactly.

New Data

The past year was an even quieter year for new data about schools than the previous one. The data from the Third International Mathematics and Science Study are due to be released soon — probably in December — but most data analyses this year were rehashes of old, sometimes quite old, material.

Threatened with annihilation by the Gingrich gang, the U.S. Department of Education finally got around to looking at what the data said about education. Even though most overall trends were up, Emerson Elliott, then-commissioner of the National Center for Education Statistics, would commit himself to saying only that "some conditions are improving, while others are not."[14] The *Washington Post*, never quick with a good word for schools, looked at Elliott's data and awarded the schools an editorial with the headline "A B+ for the Schools."[15]

Indeed, it seems a bit misleading to say only that things are getting better, except where they aren't. Most of the conditions that have showed no improvement or have worsened have to do with differences between various subgroups — the gap between the achievement of blacks and that of whites or between children of high-income families and children of low-income families, and so on. More misleading is the tendency of *The Condition of Education* to date improvements from the appearance of *A Nation at Risk* in 1983. This gives the impression that the report caused the changes that led to the improvements. Such a causal attribution would make sense in view of the furor caused by the "paper Sputnik." It would also be convenient to link changes to a concrete event, such as the publication of the report. It's all very convenient, but it's wrong: Most of the upward trends had begun before *A Nation at Risk* appeared.

One piece of good news in *The Condition of Education* is that, despite continuing immigration by people with limited proficiency in English, the difference between white and Hispanic reading scores in the National Assessment of Educational Progress (NAEP) has been declining consistently since 1975. (The difference increased from 1990 to 1992, but the change is small enough that it could be a blip.) The gap between white and Hispanic mathematics scores has also been declining since 1973.

More disturbing, the gap between the scores of black students and those of white students declined from 1975 to 1988 but increased in 1990 and again in 1992. Moreover, that gap remains large: black 17-year-olds score just below white 13-year-olds on the NAEP mathematics test.

Although the SAT does not measure school outcomes, people are interested in its vagaries, and so I note here that SAT scores rose in 1996 for the third year in a row, moving up two points on the math section and one point on the verbal. In 1996, 1,084,725 students took the test, about 17,000 more than in 1995. Although the scores are reported this year using the recentered scale only, *changes* in scores are the same as they would have been using the old scale.

As in the past two years, rising scores did not garner the media attention that declining scores have. Only *USA Today* thought the news worthy of the front page. The *New York Times* and the *Washington Times* buried the story deep in the front sections, while the *Washington Post*, as has been its custom for three years running, relegated its article to the Metro section — material of only local interest. Only the *Washington Times* thought it necessary to comment on the recentering, featuring a long quote from former assistant secretary of education Chester Finn, Jr., declaring the test "ruined."

A few words are probably needed about that much-ballyhooed recentering. Every five years or so, the makers of commercial achievement tests "renorm" them. This is essentially what the College Board did in its recentering, but it was the first such adjustment since the standards were set on the SAT in 1941 and the average raw score was assigned a scaled score of 500. The group taking the SAT in 1941, though, was by no means "average." It consisted of 10,654 white students living in the Northeast and planning to attend primarily Ivy League and Seven Sisters colleges. Sixty percent were male, and 40% had attended private college-prep schools.

Currently, 30% of SAT-takers are minorities, 52% are women, 83% have attended public schools, and 41% report an annual family income of $40,000 or less. Obviously, the 500 "average" from the 1941 elite does not represent the average score of this much more representative, much more heterogeneous, group. The College Board quite reasonably decided to make 500 represent the average score once again. This decision unleashed a torrent of irrational criticism that it was trying to hide poor performance. "The largest dose of educational Prozac ever administered," commented Chester Finn at the time. I am certain, however, that, if we could step back to 1941 and administer the SAT to a group demographically the same as those who took the SAT in 1995, the 1941 group would score substantially *lower*.

As it is, some students will actually get lower scores on the SAT math section with the recentered scale than they would have gotten with the original scale. This is because over the last 15 years there was enormous growth in the proportion of students scoring above 650 on the math section. In *The Candidate's Handbook, 1996*, a publication of the Heritage Foundation, Denis Doyle attributes this growth to Asian American students. However, even a cursory look at the data would have shown him that Asian students constitute far too few test-takers to account for such growth. In fact, 6.8% of non-Asian test-takers scored above 650 in 1981, while 10.8% of non-Asians scored that high (on the old scale) in 1995, a 57% increase. In any case, the recentering pulls some of these students down — though not by much: Students obtaining scores between 660 and 710 would have scored about 10 points higher on the old scale.

As a practical matter, the recentering means that a student who gets 500 knows that he or she is typical. On the old scale, this 500 would convert to 420 on the verbal scale and 470 on the math. These scores could well lead students to conclude that they are below average, given that 500 is considered average. But the old 500 was "average" only for the tiny elite who took the test in 1941.

Secretary Riley as Rip Van Winkle

Secretary of Education Richard Riley must have been pleased with the press coverage he got when he released trend data from *The Condition of Education*. After all, when in previous recorded history had the *Washington Post* accorded a grade as high as a B+ to the schools? Maybe Riley thought he could use the tactic again a few months later to emphasize more good news. While his tactic didn't work on the *Post*, articles turned up in a number of newspapers on June 18 and 19 reporting that, in comparison to other nations, American youngsters read very well. The *Los Angeles Times* and the *Houston Chronicle* carried the story in their front sections, while *USA Today* displayed the story prominently on the front page.[16] "U.S. High in Literacy," trumpeted the *Houston Chronicle*. One wonders whether Newt Gingrich saw the story. Clearly, IBM's Gerstner did not. At a conference in July 1996, Virginia Gov. George Allen quoted Gerstner as saying, "We can teach them work skills. What is killing us is teaching them how to read."

The reports on reading performance were true, of course. But the only reason they qualified as news was that the papers had ignored the story the first time around. When the study was actually "news," only *Education Week* and *USA Today* covered it at all, and the *USA Today* story came complete with a quote from Francie Alexander, then-deputy assistant secretary of education, dismissing the results. On the phone, *Los Angeles Times* reporter Josh Greenberg said that he and his editors were suspicious of the story, given that it was four years old, but decided to go with it anyway as no one seemed to know anything about it. In that, Greenberg and his editors were certainly right. The data were those from the 1991 International Association for the Evaluation of Educational Achievement (IEA) study, released in July of 1992 as *How in the World Do Students Read?*

The Media

Relatively speaking, the past year was a good media year for us "contrarians." Contrarians was the label affixed to me, David Berliner, Harold Hodgkinson, Harold Howe II, Richard Jaeger, and Iris Rotberg on the cover of the May 1996 issue of the American Association of School Administrators' magazine, *The School Administrator* — along with the title "The Leading Defenders of America's Public Schools." The issue celebrated the 200th anniversary of Horace Mann's birth, and we all contributed articles. AASA Executive Director Paul Houston contributed a cover essay in which he observed something with which we contrarians all agree: "American education has many challenges and failings. They just don't happen to be the ones about which most of our citizens have been told." Houston wants to expand this issue into a book.

The cover of the November/December 1995 issue of *Teacher* magazine featured large, hot-pink type against a black background, which asked the question, "Is the School Crisis a Fraud?"

The article for the most part featured Berliner's work and mine and revealed an interesting change in tactics by our detractors and by school critics in general. In the early days of our research, the critics labored arduously to ignore us. (Some still use this tactic; in her 1995 book, *National Standards and American Education*, Diane Ravitch alludes to us in several places but never mentions any of the six contrarians by name.) At the same time, they clobbered schools with ranks and numbers: "American high schoolers come in last or next to last in virtually every economic measure," said Gerstner and his colleagues. "International examinations designed to compare students from all over the world usually show American students at or near the bottom," said Albert Shanker, president of the American Federation of Teachers (AFT).[17]

These statements are typical. They show how the school-bashers once tried to use numbers and statistics to show that public schools had failed. Now that the contrarians have shown repeatedly that these numbers show nothing of the sort, the critics have shifted their ground and want to declare the numbers irrelevant. They refer to us as using "numerically driven arguments," as if this were something inappropriate or even reprehensible when it is precisely what they once did.

It is true that the more thoughtful commentators in the *Teacher* article — among them I number Deborah Meier, David Tyack, David Cohen, and Mike Rose — called attention to the qualities that numbers cannot measure. But we contrarians have done so as well. The Third Bracey Report presented Israel Scheffler's view of the defining characteristics of education, which is worth repeating:

> the formation of habits of judgment and the development of character, the elevation of standards, the facilitation of understanding, the development of taste and discrimination, the stimulation of curiosity and wondering, the fostering of style and a sense of beauty, the growth of a thirst for new ideas and visions of the yet unknown.

I offered this comment on these features of education: "The extent to which we accept Scheffler's definition is the extent to

195

which we must realize that, for all the test scores and graduation statistics presented here and elsewhere, we really do not have appropriate indices of how the system functions or doesn't."[18] But the qualities described in this definition are not the qualities being published in the *New York Times* ad with which this report began. That ad is a "numerically driven argument," and it is those numbers that we contrarians have rebutted.

At one level, it is unfortunate that *Teacher* brought in thoughtful critics, because they give the school-bashers who use numerically driven arguments — Denis Doyle, Chester Finn, Diane Ravitch, Albert Shanker, and so on — an undeserved credibility by association with genuine scholars.

Shanker, in fact, provided the most stunning example of hypocrisy in connection with numerically driven arguments. When I spoke to the Education Press Association in 1995 and presented as many statistics as I could wedge into an hour, Shanker spoke next. Shanker, who in 1993 had already written such statements as "The achievement of U.S. students in grades K-12 is very poor" and "American students are performing at much lower levels than students in other industrialized nations," now discarded all use of actual data. He recounted how he kept meeting young people who could not make change and having other "personal experiences" that repudiated my data. "Frankly," said Shanker, "I find these experiences more compelling than [waving his arm at the screen where my graphs had appeared] all those numbers that Jerry just put up there." And yet, when Laurence Steinberg and Lawrence Stedman wrote numerically driven opinions recapitulating the usual litany of charges against schools, Shanker grabbed the numbers as a drowning man grabs flotsam and used them in three of his weekly paid advertorials in the Sunday *New York Times*.

One media curiosity continued this past year and warrants a brief comment. When a report by or an article about the contrarians appears, rebutters are always brought in for "balance." When a report comes out that is critical of the schools, the media almost always play it straight, without opposing commentary. To my knowledge, only once has anyone ever called me or any of the "revisionists" to comment on such a negative report. Strangely enough, that was the conservative *Washington Times*, and it gave my retort almost as much space as the report the story was about.[19]

As for positive media coverage, the *New York Times* ran a long article on the contrarians, and *Newsweek* essayist Robert Samuelson titled one of his articles about us "Three Cheers for the Schools?"[20] In his essay, Samuelson referred to me as the "godfather" of the contrarians, which is amusing but not historically accurate. Samuelson could not bring himself to give the schools three cheers, but he did declare flatly that much of the crisis rhetoric had been overblown. Even *Better Homes and Gardens* got into the act with "The Good News About Our Schools," a surprisingly meaty and accurate piece; and I finally managed to pry open the door of the *Washington Post* op-ed page after five years of trying.[21]

In speeches and workshops, I generally excoriate the media for their susceptibility to the Worst Possible Spin Syndrome (WPSS). At the same time I tell audiences that the most balanced and most extensive coverage of education in the country appears in *USA Today*. *USA Today*, sometimes accused of rendering sound bites on paper, often includes two-page inserts on education, and for the week of 13 May 1996 it ran a weeklong series.[22]

As part of its weeklong series, *USA Today* conducted a survey of parents and children and found that, overall, both groups gave schools a grade no lower than B- on a variety of elements. (For example, parents awarded this low grade to the superintendent, the school board, the budget process, and the way students treat one another.) Indeed, 75% of parents awarded their children's schools either an A or a B. The survey did show, though, that elementary school parents are much more satisfied with their children's schools than are secondary school parents. For instance, 42% of secondary school parents said that schools did not prepare students adequately for the world of work, and 38% said that schools did not prepare students adequately for college. Perhaps because of the temporal distance of elementary school parents from these realms, these complaints were voiced by only 16% of

197

elementary school parents. Thirty-two percent of secondary school parents felt that their children were not challenged to learn, but only 17% of elementary school parents felt that way.

On the downside, fully 33% of the students said that getting good grades does not make you popular, and only 31% said that they did an hour or more of homework nightly. Forty-seven percent of the parents, despite giving high marks to the public schools, said that they would send their children to private schools if they could afford it.

Overall, though, even the editorial page of *USA Today* was surprisingly upbeat. I say surprisingly because in five years that page has never published any of the many articles and letters to the editor that I have submitted, nor had they previously said anything positive. But above a May 13 editorial three times the normal length, *USA Today*'s headline read, "U.S. Schools Can't Teach? Don't Believe the Myths." The opening paragraph read: "It's time to set the record straight. Schools have been getting a bad rap over the past decade or so, fueled by some myths that have been around so long they're often accepted as fact."[23] Tell me about it.

There are several things to take into account about the *USA Today* survey. First, it asked parents only about schools their children attend, and parents are consistently more positive about their own children's schools than about the schools elsewhere in the nation. This is probably because of two other factors: 1) people depend on the national media for information about the nation's schools, and the national media accentuate the negative; and 2) people depend much more on local sources for information about local schools.[24]

Second, it is a somewhat superficial survey. Recall that the Public Agenda Foundation in its 1995 report, *Assignment Incomplete*, found that, when the researchers started to scratch the surface of public support, it was very thin.

Third, some of the questions posed vague hypothetical situations. Would 47% of parents really send their children to private schools if they could afford it? We have no idea what kind of financial picture the respondents held in their minds when considering this possibility. Would a fully paid tuition allow them to "afford" it? Would their overall economic comfort level have to rise also? We don't know, but we do know that people often respond to hypothetical situations differently from the way they do when confronted with a reality.

My salute to *USA Today* is not meant to suggest here that the media have finally stopped bashing schools. There continued to be much "gratuitous violence" visited upon the schools. Gratuitous violence is a phrase I use to describe articles that are written about something that has nothing to do with schools but that contains a slap at the schools nonetheless.

And the media still remain prone to WPSS. Typical of WPSS was the way the media handled the NAEP history assessment released in November 1995. The *Washington Post* headlined its story "Knowing the Past May Be History, U.S. Test Reveals."[25] Rene Sanchez, the *Post* education writer, opened the story with these words: "The nation's students have received a dismal report card in American history." Sanchez' comment was mild compared to that of Lewis Lapham, editor of *Harper's Magazine*, who took to the op-ed page of the *New York Times* and began his essay as follows: "If it is true that American democracy requires the existence of an electorate that knows something about American history, the news last month from the Department of Education can be read as a coroner's report."[26]

As with Gingrich, one wonders how Lapham would have characterized American democracy a century ago, when the high school graduation rate was 3%. In a letter rejecting an article I had submitted for publication, Lapham apologized for overstating the case. Why is it that overstated charges against the schools are always made in a public forum, while apologies for the errors are made only in private?

In response to these comments, I took to the op-ed page of the *Washington Post* with this quote:

> A large majority of students showed that they had virtually no knowledge of elementary aspects of American history. They could not identify Thomas Jefferson, Andrew

Jackson, or Theodore Roosevelt. . . . Most of our students do not have the faintest notion of what this country looks like. St. Louis was placed on the Pacific Ocean, Lake Huron, Lake Erie, the Atlantic Ocean, Ohio River, St. Lawrence River, and almost every place else.[27]

This quote could have come from an article on the 1995 NAEP history report, but it didn't. It appeared in a *New York Times* article about a survey of history knowledge that the *Times* itself had commissioned. The *Times* was incensed at the outcomes, and it put the story on the front page, next to its other major headline of the day: "Patton Attacks East of El Guettar." The date was 4 April 1943.

In that wartime survey, only 3% of the students could accurately list the states of the East Coast. Asked to identify the occupation of Walt Whitman, the students pegged him as a missionary to the Far East, a pioneer, a colonizer, an explorer, a speculator, a famous cartoonist, an unpatriotic writer, a musician, the father of blank verse, an English poet, and a columnist. Hundreds of students, according to the *Times* report, listed Whitman as being an orchestra leader. Since the *Times* made no further comment on this last item, we may assume that the editors did not make the connection to Paul Whiteman, a popular bandleader of the day.

What really made these results outrageous was that they came not from high school seniors, but from college freshmen. Although the article didn't address graduation rates, the high school graduation rate at the time stood at 45%, and only about 15% of those who graduated went on to college. The *Times* survey had uncovered not just a group of ignoramuses, but an elite group of ignoramuses.

I do not tell this story here in order to defend ignorance. Yet in my book, *Final Exam: A Study of the Perpetual Scrutiny of American Education*, I showed that the last century has seen an almost unbroken march of progress in terms of how much people know (the decade from 1965 to 1975 is the lone exception).[28] But we are not a nation of learners, nor have we ever been. And if you wish to know why, just read the base of the Statue of Liberty. It does not say, "Give me your college grads, your 1,300 SAT scorers yearning to learn." Indeed, we are closer to being a nation of learners today than at any time in the past. The progress we have made with the huddled masses of the whole world is extraordinary. It is only recently that many educated citizens of other nations have begun to migrate to our shores.

In the opening paragraphs of "The Media's Myth of School Failure," I described how members of the media fell all over one another trying to get out the report of an international comparison in math and science and how not one media outlet had reported the international reading comparison released five months later — the one Secretary Riley finally touted this year.[29] Why the difference? Well, it could be that the U.S. ranks were mostly (but not entirely) low in math and science, while American students ranked second in reading among 31 nations.

Or could it be that good news is just not news to the American media? That's what it sounds like to U.S. Department of Education staffers Laurence Ogle and Patricia Dabbs. They described what happened when a generally positive geography assessment issued forth from the NAEP. "The geography press conference was attended by the President of the National Geographic Society, and the mood of almost all the speakers was clearly upbeat. . . . The reporting in the press, however, was lackluster and negative, at best. Few news agencies picked up the story." But when the history results came out two weeks later, not only did Rene Sanchez call the results "dismal" and Lapham declare them "a coroner's report," but reporters beat down the doors to get to talk with Ogle and Dabbs:

> Returning to our offices after the press conference, we found our voice mail jam-packed with media requests for additional information. News accounts were on the radio, and reports were even spotted on the Internet. Requests for additional information flooded in from radio and television stations, newspapers, and a few talk-show hosts. That evening, reports on the history results were seen on the network newscasts, public television, and later in the week, on the

political talk shows from Washington. . . . Even television's late-night comedy king, Jay Leno, spoke about (and ridiculed) the results. Clearly, the coverage of the negative news eclipsed the relatively good news about geography.[30]

This is worse than the reading versus math and science reporting I had described. In that case, the media were simply ignoring the good news. Here, they stand accused of confabulating bad news: "Students Fall Short in NAEP Geography Test," declared the front-page headline of the *Education Week* story.[31]

Unfortunately, as that *Education Week* headline suggests, it is not just the general media that are subject to capriciousness. When *The Manufactured Crisis*, by David Berliner and Bruce Biddle, appeared, *Education Week* carried a story deep inside the edition about the tome that would win the Book of the Year award from the American Educational Research Association. *Education Week* editor Ronald Wolk panned the book in *Teacher* magazine in a review that made one wonder if he had read it. He called this most compendious source of data a "polemic." Though parts of it are written in an impassioned style, it is surely data-based and certainly not a "polemic." Yet when *Beyond the Classroom*, by Laurence Steinberg and others, appeared — a book barely deserving of the word "research" — *Education Week* ran it as a front-page story.[32]

Events

The year was even quieter for events than it was for data. The event that everyone watched for with great anticipation was the "summit." In advance, people said it would probably be the most important policy-related event since the 1989 summit in Charlottesville between President Bush and the nation's governors.

The summit was tightly guarded, with each of 41 attending governors bringing along a chosen business leader to an IBM facility in Palisades, New York, provided by IBM's Gerstner. Some 30 "resource people" were also invited to attend. The list read like a Who's Who of the Right. From the beginning, it was clear that the governors were abandoning a lot of previous work. (Since few of them were sitting governors at the time of the 1989 summit, "abandon" might not be the best word for their inaction.) Claudio Sanchez, National Public Radio education reporter, described the activity with some small incredulity in his voice. Asked by the host of "All Things Considered" if the summit's outcome meant we would have 50 sets of standards instead of one, Sanchez replied that it could mean that we would have 16,000 sets of standards, one for each district. One could almost hear Sanchez shrugging his shoulders.

It might be telling that, in an advertorial just after the summit, American Federation of Teachers president and resource person Shanker felt obligated to acknowledge the charge that nothing happened at the meeting in order to deny it. Resource person Diane Ravitch was emphatic that something actually had happened, even if it was wrong:

> One theme was repeatedly sounded at the recent education summit in Palisades, New York: national standards are dead. Apparently, the United States should have 50 state standards or even 16,000 local standards. But no national standards. The governors, Democratic and Republican, said it; the President said it. And they are all wrong.[33]

After this opening subtlety, Ravitch went on to try and revive the corpse of national standards. She was joined in her effort a couple of weeks later by Shanker in another of his weekly advertorials in the Sunday *New York Times*. Whether they have succeeded or ever will is not yet clear. Education, seldom able to hold the spotlight in turbulent political times, has been muscled off stage by welfare reform and the Presidential election campaign. Whether Ravitch and Shanker can transform the corpse of national standards into a living mummy probably won't be known until after the election.

Meanwhile, at a July meeting, the governors formally agreed to construct an "entity" to provide "technical assistance in the areas of standards, assessments, accountability, and the use of technology in schools."[34] The governors did not give the "entity" a name, a staff, or a budget. Their earlier thinking was that the staff and budget would be small, but how a low-budget "entity" with only a few staff members can do all the things projected for it is not clear.

A number of events this year should have ramifications for education. But they are now percolating through the culture without any clear indication yet of what they will ultimately mean. I number among these events the Million Man March, the Stand for Children Day, and the various meetings of the Promise Keepers.

Education and Immigration

As this is written, our nation of immigrants seems intent on beating up on today's immigrants. There are few arenas in which those wishing to attain political popularity spew out disinformation more frequently than in the realm of immigration. Most people believe that immigrants are arriving in record numbers and rates (false), that most immigrants enter illegally (false), that most end up on welfare (false), that they take jobs from natives (false), and that they earn most of the doctorates in science and engineering (true). My facts come from *Immigration: The Demographic and Economic Facts*, by Julian Simon, a professor of business administration at the University of Maryland.[35] The monograph is a compilation of original work by Simon as well as other research.

Critics often use the doctorate statistic to declare that American students don't like science anymore. Actually, the number of doctorates awarded to native-born students soared between 1963 and 1972. The number then fell just as dramatically until 1983 and has been increasing substantially since then. The number of doctorates awarded in science and engineering to native-born students was just under 2,000 in 1958, just under 6,000 in 1972, just over 3,000 in 1983, and just under 5,000 in 1993. Doctorates

204

awarded to foreign-born students showed mostly slow, steady growth from 1958 (when the number was about 300), then began to surge in 1983, and exceeded the figure for U.S.-born students in 1989. Foreigners now receive about 60% of the doctorates in science and engineering. About half of these students become citizens or permanent residents.

Science and engineering are areas in which immigrants are in competition with natives. As I have reported each year since the Second Bracey Report, despite continued predictions of shortages (a hoax in itself), there is a glut of doctorates in these fields. This year, science writer and newsletter publisher Daniel Greenberg comments that "the paucity of solutions to the Ph.D. glut is surely one of the wonders of the great American university system. The common wisdom in the ivy-covered realm is that the problem will correct itself when students wise up to the grim job situation and stop coming."[36] That hasn't happened yet — for Americans or for foreigners.

Overall, fewer of the current immigrants belong to the "huddled masses." The proportion of aliens with eight years or less of education has dropped from 35% to 25%, while the proportion with 16 years or more has risen from 17% to 30%. Immigrants do constitute a larger proportion of undereducated residents than previously, however, because the proportion of undereducated native-born Americans has fallen more rapidly in the same 30-year period, from 37% to 11%.

The number of immigrants entering the U.S. has risen rapidly since 1980, and the number entering annually is now about the same as it was in 1910. The number of immigrants entering in one year peaked in 1916. The numbers declined precipitously after World War I, again at the onset of the Great Depression, and yet again as World War II began.

We call ourselves "a nation of immigrants" but forget how much more literally true this was in the early years of this century. In 1850 immigrants made up 9.7% of the population. By 1860 the figure had leapt to 13.2%. The proportion peaked in 1900 at 14.7%, and in 1990 it was 7.9%, up from a record low of 4.7% in 1970.

205

As for illegals, while it is tough to get a completely accurate fix, most estimates run from one-fourth to one-third of the total. Six out of 10 illegal immigrants enter legally as students, visitors, or temporary workers and become illegal only when their visas expire. Thus no more than 13% of all immigrants actually enter the country illegally.

For those between the ages of 15 and 65, the welfare rates for immigrants are lower than they are for natives. They are substantially higher for immigrants over 65, but that group constitutes a small proportion of immigrants. The overwhelming majority of immigrants are between the ages of 5 and 45 — most of them, between 10 and 40. Welfare rates are much higher for immigrants who are also refugees, but they are a tiny proportion of all immigrants.

Immigrants rarely have any negative impact on the availability of jobs or on the wages paid. Only in markets with high rates of immigration and stagnant economies do immigrants have an adverse impact, lowering the ability of blacks to obtain jobs or good wages.

Certainly immigration puts strains on some school systems. Districts that have to deal with large numbers of students whose native language is not English or with a student body that represents a hundred native languages unquestionably bear an extra burden. Overall, though, immigration remains a boon to the country. Simon and Stephen Moore surveyed top economists around the country — including 38 who had been either president of the American Economic Association or on the President's Council of Economic Advisers — regarding their opinions about immigration. Eighty percent said immigration had been very beneficial to the economic growth of the nation, and 20% said that it had been slightly beneficial. Asked what we should do about current immigration rates, 58% said increase them, 33% said keep them the same, and 11% said they didn't know. None said lower the rate.[37]

Education and the Economy

While immigration is an arena rife with myths, the status and future of the economy have sprouted their own collection of old wives' tales that suck in people who should know better. In the October 11 edition of *USA Today*, President Clinton and Vice President Gore co-signed a letter to the editor claiming that by 2000, "60% of all jobs will require advanced technological skills." They did not elaborate on what "advanced technological skills" meant. I wrote to Messrs. Clinton and Gore and also to Secretary of Labor Robert Reich and Secretary of Education Riley asking for a citation for the figure mentioned. My quartet of epistles produced only one response. Staff members at the U.S. Department of Education wrote to say that they were certain that the Department of Labor could provide the answer. It did not.

But it is clear that Clinton and Gore were not using job projection figures from the U.S. Department of Labor's *Employment Outlook: 1994-2005*.[38] That document shows that, while jobs requiring college education will grow at a faster rate than jobs that require less schooling, these jobs are mostly not high-tech jobs, and the occupations that account for the largest numbers of jobs remain low-skilled. Cashiers, janitors, and retail sales positions are the big three. (These findings are reported in more detail in the January 1996 *Kappan* Research column.) An earlier publication had listed retail sales as the top job and found that it would account for one-third more jobs than the 10 fastest-growing jobs combined. "Systems analyst" is the only high-tech occupation that is both rapidly growing and offering a large number of jobs.

Statistics like these don't stop people like IBM's Gerstner from running around like Chicken Little, screaming that the system is broken. Even more numerous are the people who are running around claiming that we need high standards in order to facilitate — this year's hottest buzz phrase — the "school-to-work transition."

Elsewhere I have declared that schools should not prepare students for work. I offered the following arguments.[39]

Schools should return to the civic function that Jefferson argued they should fill. "In every government on earth is some trace of human weakness, some germ of corruption and degeneracy which cunning will discover and wickedness insensibly open, cultivate and improve," Jefferson wrote in his 1732 plan for education in Virginia. Governments of rulers degenerate, and thus the power must be invested in the people. To prevent the germ of degeneracy from infecting the people, a nation must see to it that the people are educated. A nation educated as Jefferson envisioned would contain people properly suspicious of power.

Most work lacks any intrinsic value, and most workers would not choose to do it. It is dull, boring, and even dangerous, and — while that is an inescapable fact of life — schools should not collude with business to prepare children to endure job outcomes such as carpal tunnel syndrome.

A good commentary on work can be found in the comic strip "Dilbert," which already appears in 800 newspapers and is still the fastest-growing strip in the country. Dilbert and his buddies work for a company that has endless arbitrary and capricious rules, defective products, heartless accountants, and backstabbing co-workers. In one sequence, Dilbert suggests to a co-worker that they quit and set up their own business. "Why quit?" asks Dilbert's pal. "We can run our new company from our cubicles and get paid too." "Wouldn't that be immoral?" asks Dilbert. "That's only an issue for people who aren't already in hell," replies the co-worker.

Scott Adams, the creator of "Dilbert," put his Internet address in the strip and has been deluged with letters asking, "How did you know where I worked?" Apparently a lot of workers also think they're already in hell.

Study after study has found the American worker to be the most productive in the world. It is when the workers leave the workplace that they become Joe and Josie Sixpack, watch mindless television, and engage in other brain-numbing activities. Even if the current predictions about increases in leisure time (they seem to be coming true in Europe if not here yet) are wrong, schools should provide a liberal, not technical, education. Schools should educate students to enjoy a rich, thoughtful life, alone and in groups.

Incidentally, in this connection — to borrow the title of an article debunking the book promulgating the myth — *"Bowling*

Alone Is Bunk." Peter Hong of the *Los Angeles Times* visited bowling lanes and found them thriving. The creator of the "bowling alone" myth constructed it with statistics.[40] In the past, group participation had been associated with higher levels of education. But in recent years, while educational levels have been rising, group participation hasn't risen as much. Thus, statistically adjusting for education, participation rates drop, but this is a statistical outcome that is not validated in reality.

Actually, the American softball league reported a rise from 27 million to 40 million participants between 1972 and 1990. Participation in sports and professional groups grew dramatically between 1974 and 1994. Only church-related groups, among 15 types of groups, showed a large drop. Even participation in literary/art groups increased.

Business leaders are, once again, confusing training with education and asking schools to train young people. And in their arguments, they often operate disingenuously. Sam Ginn of Pacific Telesis likes to tell audiences about the time that his company gave a reading test to 6,400 job applicants — and only 2,800 passed. Ginn says this means we have to do more in schools. What Ginn doesn't tell his audiences is that he had only 700 positions to fill. His test found four times more qualified applicants than there were jobs available.

More important, Ginn doesn't tell audiences that his jobs paid only $7 an hour, which works out to a little over $14,000 a year. Does he really expect America's literati to show up for such jobs? Ginn's attitude was captured nicely in a "Frank and Ernest" cartoon in which a personnel officer tells Frank and Ernest, "What we want are people who are smart enough to pass our aptitude test and dumb enough to work for what we pay."

In his farewell speech as President, Dwight Eisenhower warned of the "military-industrial complex." Were he alive today, he would no doubt issue a new warning about the "government-industrial complex." The government sometimes appears to have forgotten that education should accomplish something other than the agenda of the National Alliance for Business, the Business

Roundtable, etc. To borrow the words of a now-infamous report, "If an unfriendly foreign power had attempted to impose" such a narrow agenda on our schools, "we might well have viewed it as an act of war."

Vocational information could be dispensed and training accomplished much more effectively at vocational centers that operate full time and to which students could go after high school (or after college, for that matter). A number of vocational educators have responded favorably when I have posed such a notion, although the *Journal of Vocational Education*, after commissioning the article containing this proposal, ultimately rejected it because the editor felt it would be too threatening to readers.

Research from cognitive psychology, especially the literature on the transfer of training, strongly suggests that general training is not effective. The lack of effectiveness of vocational training seems even more likely, given the Bureau of Labor Statistics projections that most skilled jobs will require extensive on-the-job training, no matter what the educational level of the job holder.

The fact is that schools have done a fabulous job on the supply side — providing business and industry with greater numbers of highly productive workers than they can use. Business and industry have done a poor job on the demand side. President Clinton is currently bragging about the 10 million jobs his Administration has created; but each month, as the Department of Labor announces more job creation, there is also a report that most of these jobs are in the low-paying service sector.

As has become a tradition in Presidential election years, this issue of the *Kappan* carries essays outlining the positions of the two major party candidates. This year's essays will carry the bylines of the Clinton/Gore '96 Campaign and Bob Dole. If nothing has changed since this was written in August, it would be more honest to say that the real authors were Richard Nixon and Ronald Reagan. Before he signed the monstrous welfare reform bill, President Clinton rejected others on the ground that they hurt children too much. Elsewhere, Speaker of the House Newt Gingrich has declared, "No civilization can survive with 12-year-olds having babies, 14-year-olds doing drugs, 15-year-olds killing each other, 17-year-olds dying of AIDS, and 18-year-olds receiving diplomas they can't read. All of those things are happening in America today."[41] Both parties seem focused on youth. It will be interesting to see what the next Administration brings to — or aims at — our schools.

Notes

1. Edward W. Desmond, "The Failed Miracle," *Time*, 22 April 1996, pp. 60-66.
2. Paul George, *The Japanese Secondary School: A Closer Look* (Columbus, Ohio: National Middle School Association; and Reston, Va.: National Association of Secondary School Principals, 1995).
3. Susan Goya, "The Secret of Japanese Education," *Phi Delta Kappan*, October 1993, pp. 126-29.
4. Susan Elbert, "Education in Japan Intolerant of Departures from Rigid Norm," *New Canaan* (Conn.) *Advertiser*, 7 December 1995, p. B-17.
5. Mary Jordan, "School Bell Takes Its Toll in South Korea," *Washington Post*, 7 May 1996, p. A-1.
6. Dennis Kelly, "Parents, Students Grade America's Public Schools," *USA Today*, 13 May 1996, p. 8-A.
7. Mark Buechler, *Charter Schools: Legislation and Results After Four Years* (Indianapolis: Education Policy Center, Indiana University, 1995).
8. Chester E. Finn, Jr., Louann Bierlein, and Bruno V. Manno, "Charter Schools in Action: A First Look," *Hudson Briefing Paper*, January 1996.
9. Jeffrey Henig, *Rethinking School Choice: Limitations of the Market Metaphor*, paperback ed. (Princeton, N.J.: Princeton University Press, 1994), p. 232. Charter schools are not mentioned in the earlier hardbound edition.
10. Alex Molnar, *Giving Kids the Business: The Commercialization of America's Schools* (Boulder, Colo.: Westview Press, 1996), p. 167.
11. John F. Witte, Troy D. Sterr, and Christopher A. Thorn, *Fifth-Year Report: Milwaukee Parental Choice Program* (Madison: Depart-

ment of Political Science, University of Wisconsin, December 1995), p. 14.

12. Peter Cookson, *School Choice: The Struggle for the Soul of American Education* (New Haven, Conn.: Yale University Press, 1994).

13. Kathryn Stearns, "School Choice: Survival of the Fittest," *Washington Post*, 25 November 1995, p. A-25.

14. National Center for Education Statistics, "Commissioner's Statement," *The Condition of Education 1995* (Washington, D.C.: U.S. Department of Education, 1995), p. ix.

15. "A B+ for the Schools," *Washington Post*, 26 August 1995, p. A-12.

16. Josh Greenberg, "U.S. Students Rank #2 in Literacy," *Los Angeles Times*, 18 June 1996, p. A-5; idem, "U.S. High in Literacy," *Houston Chronicle*, 19 June 1996, p. A-4; and Mike Madden, "U.S. Students Finish Second in Reading Test," *USA Today*, 18 June 1996, p. A-1.

17. Louis V. Gerstner, Jr., et al., *Reinventing Education* (New York: Dutton, 1994), p. 5; and Albert Shanker, "The Wrong Message," *New York Times*, 11 July 1993, Sect. 4, p. 7.

18. Gerald W. Bracey, "The Third Bracey Report on the Condition of Education," *Phi Delta Kappan*, October 1993, p. 110.

19. Carol Innerst, "U.S. Classrooms Fail Economy," *Washington Times*, 12 April 1995, p. A-4.

20. Peter Applebome, "Have Schools Failed? Revisionists Use Army of Statistics to Argue No," *New York Times*, 13 December 1995, p. B-12; and Robert J. Samuelson, "Three Cheers for the Schools?" *Newsweek*, 4 December 1995, p. 54.

21. Nick Gallo, "The Good News About Our Schools," *Better Homes and Gardens*, March 1996, pp. 56-58; and Gerald W. Bracey, "U.S. Students: Better Than Ever," *Washington Post*, 22 December 1995, p. A-19.

22. See Dennis Kelly, "Poll Finds Mix of Good, Bad, and Mediocre," *USA Today*, 13-17 May 1996, p. 1-A.

23. "U.S. Schools Can't Teach? Don't Believe the Myths," *USA Today*, 13 May 1996, p. 14-A.

24. Survey conducted for the American Association of School Administrators by Mellman, Lazarus, and Lake, January 1994. As *Kappan* readers are already aware, numerous Phi Delta Kappa/Gallup polls have shown similarly favorable attitudes toward local schools and especially toward the schools people's own children attend.

25. Rene Sanchez, "Knowing the Past May Be History, U.S. Test Reveals," *Washington Post*, 2 November 1995, p. 1.

26. Lewis H. Lapham, "Ignorance Passes the Point of No Return," *New York Times*, 2 December 1995, p. A-21.

27. Bracey, "U.S. Students: Better Than Ever," p. A-19.

28. Gerald W. Bracey, *Final Exam: A Study of the Perpetual Scrutiny of American Education* (Bloomington, Ind.: TECHNOS Press of the Agency for Instructional Technology, 1995), pp. 15-77.

29. Gerald W. Bracey, "The Media's Myth of School Failure," *Educational Leadership*, September 1994, pp. 80-83.

30. Laurence Ogle and Patricia Dabbs, "Good News, Bad News: Does Media Coverage of the Schools Promote Scattershot Remedies?" *Education Week*, 13 March 1996, p. 46.

31. Millicent Lawton, "Students Fall Short on NAEP Geography Test," *Education Week*, 25 October 1995, p. 1.

32. Debra Viadero, "Book That Bucks Negative View of Schools Stirs Debate," *Education Week*, 13 September 1995, p. 8; and idem, "Teen Culture Seen Impeding School Reform," *Education Week*, 5 June 1996, p. 1.

33. Diane Ravitch, "50 Ways to Teach Them Grammar," *Washington Post*, 11 April 1996, p. A-21.

34. Millicent Lawton, "Dodging Controversy, Governors OK 'Entity' Without Name, Budget," *Education Week*, 7 August 1996, p. 26.

35. Julian Simon, *Immigration: The Demographic and Economic Facts* (Washington, D.C.: Cato Institute and National Immigration Forum, 1995).

36. Daniel S. Greenberg, "Surplus in Science," *Washington Post*, 6 December 1995, p. A-25.

37. Stephen Moore, "The Case for More Immigrants," in Vernon M. Briggs and Stephen Moore, eds., *Still an Open Door?* (Washington, D.C.: American University Press, 1994).

38. *Employment Outlook: 1994-2005* (Washington, D.C.: U.S. Department of Labor, Bulletin No. 2472, December 1995).

39. Gerald W. Bracey, "Schools Should Not Prepare Students for Work," *Rethinking Schools*, Summer 1996, p. 11.

40. Robert J. Samuelson, "*Bowling Alone* Is Bunk," *Washington Post*, 10 April 1996, p. A-19.

41. Newt Gingrich, "An Open Letter to Republican Delegates," *Washington Post*, 4 August 1996, p. C-1.

THE
AWARDS
FOR 1997

Continuing the ceremony that has become a tradition, we open this report [the seventh Bracey Report] with our "Rotten Apple" Awards for the nuttiest statements about public education during the previous year. This year's list is much longer than in previous years, for the year that saw the birth of a girl whose mother will be 80 when the child graduates from high school and found antifederalist pundit George Will mulling possible governmental regulation of cats, was, unfortunately, also a banner year for inanities about our schools.

This year's winners are: Denis Doyle of Doyle Associates, a double winner this time around; David Broder, *Washington Post* columnist who lays claim to half of Doyle's second award; Herbert Walberg, a professor at the University of Illinois, Chicago; E. D. Hirsch, Jr., a professor emeritus at the University of Virginia; Pat Wingert, education reporter for *Newsweek*; Linda Kulman, a reporter for *U.S. News & World Report*; Louis V. Gerstner, Jr., CEO of IBM and a perennial contender, who must share his award this year with Richard Mills, commissioner of education for New

York (both Gerstner and Mills barely beat out President Clinton); and the Organisation for Economic Co-operation and Development (OECD).

While the journalists included in the list above get skewered, two others — Michael Lewis, author of *Trail Fever*, and Frank Rich of the *New York Times* — have earned "Golden Apple" Awards of genuine appreciation. The sections that follow tell what this year's winners wrote or said to merit their trophies.

Worst Untested Hypothesis of the Year Award

Denis Doyle garners one prize for the Worst Untested Hypothesis of the Year. In the education chapter for the conservative Heritage Foundation's *Issues '96: The Candidate's Briefing Book*, Doyle took me to task for noting in an op-ed article for the *Washington Post* that the proportion of students scoring above 650 on the SAT mathematics section was at an all-time high. In a section of his chapter alluding to me, which he called "Chicken Little in Reverse," Doyle gasped that "[Bracey] does not tell the reader who is pushing the SAT math scores higher (mostly Asian and Asian-American students). . . . Candidates for public office should not be fooled by fatuous assertions that test scores are 'climbing'."[1] Ignoring the possibility of any veiled racism in this remark, what is the point of the pronouncement even if it is true? And it is not.

Although Doyle could easily have tested his hypothesis about Asian students, he presented no data. A single phone call to the College Board yielded the requisite data, and it took me about 15 minutes to do the calculations. From 1981 to 1995, the proportion of students scoring above 650 grew by almost 75%, from 7.1% to 12.1%. If Doyle's hypothesis were correct, then removing the Asian students from the test-taking sample should cause this 75% figure to disappear or at least become very small. But it doesn't. With the Asian youngsters held out of the pool of test-takers, the gain is still 57%.[2] In 1995, 57% more black, white, Hispanic, and Native American seniors scored above 650 on the SAT-M than in 1981. It's a record. Score one for fatuous claims.

216

Stiffest Resistance to Data Award

Doyle collects his other award in the category of Stiffest Resistance to Data. In the same Heritage Foundation document, Doyle writes, "Government spending on education has skyrocketed, even as school performance and student achievement have remained static."[3] Were all these contentions not in a single sentence, they would each have won a prize. As shown by an Economic Policy Institute study, *Where Has the Money Gone?* from 1969 to 1994 new spending for education rose by 61%.[4] Hardly a Roman candle, much less a skyrocket. More important, most of that new money was spent in areas that would not lead reasonable people to expect increases in test scores, such as special education.

However, it is not the claim itself that takes the day, but its durability in the face of massive evidence to the contrary. When I debated him five years ago, Doyle made a similar contention about spending and test scores during the 1980s. He was unmoved by the data I presented then and has remained impervious to other data since. Indeed, *Reinventing Education*, his 1994 collaboration with Louis Gerstner, Jr., and others, made precisely the same claims.[5]

At the time of the original debate, Doyle mumbled something about the flatness of the SAT's — but, if demographic changes in the test-taking pool are taken into account, SAT scores have been rising since 1975.[6] Other critics have pointed to the "stagnant" scores in the various areas tested by the National Assessment of Educational Progress (NAEP).[7] However, because the NAEP has no impact on anyone and no one takes it seriously, kids practically sleep through the NAEP testing, so it's hard to say what it really measures. When the district I was working in at the time participated in an NAEP state-by-state tryout, about half of the teachers involved told me that they had difficulty keeping the children on task. In any case, what some observers have called "stagnant," others have called "stable." And no one, to my knowledge, has put forth any specific reasons why NAEP scores should be rising. Yet NAEP mathematics scores have been climbing, probably because of the larger numbers of students taking more and more mathematics courses since 1982.[8] The media have ignored these gains: Neither the *Washington Post* nor the *New York Times* reported the 1996 NAEP math results.

Silence of the Sheep Award

David Broder can claim a share of Doyle's Stiffest Resistance Award, not for what he has said, but for what he hasn't. We might call his half-award the Silence of the Sheep Award. For the last six years I have bombarded Broder with data refuting his negative columns about American public schools. Once, on the phone, I asked him what it would take to make him believe that what I was saying was true. He replied, "Other voices." In May 1996 the American Association of School Administrators adorned the cover of *School Administrator* with photos of David Berliner, Harold Howe II, Iris Rotberg, Harold Hodgkinson, Richard Jaeger, and yours truly. The text on the cover identified us as the leading defenders of the nation's public schools. All of us had articles in that issue, and at the end of each article was a short list of other pieces we had written about the schools. I sent this issue to Broder as evidence of "other voices." He has yet to reply, but then, it has only been 17 months.

Least-Valid Index of Effectiveness Award

Herbert Walberg's prize is the Least-Valid Index of Effectiveness Award. He earned it for his use of the OECD index of "reading progress" to "prove" that the U.S. teaches reading less productively than other OECD nations.[9] For its part, the OECD acknowledged from the beginning that the index of progress had nothing to do with effectiveness of teaching reading.

Although it had no definitive data, the OECD noted that "the fact that children do not all begin school at the same age may furnish an explanation for the differences among countries in reading progress, especially for 9-year-olds." In addition, the OECD reckoned that different countries might emphasize literacy in different grades. And it mentioned that France and Italy begin extensive education experiences at early ages (2 and 3 respectively), while students in the Netherlands begin school at age 4.[10] In fact, when I calculated the rank order correlation coefficient between the countries' ranks at age 9 and their progress, it came in at -.69. That is, countries whose children look good early don't show much "progress"; countries whose children show poorly at age 9 show lots of "progress." Or, put another way, the countries that start school late do poorly at age 9 but catch up by age 14. Makes sense.

The Swiss Bitter Chocolate Award

The entirety of E. D. Hirsch's book *The Schools We Need: And Why We Don't Have Them* presents a strong case for an award. The book's central thesis is an argument that, for the last 75 years, anti-knowledge progressives have held American education in such a stranglehold that they have created a "thoughtworld," as Hirsch calls it, in which educationists cannot imagine any other way of looking at their field. Improbable? Not to Hirsch. "If thousands of Marxist thinkers could have been caught for decades in the grip of a wrong socioeconomic theory, it is not beyond imagination that a cadre of American educational experts could have been captivated by wrong theories over roughly the same period."[11]

While the whole book is a towering rhetorical performance, one small section of it is so far beyond the pale that it earns the Swiss Bitter Chocolate Award. Hirsch's Swiss neighbors, says he, complain about the low quality of the public schools around the University of Virginia, where Hirsch is a faculty member. Of his neighbors' native schools, Hirsch writes, "Switzerland has one of the most detailed and demanding core curriculums in the world, with each canton specifying in detail the minimum knowledge and skill that each child shall achieve in each grade, and an accountability system that insures the attainment of those universal standards. . . . Each child therefore receives a highly coherent, carefully monitored sequence of early learnings."[12]

If this be true, then one would expect the Swiss kids to "slam dunk American students" (to borrow one of President Bush's vibrant but not-so-clear images about how our youngsters stack up against those in other countries). Where we have comparative data, though, it doesn't seem to work out that way:

	Reading		Math	Science
Age	9	14	14	14
Switzerland	511	536	62	56
United States	547	535	53	58

The 9- and 14-year-old reading results are on a 600-point scale identical to that of the SAT, while the math and science data are simply percentages of correct answers. (The Swiss percentages are simple averages of results for French- and German-speaking areas; the separate percentages don't differ very much.) The reading data, taken from *How in the World Do Students Read?* — the virtually unknown 1992 study by the International Association for the Evaluation of Educational Achievement (IEA) — show U.S. teenagers in a dead heat with their Swiss counterparts.[13] (So little attention was given this study when it was published in 1992 that Secretary of Education Richard Riley tried, with some success, to resuscitate it with a press conference in 1996.) The Third International Mathematics and Science Study (TIMSS), which began releasing data in November 1996, provides the eighth-grade math and science data.[14] (Switzerland did not participate in the fourth-grade TIMSS assessment.) Swiss students outscore American students in math, but they trail slightly in science.

With regard to the populations of the two nations as a whole, reading data for ages 16 through 65 are available from the First International Adult Literacy Survey (FIALS). The U.S. and Switzerland both have high percentages of people at the lowest levels of literacy (20.7% and 18.5% respectively), but the U.S. has a much higher percentage of people than Switzerland at the two highest levels (21.1% versus 9.3%). FIALS and TIMSS results are discussed in detail in the Seventh Bracey Report. Hardly a slam dunk. Not even a lay-up.[15]

The Media's Lack of Institutional Memory Award

Pat Wingert takes home the Media's Lack of Institutional Memory Award. In 1992 she and *Newsweek* hailed American students' math and science performance in the Second International Assessment of Educational Progress (IAEP-2) as "An 'F' in World Competition."[16] She fretted over how students in Taiwan and Korea outperformed our kids. While concentrating on the mostly low American ranks, she even tried to explain away the third-place finish of American 9-year-olds in science. (While U.S. ranks were mostly low, the scores were only slightly below the international average, and most countries had similar scores.)

One might have thought that, looking at the TIMSS eighth-grade data, Wingert would have noticed that these ranks were a lot better than those of IAEP-2. In IAEP-2, American 13-year-olds finished 13th out of 15 countries in science and 14th out of 15 in math. In TIMSS, American eighth-graders were 25th out of 41 nations in mathematics and 19th out of 41 in science.

Some of the countries that finished ahead of us in IAEP-2 did not repeat their success in TIMSS, so it wasn't as if the TIMSS testers had rounded up a bunch of patsy nations for us to beat up on. Only six or so countries that participated in TIMSS can be considered developing nations. Of the industrialized nations of Europe and Asia, only Finland and Taiwan did not participate. The 41 nations, by far the largest group ever assembled in such a study, offer a representative view of achievement around the world, although some of them didn't meet the TIMSS criteria for sampling or student participation rates. (These countries are presented in separate categories in most TIMSS documents, but few people have paid much attention to the distinction.)

It would seem logical for Wingert to check the files and compare the two studies. But no. There is no mention of IAEP-2 in Wingert's story on TIMSS.[17] Even though the TIMSS headline, "The Sum of Mediocrity," is a little less shrill, it is impossible to distinguish material from the two stories: "In math, the gap between the American and Asian countries was especially wide. Even the very best American students didn't measure up. And that's not even the worst part. Consider this as you try to figure out which countries will dominate the technology markets of the 21st century: the top 10% of America's math students scored about the

221

same as the average kid in the global leader, Singapore." The first two quoted sentences are from the 1992 story; the last two, from the 1996 edition.

Wingert fears that Singapore will "dominate" the technology markets. Each grade in American schools contains about 3,000,000 students. The island nation of Singapore contains 3,000,000 people. At least at night. In the morning, thousands of poor Malaysians cross into Singapore, do the dirty work, and return to Malaysia, sparing Singapore the task of educating their children. Longer-term "guest workers" from Indonesia and the Philippines must leave their families at home. Even some number of Singapore families of means, whose children are not making it in the Singapore schools, send their children to schools in Malaysia. Finally, Singapore will admit Malaysian students into its schools — if they score high enough on tests. Whatever the merits of Singapore's schools, a nation that can "outsource" its poverty and low achievers while importing academic aces has got a leg up on the rest of us.[18]

Meanwhile, an editor at *Education Daily* phoned in May. She had just spent a couple of days in a conference with Singapore's minister of education. He was visiting the U.S. to get ideas about how to teach children to think. He seemed to feel that he could learn something from us. And *Newsweek*'s reaction to the stellar TIMSS ranks of U.S. fourth-graders was an authorless squib inserted on the same page as a larger article on forced summer school participation of low-achieving students in such diverse places as Chicago, Denver, Niagara Falls, and Santa Paula, California.[19]

The Accuracy as a Frill Award

At least Pat Wingert, although accentuating the negative, reported the facts. Over at *U.S. News & World Report*, people were busy making stuff up. An article by Linda Kulman contended that, in the TIMSS eighth-grade science results, our kids were "on a par with science students in New Zealand, China, Iceland, and Bulgaria."[20]

A peek at the TIMSS data shows that New Zealand, indeed, had the same rank we did (19th of 41), but Bulgaria was fifth and

Iceland 30th. What on earth does Kulman mean by "on a par with"? What's more, China didn't even take part in the study. Details of this sorry reporting appeared in the June 1997 Research column, and I repeat the incident here only to illustrate why Kulman earns the Accuracy as a Frill Award.

For the record, here's an important statistic concerning Iceland and Bulgaria: the two countries are 25 ranks apart. So, did Bulgarian kids "slam dunk" their Icelandic peers? Hardly. Bulgarian students got 62% of the items right; Icelandic students got 52% correct. A 10% difference in the scores meant a 25-country gap in ranks. A 10% difference in scores often means a difference of one letter grade, seldom more, and, even in the case of grades, there is some question as to whether a 10% difference is a meaningful difference in real achievement. As was the case in the IEA reading study mentioned above, the TIMSS data show that there is not a dime's worth of difference among most nations. The press branded U.S. performance in TIMSS as "mediocre." If so, virtually the entire industrialized world is mediocre.

The Blindest to Data Award

Louis Gerstner, Jr., and Richard Mills narrowly beat out President Clinton to earn their prize, for all three have unfairly impugned the reading skills of American students. Clinton announced that "only 40% of third-graders can read independently." From later comments by Secretary of Education Riley, this appears to have been a rather liberal interpretation of the NAEP reading levels (perhaps Clinton's only "liberal" interpretation of anything during the year). Gerstner and Mills, though, went him one better. At the Education Summit, hosted by Gerstner, the CEO of IBM declared, "We can teach them job skills. What is killing us is having to teach them to read." (I was not at the Education Summit, of course; Gerstner's remark was relayed to me by Gov. George Allen of Virginia.) Mills, for his part, declared on National Public Radio's "All Things Considered" that "what we have is a shortage of young people who can read." These statements earn these gentlemen the

Blindest to Data Award (which, in future years, might be convertible to a Stiffest Resistance to Data Award).

Since both Gerstner and Mills live in New York, it is possible, though highly improbable, that they are accurately reflecting the realities of their home state. (I leave it to New York educators to let them know whether or not this is true.) Nationally, though, American students finished second in the IEA reading study.[21] Critics have contended that the IEA study tested only "basic" reading skills, and they have looked to the NAEP to provide more credible evidence that American students can't read. However, in a joint study, the U.S. Department of Education and the Pelavin Research Institute compared NAEP results with the IEA study and concluded that, while the NAEP test contains much more comprehensive and difficult material than the IEA assessment, "It seems reasonable to conclude that American students would do well as compared with students in other countries even if the NAEP test were administered [in other nations]."[22] It is the NAEP proficiency levels, initially promulgated to sustain the sense of crisis produced by *A Nation at Risk*, that lack credibility.

Best Perpetuation of a Discredited Myth Award

The OECD attains the coveted award for Best Perpetuation of a Discredited Myth for the statement in one of its publications that, "in recent years, adult literacy has come to be seen as crucial to the economic performance of industrialized nations. . . . Today, adults need a higher level of literacy to function well: society has become more complex and low-skill jobs are disappearing."[23] Although technically not eligible for a prize because it was not published during the past year, this study has been largely overlooked in the U.S. and so is granted a special dispensation.

The OECD study contains too few nations to permit correlation between its outcomes and economic competitiveness. Suffice it to say that my own analysis shows that the correlation between TIMSS eighth-grade mathematics results and economic competitiveness — as judged by the Davos, Switzerland, World Economic Forum — is +.09. That is, virtually zero.

The fable perpetuated by OECD gained currency from that monumental lie, *A Nation at Risk*. It became a very popular fantasy during the recession some six years later, a recession for which the schools were blamed in many quarters.

The myth was dispelled first by Lawrence Cremin, who noted that it was largely the President, the Congress, and federal agencies that determined U.S. competitiveness.[24] Attacking the schools was a frequent dodge of those actually responsible for competitiveness. Larry Cuban followed up with "The Great School Scam," observing that, while schools took the blame for the recession of the late 1980s, they got no credit for the boom of the mid-1990s.[25] Cuban could have noted that this scapegoating reprised history from three decades earlier. When the Russians launched Sputnik in 1957, schools took the hit; when America put a man on the moon 12 years later, no one felt that the schools had had anything to do with it.

Today, a wider audience is beginning to catch on. *New York Times* education writer Peter Applebome notes that "many educators and economists are increasingly skeptical of the notion that better schools mean a more prosperous nation."[26] Applebome points out something I have noted in many speeches and in most of the earlier Bracey Reports. If schools are linked to the economy and our schools are so bad, while the German and Japanese schools are so good, how come our economy is booming and their economies are mired in awful, long-standing recessions? Applebome also noticed that "most experts now regard *A Nation at Risk* as brilliant propaganda."[27] The sleepers awaken.

Applebome quotes Peter Capelli of the University of Pennsylvania as saying, "The link between education and the national economy is tenuous in all but the grossest sense — say the difference between developed and undeveloped countries." Capelli's comment stands in stark contrast to one by Gerstner, who in 1994 told a Vermont television talk show host that, if we didn't shape up our schools, we'd soon be a Third World economy (a comment that earned Gerstner the first of his many trophies in these pages). Gerstner made this comment about the time that the World Economic Forum ranked our economy number one. The Forum has since changed its formula, and we have now fallen all the way to fourth. The International Institute for Management, another Swiss operation, has maintained its formula, similar to the Forum's old one, and has put the U.S. in first place for the last four years.

The OECD statement also overlooks what many people overlook: technology makes jobs easier, not harder. When a new technology appears, it is true that it is hard to play with and that only a few specialists know how. As the technology matures, however, it becomes more user friendly. When I first started programming computers in 1961, I discovered that I could earn good money — about $100 an hour in today's dollars — for the simplest programming efforts. And being a somewhat sloppy programmer, I charged only half of what the more skilled programmers charged. Computers were tough to deal with, and programmers were in short supply. It took at least six months and an army of experts to set up and debug a new computer, a far cry from today's plug-and-play machines. In those days, novices who attempted to read the documentation accompanying programs were heard to mutter things like "I don't remember signing up for a foreign language." Today, the prose in user manuals is straightforward and, if it still poses a problem, there is a manual for "dummies" available for virtually every application.

Similarly, my 1973 Canon F-1 35-millimeter single-lens reflex cameras were far easier to use than the view cameras that preceded them or the other 35-millimeter cameras that had no built-in light meters. And these F-1s, in turn, were much more difficult to operate than the next generation of cameras. I still take them out occasionally. Sometimes one needs to control shutter speed and depth of field, and this calls for a machine that lets you (actually makes you) adjust shutter speeds and f-stops. Mostly, though, I use a point-and-shoot with a single lens that zooms from 38 millimeters to 135 millimeters at the push of a button, flashes when the light is dim, and does everything else automatically. There is a lot of hokum going around about how technology makes jobs more difficult.

The Golden Apple Awards

Now to the genuine awards. The award for Most Accurate Perception of a Politician Who Once Impersonated an Educator goes to Michael Lewis for his comments on Monitor Radio on 20 June 1997. Lewis is the author of *Trail Fever*, a chronicle of the 1996 Presidential campaign. While being interviewed about his book, Lewis declared that candidate and former education secretary Lamar Alexander "did something I didn't think possible in this campaign. He proved you could be too phony. This is why Clinton feared him most of all the candidates. He was so malleable. He even looks a little like putty." Attaboy, Michael.

Lewis' category also features an award for Best Supporting Column, this by Frank Rich of the *New York Times*, who wrote, "What Bill Gates is to software, Lamar Alexander is to hypocrisy."[28] Rich drew this analogy in view of Gates' $200-million donation to local libraries in poor areas while Alexander, according to Rich, was "fronting for a moneyed 'National Commission on Philanthropy' whose highest priority is not giving but ideological warfare."

Notes

1. Denis P. Doyle, "Education," in *Issues '96: The Candidate's Briefing Book* (Washington, D.C.: Heritage Foundation, 1996), pp. 261-95.
2. These calculations were necessarily made without the 2% of test-takers who checked "other" for their ethnicity and without the 9% who did not respond to the item. If Asian Americans are over- or underrepresented in these groups, compared to the whole sample, then the 57% figure would be slightly smaller or larger. Based on "National Ethnic/Sex Data" supplied by the College Board.
3. Doyle, op. cit., p. 261.
4. Richard Rothstein and Karen Hawley Miles, *Where Has the Money Gone?* (Washington, D.C.: Economic Policy Institute, 1997).
5. Louis V. Gerstner, Jr., Roger D. Semerad, Denis Philip Doyle, and William B. Johnston, *Reinventing Education: Entrepreneurship in America's Public Schools* (New York: Dutton, 1994).

6. C. C. Carson, Robert M. Huelskamp, and T. D. Woodall, "Perspectives on Education in America," *Journal of Educational Research*, May/June 1993, pp. 259-311.

7. Lawrence C. Stedman, "International Achievement Differences: An Assessment of a New Perspective," *Educational Researcher*, April 1997, pp. 4-15.

8. National Center for Education Statistics, *The Condition of Education 1996* (Washington, D.C.: U.S. Department of Education, 1996), p. 101.

9. Herbert J. Walberg, "U.S. Schools Teach Reading Least Productively," *Research in the Teaching of English*, October 1996, pp. 328-43. I discussed this topic at length in my February 1997 *Kappan* Research column and again in my response to Walberg's letter (April 1997 Backtalk).

10. *Education at a Glance* (Paris: Organisation for Economic Co-operation and Development, 1995), p. 207.

11. E. D. Hirsch, Jr., *The Schools We Need: And Why We Don't Have Them* (New York: Doubleday, 1996), p. 2.

12. Ibid., pp. 231-32.

13. Warwick P. Elley, *How in the World Do Students Read?* (Hamburg: International Association for the Evaluation of Educational Achievement, 1992). This report is available in the U.S. through the International Reading Association.

14. *Pursuing Excellence: A Study of U.S. Eighth-Grade Mathematics and Science Teaching, Learning, Curriculum, and Achievement in International Context* (Washington, D.C.: National Center for Education Statistics, Report No. NCES 97-198, 1996); Albert E. Beaton et al., *Mathematics Achievement in the Middle School Years* (Chestnut Hill, Mass.: TIMSS International Study Center, Boston College, 1996); and Albert E. Beaton et al., *Science Achievement in the Middle School Years* (Chestnut Hill, Mass.: TIMSS International Study Center, Boston College, 1996).

15. In support of his remarks about Swiss education, Hirsch does provide some data from the 1992 Second International Assessment of Educational Progress. However, only 15 of Switzerland's 26 cantons participated in that study. The failure of Swiss students to replicate that performance in the more representative TIMSS suggests that the earlier data were inflated through selectivity in the Swiss sample.

16. Barbara Kantrowitz and Pat Wingert, "An 'F' in World Competition," *Newsweek*, 17 February 1992, p. 57.

17. Pat Wingert, "The Sum of Mediocrity," *Newsweek*, 2 December 1996, p. 96.

18. These general facts come from statements made by various TIMSS officials, by *Los Angeles Times* education reporter Richard Lee Colvin, and by others. I have not been able to obtain concrete numbers for the various categories. But remember that these are numbers that dictators such as Singapore's Lee Kuan Yew do not want made public.

19. "An Encouraging Report Card," *Newsweek*, 23 June 1997, p. 67.

20. Linda Kulman, "Teach Us More, Teenagers Say," *U.S. News & World Report*, 24 February 1997, p. 10.

21. Technically, American 9-year-olds finished second among 27 countries, while American 14-year-olds tied for eighth among 31. However, the scores of top-ranked countries were so tightly bunched at the 14-year-old level that only first-ranked Finland had a score significantly higher than the U.S. Given that the chance of finding statistical significance increases with sample size and given that there were thousands of participants from each country, the lack of significance means that the countries are indeed virtually identical. The distance from second-ranked France to 16th-ranked Germany is a meager 27 points on a 600-point scale, one-quarter of a standard deviation.

22. Nancy Matheson, *Education Indicators: An International Perspective* (Washington, D.C.: National Center for Education Statistics, Report No. NCES 96-003, 1996), p. 57.

23. *Literacy, Economy, and Society: Results of the First International Adult Literacy Survey* (Paris: Organisation for Economic Co-operation and Development, 1995), p. 13.

24. Lawrence Cremin, *Public Education and Its Discontents* (New York: Harper & Row, 1989).

25. Larry Cuban, "The Great School Scam," *Education Week*, 15 June 1994, p. 44.

26. Peter Applebome, "Better Schools, Uncertain Results," *New York Times*, 16 March 1997, Sect. 4, p. 5.

27. Peter Applebome, "Dire Prediction Deflated: Johnny Can Add After All," *New York Times*, 11 June 1997, p. A-31.

28. Frank Rich, "Gift of Gab," *New York Times*, 26 June 1997, p. A-37.

THE
SEVENTH
BRACEY REPORT ON
THE CONDITION
OF PUBLIC EDUCATION

October 1997

Last year I lamented the relative absence of new data bearing on the performance of American schools. As if in response, the gates opened, and a deluge of new studies poured forth. So much so that this year space precludes more than mere mention of several interesting reports. I ignore these reports in the knowledge that they are first-year accounts of multi-year studies and that the more important data will be forthcoming later. For instance, the RAND Corporation's evaluation of the activities of the New American Schools (formerly the New American Schools Development Corporation), while interesting, will provide much more information at a later date about whether these schools are in fact able to "break the mold." Similarly, the U.S. Department of Education and the Hudson Institute are both conducting large studies of charter schools, and it is the future data that will tell us if these schools are actually keeping the promise of improved achievement that earned them their charters in the first place. Finally, more is likely to become visible from Achieve, the entity constructed after the 1996 Education Summit, which is housed by the National Governors' Association. In the meantime, there still remains a flood of new data for our consideration.

New Data: International

The data from the First International Adult Literacy Survey (FIALS) leads to a simple conclusion: if you are an American and can't read, you're toast.[1] Before delving into what this conclusion means, I need to describe this survey, because it defines literacy in a restricted — yet complex — way.

FIALS tests resemble those used in the National Adult Literacy Survey (NALS), conducted several years earlier by a group at the Educational Testing Service.[2] While NALS contained poetry and fiction, FIALS does not. It defines three types of literacy: prose, document, and quantitative — all three measured by the ability to extract and process information from text. "Adult" for the purposes of this study was defined as between the ages of 16 and 65.

One might wonder how such a study would be conducted. After all, most of the potential candidates are no longer neatly lined up in desks at schools and colleges. In the U.S., at least, the Census Bureau provided the sample of households to be contacted for NALS. ETS first contacted potential testees by letter, then followed up by phone except when a household did not have a phone. According to Kintaru Yamamoto at ETS, testers could administer the demographic questionnaire and assess no more than two people per day.[3]

Achieving comparability across international borders is even more problematic. The European nations are currently struggling to pare down a social services safety net that threatens to impede the progress of the European Union toward a single currency. For the purposes of FIALS, though, these safety nets mean that other nations' samples do not contain the extremes of poverty and illness that the U.S. sample does.

Sampling aside, imagine for a moment that you are a 40-year-old high school graduate. You have probably not taken a reading test in 22 years. You might have sat through some aptitude or personality inventory for a would-be employer, but the tests that are so pervasive in schools have been absent from your life for more than 20 years.

Now consider that the reading assessment before you looks unlike anything you ever saw — even during your school days. Some of the prose passages resemble those on the achievement tests you took in school, but those assessing what the testers called document and quantitative literacy mostly do not. For instance, one item presents an entire ratings page from Consumer Reports. It rates 19 clock radios in three categories, and much of the page is filled with those colored-in circles and half-empty circles and check marks and keys to advantages and disadvantages that have to be matched up against the comments at the bottom of the page. I imagine that, however well you read your morning paper, if you have never seen one of these ratings pages, you would be rather intimidated by the sheer quantity of unusual text and figures to deal with. Of course, most of the text on the page is irrelevant to your task, but only the testers know that. You do not.

Although the tasks are all "real-life" tasks, there is some question about how well they assess people's "real-life" coping skills. That is, will people taking a reading test with bus schedules on it be as careful as they would be if they really had to catch a bus to a specific destination by a certain time? In real life, they might well verify the schedule with someone standing nearby, particularly if that someone seemed to be a regular rider. If at home, a person might well not use the schedule at all but call the company and ask for bus departure times within a certain range. Many people no doubt possess the requisite skills that allow them to cope with tasks by means other than reading a complex document.

The results from NALS have been pounced on by school critics — who, for some odd reason, tend also to be phonics fanatics. They claim that NALS shows that many of our people can't read well. This statement is typical. "In 1993 the NALS reported that 40 million American adults cannot read or write. Another 50 million are functionally illiterate: that is, they can only read at an elementary level or can write their names, but little else."[4] Such statements totally misrepresent NALS and FIALS.

NALS and FIALS both place people in five levels of reading. Consider what people at the lowest two levels can do. At level 1, people "performed simple, routine tasks involving brief and uncomplicated tasks and documents. For example, they were able to total an entry on a deposit slip, locate the time or place of a meeting on a form, and identify a piece of specific information in a brief news article."[5]

At the next level — the level referred to in the above quote as "functionally illiterate" — people can "locate information in text, make low-level inferences using printed material, and integrate easily identifiable pieces of information. Further, they demonstrated the ability to perform quantitative tasks that involve a single operation where the numbers are either stated or can be easily found in text. For example, adults at that level were able to calculate the total cost of a purchase or determine the difference in price between two items. They could also locate a particular intersection on a street map and enter background information on a simple form."[6]

This is what people at levels 1 and 2 cannot do: "they were apt to experience considerable difficulty in performing tasks that required them to integrate or synthesize information from complex or lengthy texts or to perform quantitative tasks that involved two or more sequential operations and in which the individual had to set up the problem."[7]

This is not "Look, Dick. See Spot. See Spot run."

NALS and FIALS did not ask adults to read texts normally seen by, say, fifth-graders. They used realistic adult reading tasks. Recall that U.S. 9-year-olds finished second in the world in reading. In spite of that, one wonders how — or even what — these children would do if confronted with the Consumer Reports document mentioned above, one of whose tasks was classified as only level 2. Given the complexity of the tasks in FIALS, it is little wonder that most of the people who have difficulty with some of these tasks report that they do not have problems coping with reading in their daily lives.

FIALS claims that these people do have a reading problem and simply do not recognize it. And some of the data suggest that this claim has some validity. Contrasting the nature of the skills tested with the skills required in daily life calls to mind the title of a David Berliner article, "Nowadays Even the Illiterates Read and Write," a title Berliner borrowed from a quote by the Italian novelist Alberto Moravia.

It is worth noting in connection with both NALS and FIALS that Berliner analyzed just who the people in the lowest levels of NALS were. The lowest levels contained 76% of all people in the study who were more than 75 years of age, 67% of those who were physically or mentally impaired, 80% of those who were visually impaired, 66% of those who were hearing impaired, 72% of those who had learning disabilities, 72% of those who had a mental or emotional difficulty, 79% of those with speech difficulties, and 70% of those with long-term illnesses (six months or more). Twenty-five percent of all those finishing at the lowest level were not born in this country.[8]

Of course, as one tests older and older adults, one is moving further and further away from any results directly attributable to schooling. FIALS acknowledges that "literacy is a fragile skill, one that requires continued use."[9] This wise view of reading stands in stark contrast to the nutty notions put forward by some phonics enthusiasts, who suggest, for example, that once children learn to decode, they can read anything.

Finally, as regards the nature of NALS and FIALS, it would be wrong to think that prose, document, and quantitative literacy represent three independent skills or that the three scales are independent. The correlations between them are quite high. Still, there are some differences among the countries that suggest that the three concepts can be separated to some degree.

There are only seven or eight countries in FIALS, depending on whether you count French-speaking and German-speaking Switzerland as one or two countries. FIALS counts them as two. With these caveats and considerations in mind, here is a summary of the FIALS results.

Prose literacy, as understood by FIALS, uses three kinds of information-processing activities: locating, integrating, and generating (which often involves making inferences). Illustrative passages consisted of instructions on how to use medicines or assemble a bicycle or a description of a particular kind of cultured plant. Document literacy reflected similar activities for tables, schedules, charts, graphs, and maps. Quantitative literacy added arithmetic operations into the mix. For example, a person might be asked to determine the percentage of male teachers in Italy from a chart that provides only the percentage of women teachers.

There is bad news and good news in the basic results. The U.S. has a higher proportion of adults at prose level 1 (20.7%) than any other nation except Poland (42.6%). The U.S. also has a higher proportion of adults at level 5 (3.8%) than any other country except Sweden (6.4%). Most countries do not have even 1% of their readers at this highest level. The American proportion at level 4 (17.3%) is exceeded only by Canada (20.0%) and Sweden (26.3%). We tend to focus on the extremes, but, since the figures must add to 100%, if the proportion of people at a given level is high, some other level must perforce be low. And it is difficult to interpret the intermediate levels.

The results for document literacy resemble those for prose literacy except that the proportion of Americans at level 1 is higher than for prose (23.7%). Sweden again has the highest proportion of adults at level 5 (7.7%), and Canada also has a higher proportion of adults at level 5 than the U.S. (5.4% compared to 3.7%). This outcome might reflect American schools' emphasis on literature rather than on technical reading, although the U.S. is back in second place for quantitative literacy, with 5% compared to number-one Sweden's 8.5%.

Looking at the results by immigrant status is revealing. The U.S. has the highest proportion of native-born adults at level 1 for prose literacy (14.0%). Canada (12.9%) and Germany (12.3%) follow close behind. Other than Canada, the rest of the countries have considerably smaller proportions of native-born adults at low levels for document and quantitative literacy, again suggesting that the U.S. concentrates on literature.

The results for immigrants are even more dramatic, with 55.5% of U.S. immigrants scoring at level 1. Save for German-speaking

Switzerland, no other nation comes close. Curiously, only Sweden and Canada have higher proportions of immigrants scoring at levels 4 and 5 on prose literacy than the U.S. But the U.S. has by far the lowest proportion of immigrants at levels 4 and 5 on document and quantitative literacy. (Because such small proportions of adults scored at level 5, aside from the basic results reported above, the FIALS analyses combine levels 4 and 5 into a single figure). This might reflect how much our schools concentrate on literature, but it might also reflect the kinds of skills that other countries are looking for in immigrants.

That the selection of immigrants by skill plays a role in the scores is shown dramatically by the results from Canada. While 31% of Canada's immigrants scored at prose level 1, 26% scored at levels 4 and 5. Only 21.8% of Canada's native-born adults scored this high. This outcome clearly reflects Canada's dual immigration policy: a relatively open door on the one hand and aggressive recruiting of skilled workers on the other. This policy should be kept in mind when making any comparisons of educational outcomes in the two countries.

These results also reveal the general worthlessness of international test scores by themselves. Cultural, social, and economic contexts must be taken into account.

It is when we parse the reading scores by income that we see the condition with which I opened this discussion. The results appear in Table 1.

Table 1. Income by Prose Literacy Level in the U.S.

INCOME LEVEL	FIALS LEVEL			
	1	2	3	4/5
No income	45.2	31.3	20.6	11.9
Quintile 1	26.1	22.0	19.7	16.3
Quintile 2	17.9	20.2	19.2	16.3
Quintile 3	8.0	15.5	21.3	21.6
Quintile 4	2.6	8.0	15.1	21.8
Quintile 5	0.3	3.0	4.1	12.1

Note the relatively flat distribution of income across reading levels 4 and 5. Knowing how to read well will not guarantee you a living wage in this country. Almost the same proportion of adults reading at levels 4 and 5 report no income as report income in the upper 20% of wage earners. But not knowing how to read well will virtually guarantee you a life of poverty: 71.3% of American adults scoring at level 1 report either no income or an income that puts them in the bottom 20% of all workers. Fewer than 3% of those who score at level 1 find themselves in the upper 40% of wage earners. For the year of the study, the upper bound of the first quintile was $6,400; for the second, $14,560; and for the third, $23,000. This means that 89.2% of those reading at level 1 earned $14,560 a year or less and that 97% of all those reading at level 1 earned $23,000 a year or less.

If President Clinton gets his education plan fully enacted, a lot more highly skilled readers are going to show up in those lower income quintiles, because most of the jobs he likes to say that he has created fall in the low-paying service sector. His plan would increase the supply of good readers (perhaps) when the demand for them is already not that high (recall that the Second Bracey Report found 26% of college graduates taking jobs that require no college). Business and industry must love Clinton's plan because it is a great way to depress the wages of skilled labor.

While the patterns for most other nations are similar, in none of them is the separation of income by reading level as stark as in the U.S. Indeed, some countries show some dramatically different results. In Sweden, for example, 41% of readers at prose level 1 are in the top two quintiles of income, compared to 55% of readers at prose levels 4 and 5. Sweden does not distribute its wealth in the same way that we do. On the other hand, 41% of German readers at prose levels 4 and 5 report either no income or income that puts them in the bottom quintile. Whether this means that Germany is less far advanced along the "information highway" than the U.S. or simply reflects that nation's severe, long-standing recession, or both, is not clear.

It is probably a combination. A segment of National Public Radio's "Marketplace" that was broadcast on 4 June 1997 noted that Mercedes and BMW, both of which have recently built factories in the U.S., are taking the label "Made in Germany" off their cars. According to one German interviewee, that label now means "high costs, 100-year-old technology, and lousy service. 'Made in Germany' is no longer a boast. It's a curse." Another German commentator observed that, if Bill Gates were German, "Bill Gates would still be a mid-level technician in Siemens. Microsoft would never have happened." But, as the American Federation of Teachers never tires of pointing out, a lot more German kids pass the *Abitur* than American kids pass Advanced Placement exams. I wonder what happens to them as a result. The AFT has been silent on this.

Some data in FIALS I do find disturbing. Save for Poland, the U.S. has by far the largest proportion (23.5%) of level 1 readers between the ages of 16 and 25. Canada has 10.7% of its young adults at level 1, and the rest of the nations have less than 10% of young adults at this level. With the exception of Poland again, the U.S. has the lowest percentage of readers in the 16-25 age range at levels 4 and 5 (12.8%). Between the ages of 26 and 35, 21.6% of American readers are at levels 4 and 5, which compares favorably with all countries except Sweden at 41.7%. Between the ages of 36 and 45, 29.2% of American readers are at levels 4 and 5, a figure exceeded only by Canada (31.3%) and Sweden (31.7%). Between the ages of 46 and 55 and 56 and 65, the U.S. proportions at levels 4 and 5 (23.8% and 14.7%) are surpassed only by those of Sweden (28.2% and 16.2%).

The American age-level pattern differs from most countries. It might reflect a combination of our higher dropout rate and our higher college attendance rate for those who graduate. Still, even taking into account immigration, poverty, and the complexity of the FIALS definition of level 1 literacy, it is disturbing to find so many younger Americans reading at so low a level.

TIMSS

The Third International Mathematics and Science Study was the big hit of the year. Most educators who hold press conferences consider themselves lucky if they draw 25 people. Some 300 showed up for the first release of TIMSS data in November 1996. The number of TV cameras present made the event seem more like the streets of Los Angeles on Academy Awards night.

For the record, I repeat the major finding of eighth-grade test results: American eighth-graders placed 25th of the 41 nations in mathematics and 19th of 41 nations in science. These facts and numerous others have been discussed in my Research columns for March, April, and June, and I've made mention of several new findings from TIMSS in connection with the awards given to Linda Kulman and Pat Wingert (see pages 220-23).

The press almost uniformly pronounced the eighth-graders' performance "mediocre," forgetting that "average" is a statistic and "mediocre" is a judgment that might or might not be accurate. As I noted above, there are about 30 "mediocre" nations, because the scores of most countries were closely bunched — and close to the scores of the U.S.

The U.S. media universally considered the high finishes of the Asian participants as something to worry about and strive to match. Only *The Economist* managed to observe an important point.

> Just as western countries are busy seeking to emulate Japanese schools, schools and universities in Japan are coming under pressure from employers to turn out workers with the sort of creativity and individuality that the Japanese associate with western education. And just as American and British politicians are demanding that schools copy their more successful oriental counterparts and set their pupils more homework, the South Korean government is telling schools to give pupils regular homework-free days, so they can spend more time with their families — just like western children. Perhaps in education there is such a thing as a happy medium.[10]

The eighth-grade data might have been ho-hum, but the fourth-grade results were so upbeat that President Clinton made a last-minute decision to announce them himself. If one considers only the countries that met all the TIMSS sampling criteria, then U.S. fourth-graders were seventh of 17 nations in math. If one adds those countries that violated one or more of the requested sampling procedures, then American students finished 12th of 26. In science, these corresponding numbers are third of 17 and third of 26.[11]

If one considers the results in terms of statistically significant differences, as several reports evidently did, then seven countries had significantly higher scores in mathematics than the U.S., and five of these seven met all the sampling criteria. In science, only Korea had a significantly higher score, which apparently led some reporters to give the U.S. finish as second place. Japanese fourth-graders also finished ahead of the U.S, however, with 70% of the science items correct versus 66% for the U.S., but the difference was not significant.

I prefer to work with the raw percentage correct rather than with the scaled scores most commonly used in TIMSS documents. While I understand the need for statisticians to take account of sampling errors and other factors, these statistical machinations bother me, as does spreading the results over a 600-point scale — a scale that makes tiny differences look big. And some simply odd things happen (statistically explainable, but odd on their face). For instance, in fourth-grade science, Korean students averaged 4% more items correct than Japanese students, who, in turn, averaged 4% more items correct than American students. On the scaled scores, though, the distance between Japan and the U.S. is only nine points, while the distance between Japan and Korea is 23 points. And the scaled score for the Netherlands is nine points below that of the U.S., even though Dutch students averaged 1% more items correct than did American students. Aside from anything I might write for statistics journals, I'll stick with percentage correct.

The fourth-grade results caused the President to take to the Rose Garden to declare that we didn't have to settle for second-class standards and that the national goal of being first in the world in math and science by 2000 was at least a possibility at some grade levels. While cheering the results overall, Clinton still emphasized that the U.S. was the only country that slid from above-average in math at the fourth-grade level to below-average at the eighth-grade level. Unfortunately, he described the slide in words that suggested that the fourth-graders and the eighth-graders were the same youngsters, which sent TIMSS personnel scrambling to explain that the two grades were tested at the same time. Some observers implied that, since recent education reforms had been in place for the full four years for the fourth-graders, they might have benefited more than eighth-graders, who got their school start before some of the reforms. The implication was that, if we came back with a FIMSS four years from now, this cohort of fourth-graders would show better. Of course, this assumes that all other countries would run in place, which they won't. As one post-TIMSS paper revealed, no matter what its TIMSS score, virtually no country is satisfied with its math and science curriculum.[12]

I am stunned by the TIMSS fourth-grade science results and not necessarily cheered by them. The word I have used most often to describe elementary science instruction in this country is "haphazard." And I am not alone in this view. In an unscientific survey, I asked the people I was speaking with on the phone what they thought of elementary science instruction in the U.S. "Hit or miss" was one answer; "flaky" was another. And why not? Analyzing a school reform effort in a wealthy Boston suburb, Richard Murnane of Harvard University and Frank Levy of MIT found that some teachers there believed that we see by emitting light through our eyes. (I discuss this reform effort in more detail below.) On NPR's "All Things Considered," TIMSS Director Albert Beaton of Boston College stated that at least some countries don't make much of science in the early grades. We may be measuring their neglect more than our own success. Still, the percentage of correct answers given by American students was pretty good, and the sample questions don't look like set-ups.

People have offered various reasons for the "slide" from fourth grade to eighth grade in mathematics. I would contend that it's primarily because mathematics instruction stops for most students after grade 4 or 5. The TIMSS people found that U.S. students were still reviewing arithmetic in eighth grade; but I think that, for most kids, the review kicks in even earlier. I have only circumstantial evidence for this contention, but it certainly seems to fit.

The schools in the First in the World Consortium score high at both grades (these results are discussed in more detail below). Consortium students get a challenging curriculum, and more than half of them take algebra as eighth-graders, compared to about 15% of students nationwide. The Consortium students provide no evidence of a "slide," and that makes sense, given what they are studying.

The Asian nations, especially Japan, are often portrayed as trying to make everyone look alike in terms of achievement. "The nail that stands up gets hammered down" is the oft-repeated Japanese saying. Thus it is interesting that the variabilities of Asian nations are not that much smaller than the variability of Americans at grade 4, and, for the most part, this variability increases from grade 4 to grade 8 to become larger than the U.S. variability in mathematics. Only Singapore reduced its variability from grade 4 to grade 8. (I have already alluded to nonschool factors that increase the scores in Singapore; one would imagine that these factors would also serve to reduce variability.)

In math, the standard deviation of fourth-graders in the U.S. was 85 points on the 600-point scale; in Japan, 81; in Korea, 74; in Hong Kong, 79; and in Singapore, 104. The standard deviation in math of eighth-graders in the U.S. was 91; in Japan, 102; in Korea, 109; in Hong Kong, 101; and in Singapore, 88. In science, the standard deviation of fourth-graders in the U.S. was 95; in Japan, 73; in Korea, 68; in Hong Kong, 79; and in Singapore, 97. The standard deviation in science of eighth-graders in the U.S. was 106; in Japan, 90; in Korea, 94; in Hong Kong, 89; and in Singapore, 95.

One would expect that the U.S., which by conventional wisdom champions individual differences and tracks students, would show increasing variability over time. But three of the four Asian nations also show increasing variability. Indeed, the standard deviations for those three countries are larger for mathematics at the eighth grade than is the standard deviation in the U.S. We have so little data on these countries that we cannot even conjecture what is happening, except to say that it runs counter to the convention-

243

al wisdom about education in those nations. There's a hint of a possible explanation for Japan in an article by Susan Goya, an American who has taught extensively in Japanese schools. Goya contended that the curriculum in Japanese high schools is tough and unbending and that at the advanced levels up to 95% of the students don't know what is going on. Kazuo Ishizaka made a similar point in differentiating between the presented curriculum in Japan and the attained curriculum.[13] But both were addressing high school phenomena. Whether or not the process has begun in the middle school is not clear. A spot check of five other nations finds similar increases in variability in Australia, Austria, Hungary, and Norway, but a reduction from fourth to eighth grade in Portugal.

Various TIMSS commentators and others looking at the TIMSS data have stated that TIMSS results reveal something close to world consensus about what a math curriculum should contain and less consensus on the curriculum for science. (They've also pointed out that the U.S. math curriculum is not like that of the rest of the world.) On the other hand, TIMSS Director Beaton reminded the audience at a TIMSS symposium of the old saying that there are two things one doesn't want to watch being made: sausage and legislation. Beaton suggested that an international test might be a third. At a 1991 symposium on international comparisons, Tjeerd Plomp, an IEA official, sighed, "We can only hope that the tests are equally unfair to everyone." In 1997, Beaton restated Plomp's longing.

TIMSS did attempt to determine whether the test/curriculum mismatches affected performance. People in all countries reviewed items to determine if they were taught in that nation's curriculum. This review does not appear to have constituted a major TIMSS activity, and the degree of accuracy of these ratings cannot be known. TIMSS then looked to see how well a country did on items selected as covered by other countries' curricula and how well the other countries did on items selected as covered by the target country's curriculum. Overall, there is little variation in performance in either case.

For instance, Scottish students scored at the international average in science (56%) on the actual TIMSS test. If we look at the performance of Scottish students on items selected by other countries as covered by those countries' curricula, the Scottish percentage correct ranges from a low of 53% on items chosen by French-speaking Belgium to a high of 59% on items picked by Cyprus. Similarly, using only the subset of items selected by Scotland, other countries did not vary by more than one percentage point from their average on all items. (I did not use the U.S. for this analysis because we selected all the items, apparently as a statement of faith in the TIMSS endeavor.)

The similarities of performance among countries on any subset of items holds up at the fourth-grade level for mathematics, but there are some anomalies in science. All countries perform somewhat better on the item sets chosen by Hong Kong and Scotland and a lot better on the item set chosen by Ireland. For instance, American fourth-graders got 66% of the items right on the whole test but 78% of the items right using the Irish subset. This differential is typical across the 26 countries.

The above results seem to indicate that the TIMSS tests were "equally unfair" across nations. However, the data presented for sample items appear to refute the notion that there is a consensus curriculum. The "p-value" of an item is the proportion of students who got the item right. Not only do the p-values vary wildly across the various areas, they vary wildly across countries. For instance, consider this item from the fourth-grade math test.

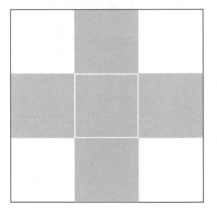

What fraction of the figure is shaded?
a) 5/4
b) 4/5
c) 6/9
d) 5/9

Eighty percent of American fourth-graders got this item right, compared to 89% of Japanese, 92% of Koreans, 94% of Singaporeans, and 96% of fourth-graders in Hong Kong. Students in the Czech Republic finished just behind the Asian nations in total score, but only 43% of Czech students got this item right. In Norway, only 25% of the students chose the correct answer, but that was better than in Portugal, where just 16% of the students picked the correct option. Why?

Or consider this item, a similar question but with the answer alternatives presented as decimals.

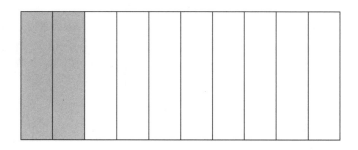

Which number represents the shaded part of the figure?
  a) 2.8
  b) 0.5
  c) 0.2
  d) 0.02

On this item, American fourth-graders fell to levels as low as Czech fourth-graders (32% and 31% correct respectively). More interesting and more problematic is the fact that in eight countries the proportion of correct answers declined from third grade to fourth. (While the results are usually reported for grades 4 and 8, there are also data from grades 3 and 7 in the TIMSS documents.) On yet another proportionality item, a tough one where the international average was only 21% correct, 25% of the students in the Czech Republic got the item right, as did 25% of American kids, but only 11% of the students in high-scoring Hong Kong aced it.

In a data representation item, students were shown a graph depicting the number of cartons of milk sold in school each day for a week. Part one of the question asked how many cartons were sold on Wednesday; the second part asked how many were sold for the week. In both parts, students had to produce the answer. Ninety-six percent of Korean students got the first part right, and 73% could add up the number of sales for the week. In Japan, though, while 94% of the students could pick how many were sold on Wednesday, only 32% could accurately find the sum for the week. American kids showed a similar drop, from 90% correct to 57%.

Such apparently capricious differences in items from country to country and the capricious changes from third grade to fourth do not seem to betoken a consensus "world curriculum" in math. For the statistically oriented reader, I say this: The point-biserial correlation coefficient between the "p-value" of items and the countries' average percentage correct would be low for a number of items.

The data for eighth-graders appear more regular (from an "eyeball" analysis), but instances of capricious variation within a country across items of the same type do occur, and there are items for which some countries show substantial increases from seventh to eighth grade, while others show no gains or even declines in the percentage of students getting the items right.

If anything, the items in science, where there is supposedly no consensus curriculum, behave more as if there were than do the items in mathematics. But items vary oddly here, too. For instance, one item shows a plain bounded on two sides by mountains. A river flows through the plain, and a farm sits near the river. Part one of the item requires students to give a good reason for putting a farm in that location; part two asks for a bad reason. The item was used in all four grades tested. At the third and fourth grades, Korea (81%, third; 91%, fourth), the U.S. (66%, 83%), and Singapore (64%, 78%) had the highest percentage of correct answers to the first part of the question. When asked for a bad reason, though, third- and fourth-graders in England and Ireland scored best, an advantage these nations maintained in the seventh and eighth grades as well, even though a smaller proportion of Irish eighth-graders than Irish seventh-graders got the item right.

On this item, Hong Kong students showed an appreciable gain between third and fourth grades, but not from fourth to seventh or eighth (45%, 65%, 65%, 70%). Of course, Hong Kong has no rivers that flood, and farms are not common to the experience of most children there, although there are farms beyond the mountains that separate the Kowloon Peninsula from the much larger area of mainland Hong Kong.

On an item asking why mountains can have snow on their tops when the snow on the lower elevations has melted, students in countries with snow-covered mountains did better than students in countries without them. (The poor performance of Austrian students was an anomaly.) TIMSS item selection techniques are designed to weed out science items that are affected by cultural or geographic features or by climatological considerations (e.g., items on seasons), but they seem not to have been wholly successful.

The TIMSS data serve another purpose — unintended, but useful. In the Second Bracey Report, I criticized the findings of Harold Stevenson and his colleagues at the University of Michigan on the grounds that the samples, at least those that Stevenson bothered to describe, were neither representative of their respective countries nor comparable to one another.[14] I also outlined a number of nonschool factors that would bias results in favor of Asian nations (e.g., fewer siblings, more parents and grandparents living with the children).

There was no direct way of showing how biased the Asian samples were, but consider this. Stevenson administered math tests to five high schools in Fairfax County, Virginia, a diverse but mostly affluent suburb of Washington, D.C.[15] (Fairfax currently contains 148,000 students with 36% minority, 20% non-native English speakers, and 17% eligible for free or reduced-price lunch.) Only 7% of the students in the highest-scoring regular high school in Fairfax County (not counting selective and specialized Thomas Jefferson High School for Science and Technology) scored as high as the average student in the highest-scoring school in Sendai, Japan; only 1% scored as high as the average student in the best school in Taipei; only about one-half of 1% scored as high as the average student in Beijing's best regular high school (not counting a special school for math prodigies). The scores of the best schools in the three Asian locales did not greatly exceed a number of other schools there.

Students in the highest-scoring regular Fairfax County high school scored at the 84th percentile on a commercial achievement test and at 591 on the SAT math section. In 1995, an SAT math average of 591 placed the average student in this high school at the 81st percentile nationally. Could Japanese students really be scoring that much better? I didn't think so but had no way of finding out.

Even at the Thomas Jefferson High School for Science and Technology, only 10% of the students scored as high as the average student in the best school in the Taiwanese sample, and only 5% attained the scores of the average student in Beijing's best regular high school. To me, this did not make sense. After all, in 1995 the average student at Thomas Jefferson scored 720 on the SAT math section — on the old scale.

The data from TIMSS make clear that, while the Japanese students maintain a sizable edge over U.S. students in mathematics — though not in science — their dominance is not nearly as great as Stevenson's results would suggest. About 24% of American fourth-graders scored as high as the average Japanese student, but only about half that many scored as high at the eighth-grade level. (Stevenson's data were from grades 1 and 5.)

Additional evidence that Stevenson's sample overestimated Japanese attainment can be found by comparing the TIMSS results for the First in the World Consortium to the TIMSS results for the various nations.[16] The Consortium is a group of 20 suburban Chicago districts that paid to have their children take the TIMSS tests. Their average eighth-grade math score was 585, compared to Japan's 605, a difference that was not statistically significant. (I report these results in scaled scores because the Consortium documents do not show percentage of correct answers.) At the fourth-grade level, third-ranked Japan scored 597 in math; the fourth-ranked Consortium, 591. In Stevenson's Fairfax County study, that wealthy suburb, even at its specialized high school, looked awful against supposedly representative schools in Asian nations. In TIMSS, the suburbs hold their own. Indeed, in science, the Consortium eighth-graders finished fourth, and no country had a score that was significantly higher; at the fourth-grade level, the Consortium outscored all nations in science, and only second-ranked Korea's score was not significantly lower. These results make sense.

Stevenson had also compared Asian schools to a sample of 20 Chicago-area schools, the latter chosen to represent all socio-economic strata in the city.[17] Yet in a comparison of two grades and two types of mathematics problems, only once did the average of the best school in Chicago surpass the average of the worst school in Beijing. In view of TIMSS data, even though China did not participate, I'd say this doesn't make sense — unless the Stevenson samples are not representative.

The performance of the First in the World Consortium raises questions about generalizations that the TIMSS staff and the U.S. Department of Education staff made about the American curricula, especially in mathematics. The math curriculum was characterized as "a mile wide and an inch deep." Yet the Consortium eighth-graders finished fifth in math, and the fourth-graders finished fourth. At both grade levels only Singapore had a significantly higher score. If the American math curriculum is superficial, how could this be? Like most generalizations about American schools, this one doesn't hold up well to scrutiny. In science, the Consortium eighth-graders were second, and no one had a higher score; the fourth-graders were first, and only Korea did not have a significantly lower score.

The performance of the Consortium is consistent with the earlier math results from IAEP-2: the top third of American schools finished one point behind top-ranked Taiwan and one point ahead of second-ranked Korea (these are NAEP scale points; a report linking TIMSS and NAEP is forthcoming).[18] The bottom third of American schools finished below last-place Jordan. There simply is no "American math curriculum."

New Data: Domestic

The NAEP mathematics scores rose for the third assessment in a row. Ho hum. At least, that's how the media reacted. Nothing showed up in the *Washington Post* or the *New York Times*. Even *Education Week* minimized the results. "More American students have upgraded their math skills," according to the page-one story, "but most still lag behind world class standards."[19]

ACT (American College Testing program) scores rose for the third year in a row. Ho hum. The *New York Times* gave one-fourth of a column to the story under the heading "National News Briefs." The *Washington Post* remained silent.

An early warning signal has arrived from Iowa. Trend lines for the Iowa Tests of Basic Skills (ITBS) in the state of Iowa and in the nation have risen and fallen in synch since the ITBS was radically revised in 1955. Thus it is a little alarming to note that the ITBS scores in Iowa have fallen the last two years, slipping from the record highs they attained in the late 1980s.[20] National data, which arrive only during the years when the ITBS is renormed, are not yet available. Why might scores be falling now? H. D. Hoover, director of the Iowa Testing Programs at the University of Iowa, thinks the reason is that we're paying too much attention to self-esteem and not enough to academics. Hoover stresses that this is only his opinion, but his is certainly an opinion worth listening to.

Education and the Economy

As I noted in giving the award to the OECD (p. 224), most people now realize that the link between education and the health of a developed nation's economy is a loose one at best. Lousy schools and all, the U.S. economy continues to soar while the economies of Japan and Germany struggle, mired for years in their worst recessions since World War II. Conditions look grim for South Korea and its high TIMSS scorers as well. American unemployment has fallen to a low that economists once thought was impossible — until it happened. (Remember, an economist is a person who can explain tomorrow why the predictions he made yesterday didn't

251

come true today.) According to NPR's "All Things Considered" broadcast of July 29, workers are so scarce in Iowa that Iowa businessmen are organizing recruiting trips to Texas.

Some new data do suggest that the productivity advantages reported in these pages and elsewhere might have been somewhat misleading. As shown in *Education Indicators: An International Perspective*, U.S. productivity has exceeded productivity in Europe and Japan since measures began in 1961.[21] Other nations have been gaining. What else would we expect as the world rebuilt after World War II? But as of 1991, only France had approached the U.S. level.

New data from the Bureau of Labor Statistics (BLS) indicate that, using the traditional measure, in 1995 the U.S. maintained its advantage over the 12 other countries studied.[22] The technique arbitrarily sets U.S. productivity at 100 and then calculates the productivity of other countries from their Gross Domestic Products (GDPs) using Purchasing Power Parities (PPPs), a formula for determining how much comparable goods and services cost in various countries. However, the BLS suggests that the traditional representation might not be the fairest. Its two new analyses include comparisons using only employed people and productivity per hour for employed people. Unemployed people don't contribute to the GDP, and Europe has lots of unemployed people these days — 13% overall as of early August 1997.

Looking at productivity per employed person, most countries gain on the U.S., but they do not overtake it, while Japan falls even further back. Using two formulas for calculating PPPs, the BLS finds that only Belgium's productivity exceeds that of the U.S., while France and Italy come close. People who might be scratching their heads over Italy should forget the Italy depicted in movies and think about the highly populous, highly prosperous, highly industrialized, and highly productive northern region. Think Milan, not Naples.

If we move from productivity per employed person to productivity per employed person per hour, Japan recedes even further, but three of the other five countries for which data exist surpass the U.S. Setting U.S. productivity at 100 in these computations, Japan finishes at 69.9, Sweden at 84.2, France at 104.6, Germany (only that which is the former West Germany) at 106.7, and Norway at 113.1. The BLS warns that, although it considers output per hour the best productivity measure, it is also the hardest to measure accurately. Most countries can't provide such data, and the BLS states that, even for those countries it considered reliable enough to put into its publication, "comparative figures on GDP per hour should be viewed with a greater degree of caution than the figures on GDP per employed person."[23]

The New Basics Redux

The first time I recall seeing the term "new basics" tossed around was in *A Nation at Risk*, and, with the exception of computer science, there was nothing new about them. They were simply a call for more: more English, more math, more science, more social studies. A few years later, Jerry Brown, former governor of California, introduced his "new basics," which consisted of "the three C's": communication, computation, and something else I can't remember. Now come Richard Murnane and Frank Levy with their six "new basics," only two of which are any different from the earlier lists.[24] To those lists, Murnane and Levy add "the ability to solve semistructured problems where hypotheses must be formed and tested" and "the ability to work in groups with persons of various backgrounds."

Murnane and Levy start from a troublesome statistic that indeed requires our attention. In 1979, a 25- to 34-year-old male with a high school diploma did earn considerably less per year than a comparable male with a college degree: $27,000 as opposed to $32,000. By 1993, however, the gap (in constant dollars) had become a chasm: $20,000 as opposed to $31,000.[25] Given the plummeting real wages of people with high school diplomas, Murnane and Levy argue that a diploma no longer unlocks the door to the middle class.

What to do? Well, we could send everyone to college. This is President Clinton's notion. Murnane and Levy, though, argue that a more effective solution is to alter the curriculum of high schools to teach more of the skills employers say they need. Murnane and Levy point out not only that the higher-paying jobs are going to college grads, but also that there is a stronger relationship today between performance in high school and later earning power even for those who do not go on to higher education. (Conventional wisdom holds that employers don't pay any attention to high school performance. Nonetheless, higher performance in high school already has an impact on later earnings.)

Murnane and Levy accept too much at face value the NAEP performance levels that have been rejected in many quarters as political tools designed to maintain a sense of crisis about schools. They use these NAEP results to contend that many high school graduates now leave schools without the reading and math skills sufficient to obtain good-paying jobs or to get the kinds of entry-level jobs that can lead up a wage ladder.

Murnane and Levy contend that, for the "new basics," math need be only ninth-grade level, which means "the ability to manipulate fractions and decimals and to interpret line graphs and bar graphs." This poses a problem for employers because, when it comes to these skills, "many recent high school graduates don't have them."[26]

Oh? In the TIMSS sample questions, 90% of American fourth-graders correctly provided a simple interpretation of a bar graph, and 57% of them successfully made a complicated interpretation. Asked what proportion of a figure was shaded, 80% of American fourth-graders got it right, a number exceeded by only four other nations. On questions where few American students got the right answer, few kids on any part of the globe got the right answer. Maybe no one is learning the "new basics," but, when one finds commonality among fourth-graders in 26 countries, I have to suspect that something other than the low quality of American schools is at work.

At the eighth-grade level, one TIMSS item showed a line graph with stopping distance on the ordinate and speed when brakes are applied on the abscissa. The question asked the students to determine how fast a car was going if it stopped 30 meters after the brakes were applied. Seventy-two percent of American kids got the item right, a success rate topped by just eight of the 40 other nations — and not by much even in those eight countries. Given a fraction and asked to write a larger one, 81% of American eighth-graders succeeded. No nation had 90% or more correct on this item.

Given the size of a gas tank, the rate of fuel consumption, and the distance driven, only 34% of American eighth-graders could accurately determine how much fuel would be left at the end of the trip, but only three of the 41 countries had more than half of their eighth-graders succeed on this question.

When one couples this performance of fourth- and eighth-graders with the data showing large increases in the proportion of high school students who are taking more math and science courses,[27] one must wonder just what Murnane and Levy mean by "many students" who lack math skills. Of course, with almost two-thirds of each June's high school graduates attending some form of higher education in the fall following their graduation, employers of high school graduates do not see many of the more academically able students.

Elsewhere, Murnane and Levy have put their thesis thus:

> For 15 years, the basic skills of high school seniors have risen slowly while the skills required for a decent job have increased radically. If schools gave tests that measured students' reading, writing, and math skills against employers' requirements, parents would see the problem and demand solutions. But few schools give such tests.[28]

In their book, they contend that "the most important problem U.S. schools face is preparing children for tomorrow's jobs."[29] This proposition — that the conditions of business have changed, so schools must change — has become so common since *A Nation at Risk* that we have grown numb to its monumental arrogance. Business conditions have changed. So what? Let 'em cope. Remember, unemployment is remarkably low. Good jobs are not going

255

abroad because, as *New York Times* economics writer Sylvia Nasar wrote a few years back, America is already the low-cost producer of many goods and services.[30] And the TIMSS data now show that only six countries demonstrate much higher math skills than the U.S.; only one country is much higher in science.

That employers are not coping was shown clearly in the Sandia Report. The Sandia engineers examined the distribution of jobs according to skill levels and the distribution of training dollars across those levels. The jobs were fairly evenly distributed across three levels: college education required, skilled labor, and unskilled labor. The dollars were not so evenly distributed. Almost 70% of all training dollars went to people with college educations. Almost 20% went to provide additional training for already skilled labor. That left less than 15% of the dollars to help unskilled labor.[31]

The Sandia engineers noted that, whereas Japanese automakers provided about 325 hours of training for new workers at Japanese factories and almost 300 hours for new workers at their American factories, American automakers provided fewer than 50 hours of training. A story on "All Things Considered" in July 1997 observed that the average training provided retail workers is seven hours.

Clearly, American industry is getting by on the cheap where training is concerned. But you wouldn't know it to read about the doleful condition of American labor. One report lamented that Lockheed Martin spends more than a million dollars a year in basic skills remedial training.[32] The report provides no citation for the figure, but let's assume that it is true. Lockheed Martin's 1995 income was almost $27 billion.[33] They're not even spending chump change on such training.

Murnane and Levy's attitude is so common in the U.S. today that we might be inclined to chisel into the stone over every high school entrance this inscription: "P.S. 139. A Wholly Owned Subsidiary of the Business Roundtable." Even we educators seem tragically in danger of equating two very different processes: education and training.

The solution proposed by Murnane and Levy suffers from another problem: The youngsters who actually lack the reading and math and "new basic" skills don't live where the good jobs are anyway. William Julius Wilson, among others, has amply documented this fact.[34] Students in the urban ghettos who graduate with "the new basics" are going to be very frustrated. Most poor urban youngsters probably already know that the good-jobs myth is a hoax as far as they're concerned, so they won't even have bothered.

Sometimes the good-jobs problem in rural settings pits the school against the family. In the early stages of its monumental reform efforts, Kentucky established the Pritchard Commission, named for the man who chaired it. Among its duties was explaining to the people of Kentucky the good things that would happen to their children as a result of reform. At one stop, the audience booed. They knew that there was no market in their area for the skills being described. They had quickly reached the logical conclusion that their children would leave. They booed because they didn't want their families to be broken up.

Murnane and Levy assume that, if the students have the skills, the jobs will be there. They won't. The FIALS data showed that many people at the highest levels of literacy had no income or earned only poverty-level wages. Bureau of Labor Statistics job-creation projects show that the current jobs boom is in the low-paying service sector: cashiers, sales clerks, janitors, waiters, and so on. (Various aspects of this situation were discussed in the Fourth and Fifth Bracey Reports and in the January 1996 Research column.) Murnane and Levy are half right: Wage prospects are bleak for people without reading and math skills — but they remain iffy even for those with such skills.

The final problem with the Murnane and Levy hypothesis is that it might well be wrong. According to MIT economist Lester Thurow, most of the job growth in the last 30 years has been in the service sector.[35] In the same period in which Murnane and Levy find the wages of high school and college graduates diverging, the number of hours worked by retail workers has fallen from slightly over 40 to 28. Retail wages, which were once comparable to

257

those in manufacturing, have declined, and the retail sector shows negative productivity growth. The declines in wages and length of work week are both the result of government policy: The government announced that employers don't have to pay benefits to part-time workers, and so they don't. The retail sector accounts for 74% of all part-time workers, including a large percentage of contingent workers — i.e., temps.

Thus not only have wages in the service sector declined, but workers in this sector have lost their benefits packages. Retail jobs account for 25% of all job generation, says Thurow. The largest single industry in the country is currently the hospitality industry, another employer of part-time, benefit-less workers. And, according to Christopher Cameron of the Southwestern University School of Law, the contingent work force — temporary, part-time, and contract workers — now constitutes 25% of all workers.[36] Although some contingent workers make decent wages as programmers, writers, or editors, most contingent jobs are likely to be held by those without college degrees. Reductions in the length of the work week and loss of benefits alone could account for much of the change in wage differentials documented by Murnane and Levy. There is no need to invoke a change in the job demands of business.

Murnane and Levy are on much firmer ground when they stick to describing school reform efforts.[37] In a *Washington Post* article, they described a seven-year reform effort in a school system in which all the odds were weighted toward success: average income $90,000 a year, parents active in the schools, 95% of the graduates attending college. Still, they found that, "in this community as in most, elementary school science, when it was taught at all, was accomplished through a method dubbed 'chalk and talk.' The teachers would lecture, the kids would take notes, and a quiz would follow." According to Murnane and Levy, the "chalk and talk" technique was used for science even by teachers who had larger repertoires of strategies for other subjects. (Once again, this makes one wonder about the meaning of the fourth-grade TIMSS data.)

Through a process of trial and error — and plenty of both — this school system changed its elementary science instruction. (This is the same district mentioned earlier in which some teachers believed that we see by emitting light from our eyes.) The reform produced a modicum of success. "As the teachers became more comfortable with the material, some formed teams to help one another organize the science lessons and assemble the equipment. They discussed how they could modify experiments to make them work better." Sounds like what we want. It took seven years.

Murnane and Levy declare the project a success.

> A happy ending, but a cautionary tale. Compared to the national landscape, this affluent community has big advantages. But even here, a serious piece of teacher retraining — a throwaway line in most task force reports on what education reforms are needed — was a hard slog with a big misstep. Most school districts start from further back.

This article by Murnane and Levy should be the office wallpaper of those who have tried to find some magic bullet of school reform, e.g., people such as John Chubb and Terry Moe, who in their book actually did call choice a panacea.[38]

Teacher Preparation (Ho Hum!)

Teacher preparation comes close to matching the weather as something everyone talks about — mostly complains about — but does little to change. Still, proposals and programs — Lee Shulman's work at Stanford, the Holmes Group, and so on — seem to have difficulty staying on the radar screen. The latest blip comes from the National Commission on Teaching and America's Future.[39] Although that group's report regurgitates the nonsense from *A Nation at Risk* in a tone-setting introduction, it does contain some important pieces of data.

For instance, students in mostly minority schools are much more likely to be taught by teachers who did not major in the field they teach (42% who did major in their fields, versus 69% in mostly white schools) or teachers who have no certification in their field (54% certified, as opposed to 86% in mostly white schools). Teachers with not even a minor in the field they teach in are much more likely to be found in schools with 50% or more free-lunch recipients than in schools with fewer than 20% free-lunch recipients.

Although not new, some of the commission's findings bear repeating: Schools have low expectations for students, there are no enforced standards for teachers, there are major flaws in teacher preparation, teacher recruitment is "painfully" slipshod, induction for beginning teachers is inadequate, and there is little reward for professional development, knowledge, or skills.

Moreover, the report is a tough-talking document.

> Although no state will permit a person to write wills, practice medicine, fix plumbing, or style hair without completing training and passing an examination, more than 40 states allow districts to hire teachers who have not met these basic requirements. Most states pay more attention to the qualifications of veterinarians treating America's cats and dogs than those of the people educating the nation's children and youth.[40]

A Coda

I drifted into education from psychology in the late Sixties. One of the first words I recall hearing was "portability." It was a problem, this portability. Educators couldn't seem to carry their successful innovations and programs from one site to another and repeat their accomplishments. The programs just weren't portable, and it was a cause of great concern. It still is.

In 1997 comes a story about how one of our most successful — and one of our most famous — teachers could not carry himself from one setting to another and how a program he left behind could not sustain its vitality without him.[41] The ultimate in failed portability. Jaime Escalante — teacher, mentor, inspiration for the movie *Stand and Deliver* — left his Los Angeles school in 1991. In that year, 143 of his poor, Hispanic calculus students took the Advanced Placement examination in calculus, and 87 of them scored high enough to earn college credit. Last year, only 37 students at the school took the test, and only seven obtained college credit for their efforts.

Escalante is now in Sacramento, attempting to replicate his success. Sadly, he can't. This year he managed to get only 11 students to take the AP calculus. Part of the reason for his earlier success appears to have been the Hispanic culture and language he shared with his students in L.A. Escalante often spoke to them in a gruff Spanish. Now, with his classes about equally divided among blacks, whites, Hispanics, and Asians, the cultural force is mostly gone.

This should be a cautionary tale for reformers. A more formal study, though, found the same thing: Local conditions prevail.[42]

What kind of year was it? Well, the year that found George Will mumbling about federal control of cats also found him discovering that schools don't have total control over children: "Between birth and age 18, a young American spends 9% of his or her time in school. What occurs in the other 91% colors, and overwhelms, the 9."[43] Bravo, George.

It was a year like all years, filled with events that alter and illuminate our lives. The U.S. posted better finishes in international studies and showed some rising test scores. And we were there. Save for Peter Applebome of the *New York Times*, though, the media were largely absent. Perhaps they'll show up next year.

Notes

1. *Literacy, Economy, and Society: Results of the First International Adult Literacy Survey* (Paris: Organisation for Economic Co-operation and Development, 1995).
2. Irwin Kirsch et al., *Adult Literacy in America* (Washington, D.C.: U.S. Department of Education, 1993).
3. Kintaru Yamamoto, personal communication, June 1997.
4. Cheri P. Yecke, *The Virginia Education Report Card* (Richmond: The Family Foundation, 1996), p. 6.
5. Kirsch et al., p. xiv.
6. Ibid., p. xv.
7. Ibid.
8. David C. Berliner, "Nowadays Even the Illiterates Read and Write," *Research in the Teaching of English*, October 1996, pp. 346-47.

9. *Literacy, Economy, and Society*, p. 87.

10. "World Education League," *The Economist*, 29 March 1997, pp. 21-23.

11. *Pursuing Excellence: A Study of U.S. Fourth-Grade Mathematics and Science Achievement in International Context* (Washington, D.C.: National Center for Education Statistics, Report No. 97-255, 1997); Ina V. S. Mullis et al., *Mathematics Achievement in the Primary School Years* (Chestnut Hill, Mass.: TIMSS International Study Center, Boston College, 1997); and Michael O. Martin et al., *Science Achievement in the Primary School Years* (Chestnut Hill, Mass.: TIMSS International Study Center, Boston College, 1997).

12. J. Myron Atkin and Paul Black, "Using TIMSS in a World of Educational Change," in *Learning from TIMSS: An NRC Symposium on the Results of the Third International Mathematics and Science Study* (Washington, D.C.: National Academy of Sciences and National Research Council, 3-4 February 1997); and idem, "Policy Perils of International Comparisons: The TIMSS Case," *Phi Delta Kappan*, September 1997, pp. 22-29.

13. Susan Goya, "The Secret of Japanese Education," *Phi Delta Kappan*, October 1993, pp. 126-29; and Kazuo Ishizaka, "Japanese Education — The Myths and the Realities," in *Different Visions of Education* (Ottawa: Canadian Federation of Teachers, 1993), pp. 116-25.

14. See Gerald W. Bracey, "The Second Bracey Report on the Condition of Public Education," *Phi Delta Kappan*, October 1992, p. 110.

15. Harold W. Stevenson, unpublished analyses conducted for Fairfax County (Va.) Public Schools, 1992.

16. David J. Kroeze and Daniel P. Johnson, *Achieving Excellence: A Report of Initial Findings of Eighth-Grade Performance from the Third International Mathematics and Science Study for the First in the World Consortium* (Northbrook, Ill.: Northbrook School District 27, November 1996); and *Achieving Excellence: A Report of Initial Findings of Fourth-Grade Performance from the Third International Mathematics and Science Study for the First in the World Consortium* (Northbrook, Ill.: Northbrook School District 27, 10 June 1997). See also Mark Hawkes, Paul Kimmelman, and David Kroeze, "Becoming 'First in the World' in Math and Science: Moving High Expectations and Promising Practices to Scale," *Phi Delta Kappan*, September 1997, pp. 30-33.

17. Harold W. Stevenson et al., "Mathematics Achievement of Children in China and the United States," *Child Development*, vol. 61, 1990, pp. 1053-66.
18. To obtain this information, I merged categories from the 1992 NAEP mathematics assessment with those from IAEP-2, which were converted to the NAEP scale by the National Center for Education Statistics and published in *Education in States and Nations* (Washington, D.C.: National Center for Education Statistics, Report No. 96-160, 1996).
19. Kathleen Kelly Manzo, "Students Post Higher NAEP Math Scores," *Education Week*, 5 March 1997, p. 1.
20. H. D. Hoover, personal communication, January 1997.
21. Nancy Matheson, *Education Indicators: An International Perspective* (Washington, D.C.: National Center for Education Statistics, Report No. 96-003, 1996), p. 181.
22. "Comparative Real Gross Domestic Product Per Capita and Per Employed Person, Fourteen Countries, 1960-1995," unpublished paper, Bureau of Labor Statistics, Washington, D.C., 1997. In addition to the U.S., the study included Austria, Belgium, Canada, Denmark, France, Germany, Italy, Japan, the Netherlands, Norway, Sweden, and the United Kingdom. (Only 13 countries are listed.)
23. Ibid., p. 12.
24. Richard J. Murnane and Frank Levy, *Teaching the New Basics: Principles for Educating Children to Thrive in a Changing Economy* (New York: Free Press, 1996), p. 33.
25. The figures for females are similar to those for males, except that women high school graduates have not lost any ground since 1979, while women college graduates have actually seen a sizable increase in wages. Whereas male college graduates lost about $1,000 in annual salary between 1979 and 1993, women college graduates gained about $6,000.
26. Murnane and Levy, p. 33.
27. National Center for Education Statistics, *The Condition of Education 1996*, p. 101.
28. Richard J. Murnane and Frank Levy, "Clinton Is Half-Right on Schools," *New York Times*, 17 February 1997, p. A-23.
29. Murnane and Levy, *Teaching the New Basics*, p. 18.
30. Sylvia Nasar, "The American Economy: Back on Top," *New York Times*, 27 February 1994, Sect. 3, p. 1.

31. C. C. Carson, Robert M. Huelskamp, and T. D. Woodall, "Perspectives on Education in America," *Journal of Educational Research*, May/June 1993, p. 296.

32. Yecke, p. 6.

33. "The Fortune 500," *Fortune*, 29 April 1997, p. F-1.

34. William Julius Wilson, *When Work Disappears: The New World of the Urban Poor* (New York: Knopf, 1996).

35. Lester Thurow, "Labor Markets, Employment, and Economic Prosperity," paper presented at an Economic Policy Institute symposium, 23 May 1997, Washington, D.C.

36. Christopher Cameron, "Why Limit Benefits to Full-Time Workers?" *USA Today*, 23 July 1997, p. 13-A.

37. Richard J. Murnane and Frank Levy, "The ABC's of School Reform," *Washington Post*, 1 September 1996, p. C-1.

38. John Chubb and Terry Moe, *Politics, Markets, and America's Schools* (Washington, D.C.: Brookings Institution, 1989), p. 217.

39. *What Matters Most* (New York: National Commission on Teaching and America's Future, 1996).

40. Ibid., p. 14.

41. Jay Mathews, "A Math Teacher's Lessons in Division," *Washington Post*, 21 May 1997, p. D-1.

42. Milbrey W. McLaughlin, "The RAND Change Agent Study Revisited: Macro Perspectives and Micro Realities," *Educational Researcher*, December 1990, pp. 11-16.

43. George F. Will, "'187': Young Men on the Edge," *Washington Post*, 10 August 1997, p. C-7.